THIS BOOK BELONGS TO

_____

START DATE

_____

12-for-12
*A Practical Guide For A Year Of
Spiritual Formation In Community*

Andy Saperstein

Published 2024 by
Vineyard Columbus
6000 Cooper Rd
Westerville, Ohio 43081

vineyardcolumbus.org

© Vineyard Columbus

All rights reserved. No part of this publication may be reproduced, stored in a retrieval system or transmitted, in any form or by any means, electronic, mechanical, photocopying, recording or otherwise, without the prior written permission of the copyright owner.

Scripture quotations marked (NIV) are taken from the Holy Bible, New International Version®, NIV®. Copyright © 1973, 1978, 1984, 2011 by Biblica, Inc.™ Used by permission of Zondervan. All rights reserved worldwide www.zondervan.com. "NIV" and "New International Version" are trademarks registered in the United States Patent and Trademark Office by Biblica, Inc.™

Scripture taken from the NEW AMERICAN STANDARD BIBLE®, Copyright © 1960, 1962, 1963,1968,1971,1972,1973,1975,1977,1995 by The Lockman Foundation. Used by permission.

Scripture quotations marked NLT are taken from the Holy Bible, New Living Translation, copyright © 1996, 2004, 2007 by Tyndale House Foundation. Used by permission of Tyndale House Publishers, Inc, Carol Stream, Illinois 60188. All rights reserved.

Cover image by jplenio1 on Freepik

ISBN-13: 978-1-947087-25-5
ISBN-10: 1-947087-25-8

First reprint with minor corrections, May 2025.

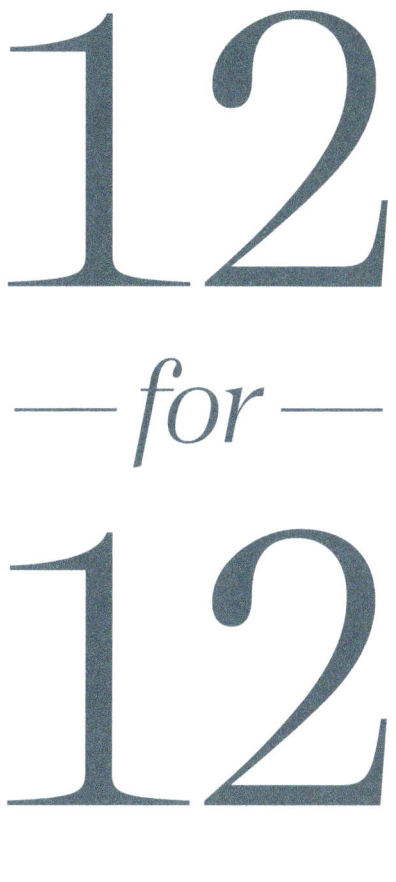

A PRACTICAL GUIDE FOR A YEAR OF
SPIRITUAL FORMATION IN COMMUNITY

First Reprint

ANDY SAPERSTEIN

There is in every person an inward sea, and in that sea is an island and on that island is an altar and standing guard before that altar is "the angel with the flaming sword." Nothing can get by that angel to be placed upon that altar unless it has the mark of your inner authority. Nothing passes … unless it be a part of the "fluid area of your consent."

HOWARD THURMAN

TABLE OF CONTENTS

ACKNOWLEDGMENTS
x

PREFACE
xii

INTRODUCTION
xiv

CHAPTER

1

Introduction to
Spiritual Formation

2

CHAPTER

2

Spiritual Formation and
Christian Community

18

CHAPTER

3

Attentiveness
to God

30

CHAPTER

4

Who is
God?

40

CHAPTER

5

Who Am I?:
Patterns of Grace

50

CHAPTER

6

Who Am I?:
Patterns of Sin

64

CHAPTER
7

Authentic Community:
Confession and Hospitality

76

CHAPTER
8

Wisdom and
Discernment

90

CHAPTER
9

Calling
and Vocation

102

CHAPTER
10

Living
Missionally

114

CHAPTER
11

Establishing Rhythms
of Grace

124

CHAPTER
12

Summing Up
and Pressing On

136

APPENDIX A:
Practices
A2

APPENDIX B:
Encounters with the Love of
God: A Visio Divina Exercise
B2

APPENDIX C:
Resources
C2

Acknowledgments

NOTHING WORTH WRITING IS WRITTEN ALONE, AND THIS book is no exception. Since forming the first 12-for-12 group in February 2010, nearly 600 individuals at Vineyard Columbus in Ohio have participated in groups led by a faithful community of several dozen leaders. Every leader and participant has shaped this book and has helped transform this curriculum from "parboiled" to "fully cooked." Thank you, dear friends and faithful leaders, for your patience, forbearance, creativity, and commitment over the years!

A smaller group of people bore particular weight in the birth of 12-for-12. Roger and Suzie Lind, our first "partners in holy crime," started leading 12-for-12 groups soon after my wife Kathryn and me. They served with us for many years on the 12-for-12 core leadership team, and significantly shaped our early groups and curriculum. Kyle and Karla Snow and Phil and Judy Niemie have also served on the core team by encouraging, sharpening, and strengthening groups, leaders, and curriculum for many years, and we count them among our dearest friends and sources of personal support. Thanks to all of you for your faithfulness, and for persevering in this work through good times and bad.

In the creation of the book itself, a few people warrant special mention. Maggie Baxter served as a faithful editor and friend, and I have come to view the abundant red ink she spills on my early drafts as a gift—thank you, Maggie, for making this book far better and for clearing away so much of the unnecessary underbrush of my prose. Lathania Butler read early chapters of the manuscript and provided crucial input in bringing far broader cultural and ethnic sensitivities to this book—thank you,

Lathania, for your keen eye and incisive ways. Casey Carmell worked diligently and patiently to create the magnificent design—thank you, Casey, for making this book far more beautiful and pleasing to read. And finally, more than anyone else, Karla Snow made this project a reality. She worked tirelessly with the content and Casey's design to lay out every section, chapter, and page and bring this project to completion. She kept me on task, provided crucial encouragement at bleak times, and believed in this project from the beginning. Thank you, Karla, for your friendship and professionalism every step of the way—this book would simply not exist without you.

Larry Warner has been a crucial advocate and encouragement for many years, and through our nearly monthly conversations has helped to keep me writing. His always gentle, often pithy counsel, his sense of humor, and the wisdom to know when to push and when not to, has kept me at my desk when I might have stayed away. Thank you, Larry, for believing in me even when I have not believed in myself, and for helping me keep the faith and bring this work to completion.

Two churches deserve special mention. In 2007, while serving on the founding team and preaching an early sermon at Elm City Vineyard in New Haven, Connecticut, I discovered the "cardinal directions of the spiritual life." Thank you, beloved Elm City, for helping me learn what the church is meant to be, and for your ongoing friendship and support and for inviting us back to serve after all these years. And Vineyard Columbus in Ohio: Kathryn and I arrived on your doorstep in August 1982. You received us gently, have walked with us ever since, and have a share in anything good we are and have become. You were our spiritual home for more than 40 years; our lives have been fundamentally shaped by your faithful care. Pastors Rich Nathan, Eric and Julia Pickerill, Daniel Nathan, Amanda Pershing, David Schermerhorn, and Paige Goslin made ample space for me to work on 12-for-12 and on this book. It is to you, and to the entire Vineyard Columbus community, that this book is dedicated.

Finally, Kathryn, wife of my youth and love of my life, you have been my chief partner in the ways of spiritual formation and outward mission in community for more than 40 years, and the chief human agent of my own formation in Christ. Thank you for your faithful love, for your consistent example of warm hospitality, and for believing in me for all these years. This book is dedicated to you, as well.

Preface

We live in a distracted age. As I write this, email notifications pop up on my screen, I hear the ping of incoming texts, I find myself tempted to check yet one more reference online, and thoughts of all I have to do at home and at work swirl in my mind. The cacophony of voices we encounter on the most ordinary of days in our own thoughts, and through the devices we put in our pockets, carry in our cars, and hook up at home, constantly vie for our attention. It is not that all of these voices are necessarily evil in themselves, though some of them certainly are. It is more that there are just so many of them, and that to give our attention to them all is to spend one of our most precious possessions—our attention—a penny at a time on things that in the end may add up to a mountain of trivialities, or at best, to something far short of the pearl of great price or the treasure hidden in a field. We want to lose neither that treasure nor our very selves to anything but what and who matters most, and the Lord's words to Martha still speak to us today: "Martha, Martha, you are worried and upset about many things, but few things are needed—or indeed only one. Mary has chosen what is better, and it will not be taken away from her" (Luke 10:41–42 NIV).

12-for-12 groups, and the curriculum you are now reading, have been developed to help 21st-century followers of Jesus, and especially Christian leaders within 21st-century churches and organizations, to reorient their lives in practical ways back to the pearl of great price and to the one necessary thing that Mary had found and that Martha in her distraction was in danger of losing. It would be nice if the church was somehow immune to the movement of currents in the cultural ocean that surrounds us, but alas, we are not. And unless we take intentional steps to retrain ourselves and the people in our churches—especially our leaders—we will be cast adrift—"tossed here and there by waves" (Eph. 4:14 NASB)—and will become indistinguishable from the ocean on which we float.

Taking practical and intentional steps to deeply reorient our lives around Jesus is a revolutionary act. When we do so, we carry the aroma of Christ not only within our churches and organizations, but also beyond them to the people and communities around us. The simple practice of having a monthly, quiet, attentive conversation with about a dozen people in the presence of the Lord is itself profoundly countercultural. And with God's help it sets a tone and trajectory for our lives even in between monthly meetings. Though the resources and practices covered during a year of 12-for-12 are varied, and seek to draw from a range of genres and cultural voices, virtually all of them involve a challenge to simply *pay attention*—to pay attention to God, to pay attention to our own lives and our own hearts, to pay attention to other people, and to pay attention to the world around us and to the work that God is calling us to in that world. The Danish philosopher Søren Kierkegaard wrote a little book entitled *Purity of Heart is to Will One Thing*, and 12-for-12 is designed to help us do just that—to rein in our own flitting gaze to a place of settled attention on that "one thing"—Jesus, who we, as did Mary, know to be the only true reference point for our entire lives.

Howard Thurman, perhaps the most celebrated African American contemplative of the 20th century, puts it this way:

> *There is in every person an inward sea, and in that sea is an island and on that island is an altar and standing guard before that altar is "the angel with the flaming sword." Nothing can get by that angel to be placed upon that altar unless it has the mark of your inner authority. Nothing passes . . . unless it be a part of the "fluid area of your consent."*
> — Howard Thurman, *Meditations of the Heart*

As you meet this year with your 12-for-12 companions and turn your attention more fully to the things of God between your monthly meetings, may the Lord strengthen you in your inner authority, may he simplify your gaze, and may he make you better able to guard your inward altar as you walk forward with him.

ANDY SAPERSTEIN

April 2024

INTRODUCTION

Twelve Facets of Our Spiritual Formation:

A month-by-month guide to 12-for-12 groups

Introduction

What is 12-for-12?

12-for-12 is a communal approach to spiritual formation that brings together 8–12 committed disciples of Jesus for 12 months of intentional and focused spiritual growth—hence the name: 12-for-12. The aim of every 12-for-12 group is threefold:

1.

TO FOSTER
in each member a deeper moment-by-moment connection with God.

2.

TO ESTABLISH
habits of living that lead to increased conformity to Christ and flourishing in all areas of life.

3.

TO INCREASE
in bearing the fruit of God's kingdom in the world.

Every 12-for-12 group exists to be a community of spiritual companions who covenant together to orient themselves more completely to God in all things; to grow in knowing and loving God, others, and themselves more truly and deeply; and to develop and walk more fully in the particular graces and calling he has conferred upon each member. While particularly well-suited to mature followers of Jesus actively engaged in service, leadership, and ministry, 12-for-12 groups can be of great value to anyone willing to embrace the group commitments and reinvest in others what they have gained through the group. These yearlong groups work best when each member fully embraces their part in this new spiritual community of fellow pilgrims.

Why 12-for-12?

21st century life, both within and beyond the church, draws us in many directions. Media and messaging permeates every corner of our lives. Endless images, requests, notifications, and expectations hinder our ability to simply be still and listen to God and to one another.

Our lives are overstuffed to such an extent that the art of quiet reflection and attentive listening gets pushed to the margins of our lives, sometimes even to the point of disappearing entirely. 12-for-12 groups serve to create space in participants' lives for the increasingly countercultural activities of quietness and focused listening to God, one another, and the inner conversation that is constantly shaping our own hearts. This is an invitation and entry point to a new, more attentive, and more intentional way of life.

This said, a 12-for-12 group is more than an invitation; it's also a very real yearlong commitment of time, resources, effort, and attention on the part of every group member. Every attempt is made to make this commitment sustainable even for people otherwise engaged in significant family, vocational, church, and ministry responsibilities beyond the group. Most homework can be undertaken during regular devotional times. Meetings are scheduled to be as minimally intrusive to members' lives as possible. Consider this 12-for-12 year both a challenge and an opportunity to establish, or reestablish, both during and outside of the monthly gatherings, habits and rhythms that deepen your life with God and positively impact your way of being overall.

What is the tone and atmosphere of 12-for-12 gatherings?

A successful 12-for-12 group depends crucially on the way you frame your relationship with God and one another when you meet together. Though much of the work of a 12-for-12 group occurs outside of group meetings when you are alone with God or going about your daily life, the ways you relate with God and one another when you meet together play a crucial part in this year of communal spiritual formation. The tone and atmosphere of your meetings will prove to be a vital part of all you will do together this year, and it is the responsibility of group leaders and every group member to nurture and protect that tone and atmosphere.

WHEN YOU MEET, THERE ARE A FEW THINGS YOU CAN EXPECT:

A typical 12-for-12 meeting is informal and relaxed and takes place in someone's home. While groups can meet any time of day, meetings often take place in the evening, when more people tend to be free. Members agree in advance on whether to pitch in on carryout food, contribute to a potluck meal, or take turns cooking. Meals may be around a large table or sitting around the living room with paper plates—either way, the food is typically simple and the fellowship warm to set the tone for the meeting time described below, which typically begins 30–45 minutes into your time together, right after the meal.

So first, after sharing a meal together, you will often begin your formal meeting time with several minutes of silence—silence and stillness will help you to quiet your own "inward fidgeting," and will prepare you and your group to be more attentive and receptive to both God and one another. Something else you will notice that's different from a more traditional small group: musical worship will often not be part of your meeting time. Connection with and worship of God will occur in other ways, including responsive readings, liturgical prayers from various traditions, and other spiritual exercises and practices.

Second, vulnerable, authentic sharing and attentive listening will form a crucial part of each 12-for-12 gathering. While there will be times of open discussion in your group meetings, most of your sharing will be one at a time, with your fellow group members simply attentively listening, receiving one another's words, and moving on to the next person after your leader has thanked them for what they have shared. Though you may be moved to immediately respond to what each person shares—to comfort, to counsel, to make a witty remark, or to otherwise respond in some way (this kind of back-and-forth interaction is sometimes referred to as "cross-talk"), your normal practice will be simply to receive one another's authentic expressions as a sacred gift and to hold them quietly together before God without comment. Often, after one or more group members have shared, you will pause silently for a few moments to recall and more deeply receive the gift of one another's spoken words and shared experiences. This practice of transparent, authentic sharing; quiet, attentive listening; and intentional recollection long stands as one of the most transformational rhythms for those who participate in 12-for-12 groups. It is intended to help build a quiet, even revolutionary space of deep encounter with each other and with God in the swirl of our often loud, cluttered, digitized world.

As you seek to vulnerably and authentically share your life with other group members, there are a couple things to keep in mind. First of all, vulnerable, authentic sharing takes courage. Your group leader will normally lead out in setting the tone and substance of courageous, transparent sharing of their own experiences, thoughts and feelings, joys, failures, etc. We share in this way knowing we can only truly come before God as we actually are—not as we wish we were, or once were, or hope to be—but as we are. As you cultivate the courageous practice of sharing with your fellow 12-for-12 companions the reality of your inner and outer life, you take small steps toward honestly presenting yourself more fully to God and his transforming work in your life.

Also, it is important to keep in mind that when group members vulnerably share experiences, especially of trauma connected to race, ethnicity, gender, age, socioeconomics, etc., it is particularly important to maintain an atmosphere of safety and shelter in the group, and to minimize the possibility of people unnecessarily experiencing past experiences of trauma through their present sharing. To share in the first person (i.e. this is how *I* felt, this is what happened to *me*, this is what God is doing in *my* life, etc.) about our own internal and external experiences (as opposed to simply reporting what others think or feel) is both a sacred and tender undertaking; it requires commitment and care for all involved, and motivates our overall commitment to confidentiality in the group.

What are the priorities of 12-for-12?
The cardinal directions of the spiritual life

All that you do in your 12-for-12 group will relate in some way to "the cardinal directions of the spiritual life": upward, inward, one another, and outward. In the lifelong process of "growing in every way more and more like Christ" (Eph. 4:15 NLT), these four key orientations consistently characterize our lives. No matter where we find ourselves in our journey with Jesus, it's always a good time to establish rhythms that will strengthen and sanctify these four cardinal directions. In this group, we will regularly refer to the four cardinal directions of the spiritual life, and we will together seek to cultivate and internalize deeper and fuller rhythms in their regard. The four cardinal directions are defined as follows:

ORIENTED UPWARD TO GOD: ATTENTIVENESS TO GOD

Of the four cardinal directions, our orientation *upward* to God is the one without which none of the other orientations are meaningful or possible. Jesus states in John 15 that unless we abide in him, and he in us, we will bear no fruit, and we will in fact be able to do nothing. Paul speaks in his letter to the Ephesians of "the summing up of all things in Christ, things in the heavens and things on the earth" (Eph. 1:10 NASB), for he understood that the central focus of all history, of all Scripture, and certainly of our own lives is and must be the person of Jesus Christ. Through Christ, and through the Holy Spirit who is given to each of us, we have access to the Father, and in the end, it is God—Father, Son, and Holy Spirit—who will be the chief aim and end of this group, and of our lives.

Together we will seek to cultivate this "godward" orientation in a number of important ways, with an emphasis on expanding the ways we encounter God both through his word and through prayer, through close community with others, and by cultivating a lifestyle of attentiveness, observation, and reflection aimed at making us more aware of God's presence and activity at all times, in all places, and in all things. In these ways we will seek God's help in building a life seamlessly connected to and yielded to him in every aspect of our lived experience. This commitment to living "godwardly" will stand as the primary focus of the group.

ORIENTED INWARD: ATTENTIVENESS TO OURSELVES

The greatest commandment, Jesus says, is to "love the Lord your God with all your heart, and with all your soul, and with all your mind, and with all your strength," and to "love your neighbor as yourself" (Mark 12:30–31 NASB). He calls us to engage in a life of loving God, ourselves, and others with all that we are and all that we have. To do so, we must know and pay attention to ourselves, for if we are completely unaware of ourselves—if we do not take the time to look inwardly—then we will be significantly hindered in our ability to rightly steward the gifts and graces God has placed in us for his glory. We will be similarly hindered in our ability to identify, avoid, and put to death obstacles to God-given gifts and graces—namely our own sinful ways of being—that get in the way of his work and purposes in and through us.

Paul says to Timothy to "pay close attention to yourself and to your teaching" (1 Tim. 4:6 NASB). And in Chapter 1 of his *Institutes of the Christian Religion*, John Calvin asserts that, "Without knowledge of self, there is no knowledge of God. Our wisdom, insofar as it ought to be deemed true and solid wisdom, consists almost entirely of two parts: the knowledge of God and of ourselves" (Calvin and Beveridge 2008, Ch. 1, 1:1). Without a regular inward gaze, our spiritual lives will never fully grow and flourish as God intends.

The idea of paying attention to ourselves has often been viewed with suspicion as somehow selfish. American culture, including American church culture, is often partial to action and extroversion. The idea of slowing down to become aware of our inner thoughts, feelings, and motivations strikes some as frightening, as a waste of time, or as inordinately introspective. But it is to our own peril and at real cost to those around us and to the progress of God's kingdom, both in and through us, that we ignore ourselves—both the gifts and graces given to us, and "the sin that so easily entangles us" (Heb. 12:1 NASB). We will therefore make it our aim in this group to pay appropriate attention to our inner lives as a sacred gift from God to be attended to, developed, and stewarded with great care.

ORIENTED TO ONE ANOTHER: ATTENTIVENESS TO CHRISTIAN COMMUNITY

Paul's letters primarily address the church. In his letter to the Ephesians, for instance, it is only after his appeal for unity in the church, and for the ways of being and speaking that make for that unity, that Paul addresses families and the broader community. This is not to diminish the importance of family and community relationships in any way, but merely to note the central role that our relationships with one another as the people of God plays in our growth as disciples and in our full participation in the work of joining with God in bringing his kingdom to the world.

For this reason, the third cardinal direction of the spiritual life is our orientation toward *one another*—it is only in relationship with one another that any of us can hope to "become mature, attaining to the whole measure of the fullness of Christ" (Eph. 4:13 NIV). Therefore, we can expect God to work in significant ways as we attentively listen and faithfully intercede for one another in the course of a yearlong journey of spiritual formation. This "one another" orientation, however, is of course not limited merely to the relationships we share within a yearlong 12-for-12 group. The larger community of faith, the church, a body whose very identity is rooted in the love of God, is the environment in which we best learn to enjoy God's love and share it with others. It is here that we ought to receive real-time feedback regarding how to grow in self-understanding and understanding of others. Christian community is a many-faceted mirror where we see both ourselves and God reflected in and through our relationships with one another, and without this "one another" orientation, we become increasingly blind to our own selves, as well as to the One who has created us.

ORIENTED OUTWARD: ATTENTIVENESS TO GOD IN BRINGING HIS KINGDOM TO THE WORLD

We serve a God who sends us on a mission to "make disciples of all the nations... teaching them to observe all that I commanded you" (Matt. 28:19–20 NASB). Jesus taught us to pray, "Your kingdom come, your will be done, on earth as it is in heaven" (Matt. 6:10 NASB). Thus, our lives are not merely meant to be oriented toward God, ourselves, and one another, but also to the world where we are called to join him in bringing his kingdom. In this 12-for-12 group we will help one another better identify and more fully walk in the particular gifts, callings, vocations, and opportunities given to each of us for the sake of the kingdom. For as a lake that has no outlets soon dries up or becomes stagnant, we too become spiritually dry and stagnant if we do not give away the gifts we receive from God and others. In this vein, as a member of a 12-for-12 group, one of our commitments (outlined below) is to intentionally give away to others what we have gained through this group. While in many ways we will naturally pass along aspects of our transformation to others both within and beyond the church, we are also called to be intentional about giving away what we have gained. This might involve loaning an assigned book to someone, teaching another person how to pray or engage the Scriptures in a different way, incorporating some of what you've learned into your small group, or perhaps even leading your own 12-for-12 group in the future.

As we do so, we rejoice that God's kingdom is multiplicative. When a seed falls on good soil—in the heart of a person "who hears the word and understands it"—it "produces a crop, yielding a hundred, sixty or thirty times what was sown" (Matt. 13:23 NIV). Paul urges Timothy, his beloved young companion in the gospel in this way: "the things you have heard me say in the presence of many witnesses entrust to reliable people who will also be qualified to teach others" (2 Tim. 2:2 NIV). Paul elsewhere asserts that the gospel is "constantly bearing fruit and increasing" (Col. 1:6 NASB), and we are called to join God in effecting that exciting and unstoppable outward progress of his kingdom in the world.

What are the basic 12-for-12 commitments?

Participating in a 12-for-12 group involves a number of important commitments. While there may be some variation from group to group, the commitments that follow are consistent for all 12-for-12 groups and stand as a covenant created and maintained in an atmosphere of grace by every 12-for-12 member. While for a variety of reasons we may not fulfill every aspect of this group covenant, each member enters into it with a good faith commitment to do so. As we give our word to God and to one another, each member joins the group with a sense that God has given them grace in the season ahead (in the form of time, motivation, vision, discipline, etc.) to undertake all that it entails. Thus, all 12-for-12 members commit to the 12 commitments summarized on the facing page.

A successful 12-for-12 group crucially involves your physical presence at monthly gatherings. As with many commitments, a big part of keeping your 12-for-12 commitment is simply to show up. And while the work you will do between meetings is critical, those who consistently get the most out of 12-for-12 groups and most impact their companions on the way are those who faithfully attend the meetings. In short, *please come to every meeting*.

Generally, all 12 meetings will be scheduled before your group even begins, which gives you a chance to check for schedule conflicts before committing to the group. It's especially important to avoid missing meetings early on in the life of your group, as those are the months when you will share your life stories with one another and build relationships that will create an environment of trust that will carry through your year together. If you know in advance that you will miss two or more meetings during the year, especially during the first several months, it is generally best to opt instead for a different group that better fits your schedule.

TIP Put all of the year's 12-for-12 meetings on your calendar in advance to avoid unnecessary schedule conflicts.

Unexpected circumstances and unavoidable schedule conflicts may certainly arise—weddings, funerals, babies, graduations, illness, etc.—and you should by no means miss an important and immovable life event in order to attend your group or attend when you are sick. But part of your commitment to your group is to avoid planning discretionary time away or accepting other invitations or opportunities when they conflict with already-scheduled 12-for-12 meetings. By embracing this commitment, you present a gift both to yourself and to your fellow group members; it will increase the emotional and relational safety in your group, allowing members to be more vulnerable, and it will create a settled and consistent environment for the duration of your year together.

ALL 12-FOR-12 MEMBERS COMMIT TO:

1. Make every effort to attend all group meetings.

2. Make every effort to do all assigned homework.

3. Buy or otherwise acquire assigned books and materials.

4. Pray regularly for your fellow group members.

5. Share transparently and authentically during meetings.

6. Attentively listen to others during meetings.

7. Hold in confidence what others share during meetings.

8. Contribute food or money for meals at monthly meetings.

9. Contribute to a group childcare fund for meeting time.

10. Actively seek God's transforming work in your life this year.

11. Give away to others what you gain from this group.

12. Give and receive grace when you or others fall short in these commitments.

What recurring practices and homework are involved in 12-for-12?

As a core part of 12-for-12, you will engage in spiritual "exercises" and other practices designed to help you slow down and be attentive and attuned to God in every aspect of your life and experience. Many of the exercises and practices are time-tested practices drawn from the great traditions of the Christian church. Others are more modern and experimental. But all are designed to be accessible, low cost (you can also consider borrowing resources from the library, or from former 12-for-12 alumni, to further reduce costs), and are designed to help you cultivate a deeper and richer life of connection with God and others in all things.

Most of the assigned exercises and practices can be done as part of your regular devotions or seamlessly incorporated into other aspects of your daily life. Others may require setting aside a bit more dedicated time. But all are likely to bear fruit in your life with God as you engage in them over the course of each month and will give you more "tools in your toolbox" to help you connect with and serve God in the future. The intentionally broad range of practices is aimed at accommodating a similarly broad range of learning preferences and capacities. You will undoubtedly enjoy some practices more than others, and some practices will likely prove to be more beneficial to you than others. But maintain a posture of openness and a willingness to give every practice a sincere try and you won't be disappointed.

Finally, much of what we do in 12-for-12 will focus on solitude and silence, ways of praying, ways of engaging with God's word, and intentional reflection on our own lives with God, and is described in greater detail below.

REFLECTION AND JOURNALING

Both traditional Christian spirituality and modern neuroscience testify that the act of intentional reflection on our lives—on our experiences, memories, observations, etc.—accompanied by physically writing the reflections and observations down on paper assists in a demonstrable process of growth and integration. In more classical Christian terms this growth might be referred to as sanctification. Therefore, an important part of our 12-for-12 homework

TIP If you don't plan to purchase all the books, look a month or two ahead in the homework to leave time to identify and reserve any books you might need from your local library.

... much of what we do in 12-for-12 will focus on solitude and silence, ways of praying, ways of engaging with God's word, and intentional reflection on our own lives with God ...

consists of reflective journaling. While you may choose to journal electronically, you are encouraged to consider a good old-fashioned paper journal to accompany you on this year of intentional formation. For those who think in pictures, unlined paper presents an opportunity for "outside-the-lines" journal entries comprised of sketches, drawings, doodles, and the like. God can and will use these forms of expression to open you up to him in unexpected ways. Overall, journaling what we notice and discover as we engage with God and his word and consider our lives before him will form an important part of 12-for-12. We will often share with one another from our journal entries, so be sure to bring your journal with you to every group gathering.

"WORD IMPLANTED" TEXTS

James 1 speaks of receiving "the word implanted, which is able to save your souls" (James 1:21a NASB). Through regular engagement with what we call "Word Implanted" texts, interacting with God's word will be a central part of our 12-for-12 rhythms. Every month, you will be assigned several biblical texts, and over the course of that month you will read each passage aloud at least several times a week. And while different leaders may vary other assignments in ways particular to their groups, the Word Implanted texts provide a fixed biblical mooring for all that we do, and anchor us as God's people in the sacred text that frames our understanding of everything else.

As you engage with the Word Implanted texts, read the passages out loud slowly, and with varying inflection and emphasis. Regular oral reading of biblical texts may be an unfamiliar practice, but it was a regular practice in the ancient and medieval world and in many monastic communities, and it will help you engage with God and encounter his word in refreshing and soul-strengthening ways. American President Abraham Lincoln routinely read out loud, explaining the practice by saying, "When I read aloud, two senses catch the idea: first, I see what I read; second, I hear it, and therefore I can remember it better" (Herndon and Weik, 2021, p. 238). The Word Implanted practice is a gentle way to internalize and even memorize God's word in order, in the words of the Apostle Paul, to "let the word of Christ richly dwell" within us (Col. 3:16a NASB).

TIP If you are ambitious, you might even consider reading aloud at least some of the Word Implanted texts in more than one Bible translation throughout the year. Different translations often highlight different aspects of the same text and can help you notice things you might otherwise miss.

Regarding which Bible translation to choose, it is generally best to choose a version and stick with it. New American Standard (NASB), New International Version (NIV), and New Living Translation (NLT) are three versions that you might consider choosing from. While all three are considered to be faithful renderings of the original texts, they often serve to bring to light different aspects of God's revealed truth. You might consider trying all three translations toward the beginning of this year together, and then deciding which translation you will focus on going forward. Or, if you prefer, you can choose another translation and go with that. Note: While clearly useful for many devotional purposes, remember that paraphrased versions of the Scriptures such as *The Living Bible* or *The Message* allow a great deal more deviation from the original manuscripts than do traditional translations, and may therefore not be a best first choice for this practice for the simple reason that it's probably best to memorize a text closer to the original inspired intent of the passage.

No matter which translation you choose, you will find that as you engage with the regular, repeated, oral reading of Scripture, God's word will become more and more a part of your inner life and dialogue, and you will begin committing more and more of it to memory. Finally, for your convenience, you will also find in Appendix C a complete listing of all Word Implanted text references, organized by month.

ANCIENT AND MODERN SPIRITUAL PRACTICES AND EXERCISES

When we meet together, and as part of our monthly homework, an important part of 12-for-12 will be to engage in a range of exercises and practices designed to help us more fully develop in the cardinal directions of the spiritual life: upward, inward, one another, and outward. Some, such as the prayer of examen, have been practiced for hundreds of years; others are much more recent. But whether ancient or modern, all are intended to develop us in one or more of the cardinal directions. For example, *lectio divina*, or reflective reading of Scripture, helps us cultivate greater attentiveness to the Holy Spirit in our reading of God's word. The prayer of examen is intended to help us become increasingly aware of the inward ebb and flow of our own hearts before God. "Remembering the Saints" helps us cultivate a greater awareness and appreciation of the many sisters and brothers God has used to shape our lives with him over the years. The "Core Calling" exercise helps us to identify and steward the graces and gifts God places in us as part of our outward calling and vocation. Taken as a whole, the sum of these practices is intended as good spiritual "cross training," where we intentionally seek God to help us strengthen every aspect of our spiritual lives.

... as you engage with the regular, repeated, oral reading of Scripture, God's word will become more and more a part of your inner life and dialogue, and you will begin committing more and more of it to memory.

SELECTED READINGS

Reading assignments over the course of the year together may include non-fiction books, novels, short stories, essays, poems, and other writings. In many cases, you will be given a list of possible readings to choose from; in others, specific readings will be required for all group members; but generally, the reading assignments will not exceed around 100 or so pages a month. Questions and prompts will often be provided to help you engage more fully with the works, though you will generally only spend limited time discussing the readings together when you meet. You will be responsible for purchasing or borrowing books that are still in print (many are available through public libraries or for free online)—your leader may otherwise provide print or digital copies of shorter works, out-of-print resources, etc. 12-for-12 readings are carefully selected to expose you to a diverse range of voices and perspectives that present a tapestry of expressions and methods of orienting ourselves within the four cardinal directions of the spiritual life. While leaders may occasionally choose additional or alternate readings, most groups will largely follow the list of readings each month.

FILMS FOR FORMATION

For many months this year, you will find a recommended film or films listed, generally along with several questions for reflection. Because watching movies is already part of many people's normal rhythms, and because movies afford a remarkably efficient way to cover extensive subject matter, films provide excellent and accessible material for deep and broad reflection and are particularly well suited to the aims of 12-for-12. Movies also provide an approach to learning that suits those of us who are more visual or auditory in our learning style and also leverage the power of storytelling, which was one of the Lord's preferred approaches to teaching.

TIP Consider gathering with other 12-for-12 group members for an occasional movie night over the course of the year.

The films are not explicitly Christian, per se, but are selected with an eye to the way they illustrate or draw upon one or more of the cardinal directions of the spiritual life, as well as upon the other central themes and priorities of 12-for-12. To commit some of your existing "screen time" to making an intentional and reflective contribution to the ongoing process of your own spiritual formation makes real sense in our increasingly video-saturated age. This said, knowing that sensitivities of group members will vary, it will always be noted whenever the content of a given film may be difficult or objectionable for some group members, or whenever a recommended film is rated PG13—no R-rated films have been included. If you have any doubts about watching a given film, please do your own research before deciding whether to watch it. IMDb is a particularly helpful website for this, especially in the content advisory within the Parents Guide section.

COMMUNAL ACTIVITIES

While your 12-for-12 companions are not meant to become your sole spiritual community, and you will continue to maintain other, and perhaps even more foundational spiritual communities in your life during the course of this group, the communal dimensions of this group are nonetheless crucial to its success. Here are some activities to expect:

- You will generally share a meal together whenever you meet. This simple time of hospitality and breaking bread together helps establish an atmosphere of informality and warmth.

- You will commit to praying regularly for one another. This act of lifting each group member up to God will help you not only to partner with him in the work of transformation in others' lives but will also serve to knit your hearts together.

- In between monthly gatherings, you may occasionally meet in smaller groups for confession and prayer and/or possibly to check in with one another by text, phone, or in person. Similarly, you may also occasionally break into smaller groups during regular monthly meetings.

- You are also encouraged to informally connect between meetings if you are able—watch the assigned film together, reflect on the homework, discuss your progress in the group, etc.

TIP Early in your 12-for-12 year consider setting up a text or WhatsApp group to help you coordinate and stay connected between meetings.

You will likely find the community dimensions of this group both significant and enriching as you walk together with your companions through this year of spiritual formation. As your 12-for-12 companions open their lives to you during the course of the year, recognize that they are placing before you a sacred trust to be handled with care. Commit to carrying that trust gently and intentionally, making yourself available to speak a word of encouragement, reaching out to one another between meetings, and considering one another after the group has come to an end. The shared experience of 12-for-12 just might lead to some new and lasting friendships.

MONTHLY POEMS

Finally, to close out each chapter, a poem has been included—some are old, some are new, and some are original to this book. While not technically part of the homework, the poems have been selected to correspond to and shed light on each month's topic. Try to spend a little time with each poem—read it out loud a time or two, as poetry, like Scripture, often comes alive when read aloud. Sit with the language, rhythm, and imagery in each poem—open yourself to God and let him speak to you. If you find yourself moved and inspired, explore other poetry by the same or other authors, or try your hand at writing some poetry of your own.

What roles do grace and resistance play in 12-for-12 groups?

Grace is the order of the day in 12-for-12 groups, and leaders and group members alike should commit never to employ shame or pressure on one another regarding group commitments. This said, the extent to which you engage with the homework and the group commitments often bears directly on the benefits gained and fruit borne in your life as a result of the group. In stepping into 12-for-12, each of you has agreed to certain commitments, and if you find yourself either consistently resistant, unwilling, or unable to act on the commitments you have made—assigned homework, readings, exercises, films, Word Implanted texts, etc.—it may be worth seeking God to discern the reasons for your resistance. Sometimes, circumstances beyond our control get in the way, but other times, factors within our control end up impeding our progress and level of our participation. It is worth seeking God regarding the reasons we may be resisting or procrastinating.

In some cases, perhaps certain practices make us feel awkward for one reason or another, in which case it is often worthwhile simply to acknowledge and reflect on the reasons for our discomfort even as we seek to engage with the practice. Perhaps we feel too busy to fully engage with the homework and practices, but a careful assessment instead reveals we are prioritizing other things. Noticing this can in its own right help us to gain a deeper understanding of the state of our overall spiritual lives, the reasons for the choices we make, and our need for formation. As we seek to grow in grace and connection to God, there is often much to learn from both our participation as well as our resistance to that participation, so be sure to pay attention to currents of resistance in yourself, as well as to times when it is easy to follow through on group commitments. Believing there is no true Christian growth apart from freely embraced obedience to Christ, we seek to cultivate an atmosphere of freedom and grace in all we do, and to avoid any and all manipulative or coercive ways of relating to or motivating one another, intended or otherwise.

Believing there is no true Christian growth apart from freely embraced obedience to Christ, we seek to cultivate an atmosphere of freedom and grace in all we do, and to avoid any and all manipulative or coercive ways of relating to or motivating one another, intended or otherwise.

# Homework

As you take these initial steps into this year's homework, pause for a few moments to settle yourself before God. Ask God for grace and perseverance to actively engage in this year's work, both with assignments that are resonant and easy for you, as well as with those where you sense resistance in yourself. End with a brief prayer of commitment to God—not anxious and under pressure, but settled and hopeful, giving yourself to this year's work in faith that as you do so, God will meet you and make you able both to complete and find genuine profit from it in your life with him.

READING

Before your first meeting, take some time to read through Chapter 1, to look over the Chapter 1 homework, and to familiarize yourself with the contents of this guide, including the Table of Contents, the chapters, and the appendices.

REFLECTION AND JOURNALING

Consider the following questions and jot down some brief answers in your journal. Try limiting your responses to one or two fairly short sentences and be ready to share them with your group for 4–5 minutes at your first meeting.

- What are a few basic facts about your life right now? Stick to very simple statements if you can, e.g. "I am in the midst of a career change," "I am raising young children," etc.

- What is your mind preoccupied with lately?

- How have you been feeling lately emotionally?

- How have you been feeling lately physically?

- What is one question you find yourself asking God lately?

- What is one recent situation or activity where you have most experienced God's presence and pleasure?

- What is one hope and one question you have regarding this group?

PRAYER

Take a few minutes to pray for the other members of your group. Ask God to open your heart in love to each person, to bless them, to give you all courage to open yourselves to God and to one another this year, and for grace to joyfully embrace the shared commitments of the year ahead.

12-for-12

GROUP MEMBERS TO PRAY FOR:

CHAPTER 1

Introduction to Spiritual Formation

> My dear children, for whom I am again in the pains of childbirth until Christ is formed in you . . .
>
> GALATIANS 4:19 NIV

> I am the vine; you are the branches. If you remain in me and I in you, you will bear much fruit; apart from me you can do nothing.
>
> JOHN 15:5 NIV

CHAPTER 1

Introduction to Spiritual Formation

The Inevitability of Spiritual Formation

Every one of us, whether or not we are consciously aware of it, is being formed and shaped every minute of every day. Voluntarily or involuntarily, actively or passively, we are subject to influences from within and without that shape the kinds of people we are and are becoming. All that we see and hear, eat and drink, read and watch, and think and feel, as well as all we choose to do and not do, impacts each of us and contributes to our ongoing formation as persons. The people we know, the places we live and work, our families of origin, our present living situations, and our vocations do the same. And each of us has a role to play in determining the ways each of these factors form and shape us.

As followers of Christ, we recognize that our relationship with God—Father, Son, and Holy Spirit—ought to determine the ways that we allow ourselves to be formed. Prior to life in Christ, our ways of allowing influences to form us missed the mark. When we repent, which is really nothing more than admitting that we have let ourselves be shaped and formed by all the wrong things, we freely yield ourselves to Jesus and receive his forgiveness for our failure to let him shape our lives. We then commit to give him primary say regarding how our lives are shaped and formed going forward, and we look to him as our primary model for all that we commit to be and become. By turning away from our old way of life—often fundamentally shaped in our families of origin and the early years of our lives—and freely embracing a new way of life modeled after Jesus and empowered by God's Spirit, we are made into disciples. Thus begins a lifelong re-formation patterned after him.

Dallas Willard describes the life of the disciple as the life of an "apprentice (disciple/student) of Jesus," a life of being with Jesus and of "learning to live the life that he would have lived if he were I" (Willard 2002, p. 241). When Jesus tells us to take his yoke upon us and to learn from him (Matt. 11:29), he paints a picture of how we as disciples are called to be bound together with Jesus and to walk alongside him as he teaches us a new way of living. This is the path of our spiritual transformation—*the freely embraced process by which we, as disciples of Jesus Christ, participate with God through the work of his Spirit and the activity of his grace, in becoming conformed to the person and ways of Jesus in every aspect of our lives.*

Freely Embraced Obedience

A wise man once said that you can't make a tree grow by pulling on the leaves. If a tree is to grow it must "want" to grow. Similarly, spiritual formation in the way of Jesus can only be undertaken freely by those who desire growth and change—the benefits and fruits of transformation require our willing obedience. None of us can expect much transformation if we are acting out of manipulated consent, or are under duress, or are subject to oppressive leadership. Freely embraced obedience is our most important contribution to the spiritual formation process.

We enter into the process of transformation because we want to. We say, along with the Apostle Peter, "Lord, to whom shall we go? You have words of eternal life" (John 6:68 NASB). Persuaded that it is the fullest, richest, most grace-filled, and best way to live, we enter into the life of the disciple and the life of transformation. Upon pledging allegiance to Jesus, our King, it is the only fitting life to live.

But this grace-filled way of living is not without cost. Dietrich Bonhoeffer said the life of the disciple "is costly because it costs a man his life, and it is grace because it gives a man the only true life" (Bonhoeffer 1995, p. 45). Jesus puts it this way:

> "Whoever wants to be my disciple must deny themselves and take up their cross and follow me. For whoever wants to save their life will lose it, but whoever loses their life for me and for the gospel will save it." (Mark 8:34–35 NIV)

These words were not a riddle to be solved only after Jesus' death and resurrection—the meaning was clear to those who first heard them. The cross was a brutal instrument of execution used by the Roman authorities, and its use was fairly common in Jesus' day. Many people died on a cross before Jesus did. A man sentenced to die on a cross was forced to carry his own instrument of death to the place of his execution. And unlike most modern-day executions, this happened in full public view, undoubtedly in order to send a clear public message to think twice before resisting Roman authority. The sight of a man carrying a cross could mean only one thing—that man's life was over. A person must give up one's life in order to become Jesus' disciple—not literally on a cross, but in such a radical way that it was likened to it. We must allow God

...the freely embraced process by which we, as disciples of Jesus Christ, participate with God through the work of his Spirit and the activity of his grace, in becoming conformed to the person and ways of Jesus in every aspect of our lives.

to put an end to our life as we know it—the one where we are on the throne and where our own will is our supreme authority. Jesus spoke of a life wholly surrendered to him, one emptied of itself so that it can be filled with him.

Those who go far in spiritual formation into conformity with Christ understand and seek to live out Jesus' teachings on the surrender and abandonment of their lives, exchanging their way of life for his. They wholly embrace and deeply identify with these words of the Apostle Paul:

> I have been crucified with Christ and it is no longer I who live, but Christ lives in me. (Gal. 2:20 NASB)

Participating with God

But as we take Jesus' yoke upon us and begin walking beside him and learning from him, how can we expect this promised transformation to actually take place? *How* will we be changed? Is this something we must do, or is it something God does for us? Or is it something done in partnership with God? Is it like our salvation—a free gift of grace—or must we actually *do* something to earn it? Metaphors from the natural world help us better understand the process of spiritual formation:

1.

A SUNFLOWER does not *earn* sunlight by turning towards the sun, but if it does not bend toward the sun, it receives no light.

2.

A SQUIRREL does not *earn* acorns by gathering what the oak provides, but if it never leaves its nest to gather nuts, it will starve.

3.

A CHILD does not *earn* the milk from its mother's breast, but if it does not reach for her breast and nurse, it receives no sustenance.

All of nature is *participatory*—it is always responding to what God initiates and provides. This in no way translates to nature *earning* anything from him—everything is a gift of grace from God, and we, like the Israelites of old, are merely gatherers of manna that would otherwise rot on the ground. And throughout the Scriptures—in the life of the Patriarchs, the Prophets, the Apostles, and myriad others of God's people over the centuries, we see people who encounter God in the midst of often challenging lives and circumstances and *participate* with him in "working out [their] own salvation with fear and trembling" (Phil. 2:12 NASB).

Yet sadly, we often hold a distorted understanding of the relationship between grace and works. Salvation in Christ certainly involves receiving forgiveness as an unearned gift through faith in his death and resurrection, and it involves us turning away from our own way of living to give Jesus primary say over the way we live. The starting point of faith does not involve any work on our part—it consists simply of turning ourselves toward God to receive his mercy and to submit our lives to Jesus, our King. Thus, we may find ourselves later wondering that if grace is a free gift, won't it simply impact my life going forward without me doing anything? Isn't it wrong to exert myself in pursuit of something that only God can accomplish in and through me?

FOR REFLECTION
Consider everyday activities where you exert effort to lay hold of gifts from God—eating and sleeping are good examples. Do these efforts count as you earning anything from God?

Dallas Willard said, "Grace is not opposed to effort, it is opposed to earning" (Willard 2006, p. 61). In order to lay hold of the grace given to us for transformation, it will require serious effort on our part. The process of spiritual formation is profoundly participatory, but never a matter of earning anything from God—all is gift. Olympic athletes devote themselves to years of rigorous training in order to steward and develop natural athletic gifts and other opportunities afforded to them. They have no say regarding whether or not they receive those gifts in the first place—they are *gifts*, freely received. Yet, none of us expects an athlete to reach elite-level abilities without first subjecting those gifts to a lengthy and disciplined process of training and practice. Only then do the natural gifts take on the qualities and abilities of a world-class athlete. You don't long jump 25 feet, take gold in Olympic figure skating competitions, or win marathons by sitting around waiting for it to happen.

Spiritual formation will simply not take place in an environment of passivity. Only those who invest significant personal effort and attention in the process tend to make significant progress. To assist in that effort, over the course of this group we will engage in a range of practices and disciplines, including:

- Assigned readings
- Journaling and reflection prompts
- Different ways of praying
- Different ways of encountering God's word
- Watching and reflecting on assigned films
- Yielding our lives to God moment by moment

This intentional engagement with God and one another is intended to impact the way we live every minute of our lives, not merely our "quiet times." We will participate with God—in sometimes challenging ways—as we seek to model our lives after Jesus and lay hold of our own transformation. And we will do so with the same sense of expectation and hope as the child who reaches for its mother's breast, the sunflower that turns itself toward the light, or the squirrel who leaves its nest and searches the forest floor for acorns. The ways of discipleship and transformation are only and always works of God's grace, imparted to us moment by moment through the work of the Holy Spirit as we yoke ourselves to Jesus and walk forward with him.

Conformed to Christ in All Things

Conforming to the person and ways of Jesus impacts every moment and aspect of our lives as human beings. It involves what we do with our capacity to think, to feel, to speak, and to engage in relationship with others. It involves the choices we make and the way we make them. It involves what we do with our physical bodies and all of our senses. It involves all of the ways we engage with the world around us, whether at work, play, or rest. Because we are created in the image of God, spiritual formation is decidedly *holistic*. This truth is found throughout Scripture. We see it in Mark 12, when Jesus spoke of the most important commandments:

> Love the Lord your God with all your heart and with all your soul and with all your mind and with all your strength. The second is this: 'Love your neighbor as yourself.' There is no other commandment greater than these. (v. 30–31 NASB)

And the Psalmist declares:

> The earth is the Lord's, and all it contains, the world, and those who dwell in it. (Ps. 24:1 NASB)

The whole of our existence as persons created in the image of God and the whole of the created order make up the grist for the mill that is our formation in Christ. We are not at liberty to ignore or overly favor any one facet of our lives, be it the emotional, physical, intellectual, or any other aspect as we seek to be formed in Christ. Nor is it wise to neglect or inordinately focus on one aspect of human experience or the created order at the expense of all others. To the extent that we favor or neglect some aspect of our own lives, the created order, or the full counsel of God, our own spiritual formation will become similarly distorted. The formation that God intends for us is rooted in a holistic view of ourselves and of the world.

The work of spiritual formation ... often happens in the earthy context of real lives lived out among real people in the real world ...

God himself, our true north, is the one around whom we orient our lives *upwardly* and from whom we receive the power to do so. When we orient ourselves upwardly, God makes transformation possible in every other domain. This takes place first in our own lives—the *inward* of the cardinal directions—in our heart, soul, mind, and strength. God also calls us to love our neighbors as ourselves, which hearkens back to both the *one another* and the *outward* cardinal directions. We are called to love our neighbor as ourselves; the Prophet Micah calls us to do justice, to love mercy, and to walk humbly with God (Mic. 6:8); and Jesus commissions his followers to "make disciples of all the nations" (Matt. 28:19 NASB). As we are transformed, we increasingly become agents of God's purposes, able to do all these things and more, both among our fellow believers and *outwardly* in the world. In these relationships and contexts we experience even further transformation.

Through the exercises and practices of 12-for-12, we will cultivate habits of being and doing that we can incorporate into each facet of our lives. The work of spiritual formation and the fruit of our active participation with God's grace and the activity of his kingdom often happens in the earthy context of real lives lived out among real people in the real world, outside the controlled environment of our church sanctuaries and devotional closets. "The earth is the Lord's and all it contains" (Ps. 24:1 NASB)—thus every situation is a potential "potter's wheel" on which we can participate with God as he continues to form and shape us in his image.

Drop by Drop a River is Born

Habits are often small, repeated patterns of being and doing that over time form larger patterns of living that ultimately define the kind of people we become and the way we spend our lives, and much of the work of our own transformation is accomplished in seemingly imperceptible steps and in the most ordinary of circumstances. Just as a traditional Afghan proverb affirms that "drop by drop a river is born," spiritual formation takes place when small habits of heart, soul, mind, and strength lead to our own transformation, as well as contribute to the transformation of the world around us. The Apostle Paul provides a good description of this process in Ephesians 4:

> But you did not learn Christ in this way, if indeed you have heard Him and have been taught in Him, just as truth is in Jesus, that, in reference to your former manner of life, you lay aside the old self, which is being corrupted in accordance with the lusts of deceit, and that you be renewed in the spirit of your mind, and put on the new self, which in the likeness of God has been created in righteousness and holiness of the truth. (vv. 22–24 NASB)

It is this process of *laying aside* one's old self, of being renewed in the mind, and of *putting on* the new self that defines the process of our spiritual formation. This is a lifelong pattern: we repeatedly cast off our old ways of being; we allow God to renew us in the ways we think, feel, choose, and act; and we cooperate with God as he clothes us in Christlikeness. Paul's use of certain Greek verbs in this text reveals something about the way this process works:

- "Lay aside the old self" is written in the *active voice*—it is something *we* are called to do.

- "Renewed in the spirit of your mind" uses the *passive voice*—it is something we allow God to do to *us*.

- "Put on the new self" is expressed in the *middle* voice, which can either mean something we do to ourselves (e.g., *clothe yourselves*), or something we allow to be done to us (e.g., *be clothed*).

This journey of surrender, renewal, and transformation involves every aspect of our lives—what we think and feel, the words we choose to say and not to say, and the ways we use wealth and material possessions. It involves the ways we cultivate and express sexuality, how we approach work and play, and the ways we engage in relationships. It involves how we develop and constrain desires and appetites, the things we choose to create, and the things we count as beautiful—every aspect of what it is to be human comes into play in the process of our spiritual formation.

But practically speaking, how do we cultivate these habits of heart, soul, mind, and strength? How do we make real new patterns of living in keeping with our new self? Dallas Willard speaks of the necessity of vision, intention, and means—VIM (Willard 2002, ch. 5)—as the three essential ingredients in spiritual formation. We have already discussed the vision—increasing conformity to the person and ways of Jesus in every aspect of our lives. We seek to bring this vision to life by choosing to take steps of freely embraced obedience—this is our intention. But what are the means by which we get there? What are the actual tools in our formational toolbox? Among the most important are spiritual disciplines.

The Role of Spiritual Disciplines

Spiritual disciplines are to spiritual formation what an athlete's training regimen is to her development as an athlete—they are not the end in itself, but the means to the end, which is whole-life conformity to Jesus. A number of modern classics have led the church to rediscover the spiritual disciplines that saints of past centuries found indispensable in the process of spiritual formation. Richard Foster's *Celebration of Discipline* (Foster 1978), Dallas

Willard's *The Spirit of the Disciplines* (Willard 1988), and Ruth Haley Barton's *Sacred Rhythms* (Barton 2006), are among the best known and most helpful.

In general, spiritual disciplines consist of various "spiritual workout" exercises. Some are undertaken in the privacy of "devotional closets" while others are portable and well-suited to communal and public settings. In keeping with Paul's Ephesians-4 language of laying aside the old self, being renewed in the spirit of our minds, and putting on the new self, we can divide the disciplines into two groups—abstinence and engagement.

Disciplines of abstinence involve laying aside something in order to heed Paul's call to lay aside our old self, to more fully open the "spirit of our mind" to God that he might renew it, and to make us better able to put on our new self. Disciplines of abstinence include solitude, in which we lay aside social interaction for a time in order to more fully engage with God; silence, in which we step away from the cacophony of our life's noise so that we might better hear God's voice; fasting, in which we deny ourselves food (or something else) for a time, in order to turn ourselves toward God and learn how to better master our desires; and secrecy, in which we resist the temptation of seeking public praise by keeping our good works hidden.

Disciplines of engagement are those we actively take on to facilitate connection with God and other people, and to further the process of laying aside our old selves, renewing our minds, and putting on our new selves. Some of these disciplines are Scripture-centered—study, reading the Bible aloud, and Scripture memorization. Others, like confession and fellowship, bring believers together in intentional ways in order to invite God into both our private and communal lives. Disciplines of worship and celebration foster joy, gratitude, and the fear of God. Other disciplines of engagement include reflection and self-examination, moment-by-moment attentiveness to God, and various ways of praying.

The fruit borne in practices of abstinence helps us to lay hold of the benefits of practices of engagement. By temporarily removing some things from our lives—even good things—to make room for even better things, we cultivate qualities of character that render us, in the Apostle Peter's terms "neither useless nor unfruitful in the true knowledge of our Lord Jesus Christ" (2 Pet. 1:8 NASB).

Spiritual disciplines are to spiritual formation what an athlete's training regimen is to her development as an athlete—they are not the end in itself, but the means to the end, which is whole-life conformity to Jesus.

Some spiritual disciplines vary in their utility from person to person and from season to season. A discipline that bears much fruit in one person may bear little in another, and a discipline that in one season leads to much growth and change may in another season of life bear little fruit. A discipline that helps us overcome a particular pattern of sin during one season may prove ineffective in another season. Some disciplines, particularly those involving silence and solitude, engaging with Scripture and prayer, and practices of fellowship, worship, and confession, should be present in one form or another in every person's life regardless of season. Other disciplines, such as fasting, may fill a more occasional place in our lives. In general, however, familiarity with a wide range of spiritual disciplines ensures that whoever we are, and in whatever season we find ourselves, we have tools at hand to help us fully participate in the ways of transformation that God makes available to us.

A Word of Encouragement

The way of spiritual formation is lived out in an atmosphere of patience and hope. To encourage scattered first-century believers to persevere in the face of manifold challenges, James put it this way:

> Therefore be patient, brethren, until the coming of the Lord. The farmer waits for the precious produce of the soil, being patient about it, until it gets the early and late rains. You too be patient; strengthen your hearts, for the coming of the Lord is near. (James 5:7–8 NASB)

To encourage the Roman church to persevere in the face of difficulties, the Apostle Paul says:

> ... but we also exult in our tribulations, knowing that tribulation brings about perseverance; and perseverance, proven character; and proven character, hope; and hope does not disappoint, because the love of God has been poured out within our hearts through the Holy Spirit who was given to us. (Rom. 5:3–5 NASB)

The road of transformation is long, and there will inevitably be setbacks. But the Father gazes tenderly upon us every step of the way, encouraging us whenever we fall and when we get back up, determined to continue on in the way of his Son. "All discipline for the moment seems not to be joyful, but sorrowful," says the author of the letter to the Hebrews, "yet to those who have been trained by it, afterwards it yields the peaceful fruit of righteousness" (v. 12:11 NASB). The fruit will come, sisters and brothers, the fruit will come, as we abide in the Vine, who is Christ our Lord!

And so we set out together on a year of spiritual formation, opening ourselves to God and to one another along the way, persuaded that together we will cover more ground than we would by ourselves, and confident in the Lord's closing words to the Twelve:

> "... and lo, I am with you always, even to the end of the age."
> (Matt. 28:20 NASB)

Let the journey begin!

Homework

Before starting any of the homework listed below, first read through the entire list of homework exercises. This will help you to get a better sense of what to incorporate into your daily rhythms this month and to begin establishing those rhythms from the outset. May God bless you and meet you as you seek him through these assignments.

READING

1. *Sacred Companions,* by David Benner (2002)

    Read the Preface, and chapters 1–3. In *Sacred Companions,* Benner does an excellent job of first discussing in broad terms what he calls "the transformational journey," which is in essence the process of spiritual formation, and he goes on to frame that journey in the context of a group of spiritual friends. Benner's discussion in these chapters of spiritual formation in community also does an excellent job of describing the intended dynamics of a healthy 12-for-12 group, and therefore serves as a fitting introduction to the spiritual and relational dynamics you are encouraged to cultivate with God and one another as you walk forward together this year.

    Chapters 4–9 are optional. While much of the content in these chapters focuses on what it means to be and become a spiritual director, Benner also speaks constructively to the roles we will play in one another's lives this year and the contours of what spiritual friendship can look like even apart from formal spiritual direction.

AS YOU READ, CONSIDER THE FOLLOWING:

a. In discussing the transformational journey, Benner outlines the way a number of different authors and Christian traditions describe and lead people along the path of spiritual formation. Are any of these ways of describing the journey particularly helpful for you? Is there anything about the transformational journey as Benner describes it that makes you feel uncomfortable? Why?

b. Note Benner's discussion of becoming a great lover, becoming whole and holy, and becoming our true self-in-Christ. Which of these three notions do you find particularly helpful as you press into the transformational journey with this group? Why?

c. Benner says that three of the greatest gifts we can offer to one another in spiritual friendship are the gift of genuine hospitality, the gift of genuine presence, and the gift of genuine dialogue. What are some of the ways you sense God leading you to offer these three gifts to others? In what ways do you find yourself resistant to offering one or more of these gifts to others?

d. On p. 57, Benner speaks briefly about our role in "mediating grace" for one another in our spiritual communities, and he says that "the most important thing I can do is help the other person be in contact with the gracious presence of Christ." How do you sense God inviting you to "mediate grace" as you participate both in this group and in the other communities you are part of?

e. Benner lists five qualities that form the essence of spiritual friendship—love, honesty, intimacy, mutuality, and accompaniment. How are these five qualities expressed in the Trinity of Father, Son, and Holy Spirit? Of your own spiritual friendships, both past and present, which have best expressed these qualities? Which have failed to embody these qualities? What is God calling you to notice about these friendships?

f. On p. 26, Benner says, "The essence of Christian spirituality is following Christ on a journey of personal transformation." In light of the cardinal directions of the spiritual life (see Introduction, pp. xix–xxi), do you think there is anything missing from Benner's statement? What might you add?

2. If time permits, look over Chapter 2 and its homework before your next meeting.

REFLECTION AND JOURNALING

Map out your own "spiritual autobiography," with an eye to what will most help you and your 12-for-12 companions understand who you are now.

3. Begin by listing some basic facts about your life—where you were born and grew up, who your parents were, your siblings, how you came to faith, your current family situation, your education and profession, etc.

4. Then write down some of the most formative events, circumstances, seasons, or transitions in your life, whether they were positive or negative experiences.

Within the first few months of meeting, each member of your group will have 10 minutes to share along these lines—you won't be able to share everything, but when you do share, plan to spend 1-2 minutes on the "basic facts" part and the remaining time on the "formative events" part of your story.

As you each take courageous steps to share authentically and vulnerably, and to listen sympathetically and attentively to one another's autobiographies, you will lay an important foundation concerning the tone and the character of your interactions with God and with one another over the course of the next year.

TIP Of all this year's homework, the Word Implanted is among the most foundational. If you ever find yourself unable to complete most or all of the homework, try at very least to rest in the grace of reading God's word aloud in his presence.

THE WORD IMPLANTED

Several times each week, read the following texts *slowly* and *out loud*. It is generally best to choose one translation and stick with that same version for each of the texts, as repeating the same words out loud will help to more deeply implant them in your mind and heart and will over time help you to commit more and more Scripture to memory.

- Ephesians 4:21–5:2
- Philippians 2:12–16
- 2 Peter 1:1–8
- Psalm 16
- 2 Corinthians 4:6–11
- Mark 12:28b–31

TIP Put reminders on your calendar to help you weave these practices into your rhythms this month. This is an excellent way to begin forming habits that at some point you will likely remember more spontaneously.

TIP As you step into this year's homework, a helpful rule of thumb is this: "Do what you can and not what you can't." Be diligent and focused, to be sure, but when circumstances make it harder to complete some of the work, turn your gaze to God and savor his gracious gaze on you—"He himself knows our frame; he is mindful that we are but dust" (Ps. 103:14 NASB).

OTHER EXERCISES AND PRACTICES

5. As first steps in establishing our 12-for-12 rhythms, the three practices below all focus on cultivating silence and stillness in our lives—slowing down, quieting down, eliminating distraction, and learning to pay attention. You can find further details in "Silence and Stillness," Practice 1 in Appendix A.

    a. Practice "Five Minutes of Stillness." You can do this practice during your regular time with God, or perhaps at another time—consider making it one of the first things you do in the morning or the last things you do before bed. Whatever you decide, practice it several times per week if you can, paying attention to what stands out both in yourself and in the environment where you choose to give it a try.

    b. Eat a quiet meal alone with God. At least a few times over the next month, untether yourself from the usual distractions in order to enjoy a meal with a more conscious awareness of God's presence. Do not listen to, watch, or read anything while you eat. Silence all digital devices and place them in another room. Then, simply sit down in a quiet place alone to eat your meal slowly and silently in the presence of God. Savor the taste and texture of your food, the physical environment around you, and your experience of God's presence with you as you eat. As you enjoy your meal, silently express gratitude to God for your food and for his presence and rest in the quiet simplicity of this very ordinary but also truly sacred time with God.

    c. Take a quiet walk alone with God. Either in your own neighborhood, or perhaps in a park or other quiet, natural place, take at least two walks alone with God this month. Pay attention to sights, sounds, and smells as you walk. Leave your cell phone off or at home, don't hurry as you go, and gently turn your attention to God as you walk, quietly enjoying both his presence and the world around you.

6. Pray for other group members. Hold your 12-for-12 companions before God at least once a week. ✢

Primordium

Grace is a place where what is broken is mended,

where despair is ended,

where what is lost is covered over by the leaves and tendrils not of forgetfulness,

but of a forward remembering,

where hope buds,

and where there is present in ways beyond words
One who in time will bring forth sweet fruit,

even joy,

to hang down in great clusters from the starkest of vines.

ANDY SAPERSTEIN

CHAPTER 2

Spiritual Formation and Christian Community

How good and pleasant it is when God's people live together in unity! . . . For there the Lord bestows his blessing, even life forevermore.

PSALM 133:1, 3B NIV

A new commandment I give to you, that you love one another, even as I have loved you, that you also love one another.

JOHN 13:34 NASB

CHAPTER 2

Spiritual Formation and Christian Community

Our Father who is in heaven,

Hallowed be Your name.

Your kingdom come.

Your will be done,

On earth as it is in heaven.

Give us this day our daily bread.

And forgive us our debts, as we also have

forgiven our debtors.

And do not lead us into temptation, but

deliver us from evil.

MATTHEW 6:9–13, NASB

The Communal Orientation of the Spiritual Life

The Lord's Prayer is profoundly communal in its orientation. Though Jesus encourages us to avoid making a public spectacle of our prayers, and rather to pray in secret to our Father in Heaven (Matt. 6:6), the prayer that he teaches us to pray is ever mindful of the fact that when we come to our Heavenly Father in prayer, we are not alone; we always come as part of his family—the church. We are integrally bound up with the people of God, and so we pray, "*Our* Father... give *us* this day *our* daily bread... forgive *us our* debts as *we* also have forgiven *our* debtors... and do not lead *us* into temptation, but deliver *us* from evil..."

Though we all are part of many groups and communities, we have chosen this year to covenant together as a group of pilgrims traveling along a similar path of spiritual formation. The Psalmist proclaims just how good and pleasant it is when God's people dwell together in unity (Ps. 133:1); the Lord himself assures us that where two or three are gathered in his name, he is present in our midst (Matt. 18:20); the Apostle Peter refers to us as once no people, but now God's people (1 Pet. 2:10); the Apostle Paul exhorts the church in Rome to "be devoted to one another in brotherly love" (Rom. 12:10 NASB); and the author of Hebrews admonishes us not to forsake our assembling together but to encourage one another (Heb. 10:25). In light of both these exhortations and these promises, we commit ourselves in this group to be intentionally aware of one another's lives—to think about one another, meet with one another, pray for one another, confess our sins to one another, reach out to one another between meetings, and to care for one another. This intentionality is one of the chief ways we will strengthen the "one another" cardinal direction in our spiritual lives.

Given these commitments, our assigned readings this year include two books that speak to the communal orientation of 12-for-12 groups:

1.

LIFE TOGETHER
BY DIETRICH BONHOEFFER
An extended meditation on the nature of true Christian community, which Bonhoeffer wrote in 1938 during the dark days of the Confessing Church in Nazi Germany.

2.

SACRED COMPANIONS
BY DAVID BENNER
While written during much less fraught times, this book is nonetheless rich in wisdom regarding the character of the community we hope to form during this year of 12-for-12 together.

The Reality of Christian Community

In *Life Together*, Bonhoeffer asserts that Christian community is first a gift—a privilege, not a right. Throughout the ages, and around the world today, many followers of Jesus live in isolation from other believers due to political or social realities, illness, aging, persecution, imprisonment, and other conditions. Meanwhile, rather than thanking God for the gift, those of us who *do* have access to Christian community often find ourselves focusing on ways it falls short of the idealized notions of community that we entertain in our own imaginations.

Clearly we must cultivate a godly commitment to making our Christian communities better, to addressing legitimate grievances, and to ensuring that toxic and abusive communities are held to account. But Bonhoeffer helpfully calls attention to our idealized notions of Christian community—a "wish dream," in his terms—which often keeps us from embracing and experiencing the objective reality of Christian community as described in the Scriptures: "where two or three have gathered together in My name, I am there in their midst (Matt. 18:20 NASB)", and the fact that "you yourselves are God's temple and that God's Spirit dwells in your midst" (1 Cor. 3:16 NIV). Christian community is the very dwelling place of God, and a sustained, habitual acknowledgment of this reality transforms our perspective. The most ordinary gatherings of God's people become sacred assemblies—they are the context in which we participate with God in the ongoing transformation of ourselves and of the world.

▼

FOR REFLECTION

Have you, out of disappointment or criticism, allowed yourself to pull away from regular participation in Christian community? Is God inviting you to re-engage more fully in the life of the church?

Thus, our eyes are open to and prepared for the fact that the community we experience will be imperfect in very real ways. We are likely to disappoint and offend, or at very least fail to be attentive spiritual companions. At times, hard conversations and spiritual disciplines of confession, repentance, forgiveness, establishing healthy boundaries, accountability, and reparations may be required. Our community will only approximate, but never fully realize, both God's and our own ideals.

Within these tensions, however, we can still look for God's presence and activity in one another's lives and help each other notice and participate more fully in his work of transformation. We join together in hope, for God is in us, among us, and with us. Though we only imperfectly apprehend his grace as we journey together, and only imperfectly love one another, we nonetheless commit ourselves to get up when we fail, dust ourselves off, and together press on once again toward Jesus.

This collective commitment to live godwardly means we will learn over time to better love and support one another. And it means we can help one another identify gifts and graces God has given each of us in order to more fully contribute to his work in the world. We will also learn to notice, admit, and address our failures, both in and beyond this spiritual community, and to extend grace and forgiveness to one another as we do so. Each time we gather and in all of these endeavors, we recognize that God's presence is the heartbeat of all real Christian community, and by faith we trust that we will indeed encounter him whenever we are among the Lord's people.

God's presence is the heartbeat of all real Christian community...

The Value of Spiritual Friendship

FOR REFLECTION

Take a moment to call to mind one or two people who have helped you on your way with God and who perhaps have even become true spiritual friends.

However long you have followed Jesus, you can undoubtedly list at least a few people who have played an important role in your formation as a disciple of Jesus. Several years ago on a long mountain hike I found myself singing a refrain of recalling people who helped me remain on the road with Jesus—"O, Lord, my God, I lift up my heart to you; O, Lord, my God, your people rejoice in you. Thank you for . . ." And beginning with the early days of my life with Jesus in 1979, I sang in thanksgiving for all the people I remembered who had helped me on my way with God. I walked for hours, repeating the song again and again, and calling to mind dozens, if not hundreds of people. Some were simply acquaintances; others were those who deeply shaped my life and accompanied me through longer and more formational seasons. And while even relatively casual acquaintances contributed to my spiritual life in very real ways by virtue of the objective reality of Christ among us, some of the people I sang of stood out as being true spiritual friends. These are people who, according to David Benner, helped me to "discern the presence, will, and leading of the Spirit of God" (Benner 2002, p. 27) in significant and often sustained ways.

Benner describes spiritual friendship as involving three basic gifts that we offer to one another: the gift of *hospitality*, the gift of *presence*, and the gift of *dialogue* (Benner 2002, Ch. 2). The twentieth century French Catholic philosopher, Gabriel Marcel (Marcel 2011, pp. 6–7, 19, 41 ff.), sums up these three gifts with the French word *disponibilité*, best translated in English by the word *availability*. Availability involves an opening of ourselves to God and to one another in both welcome and vulnerability—when we make ourselves truly *available* to one another, we both disclose our true selves to God and to one another and we make it easier for others to do the same. We are permeable to God and to one another, allowing deep and real exchange to occur in both our earthly and our heavenly relationships. In practicing the things that make for mutual availability, there is perhaps nothing more important than good listening—patiently and attentively opening ourselves to deeply receive what we share with one another. Such mutual availability in spiritual friendship requires what Benner calls *mediating grace* (Benner 2002, p. 57), for without the abiding presence of Christ in our midst through his Spirit, we cannot even begin to live out the kind of relationships that approach God's ideal. When Jesus is the gracious mediator at the center of friendships—both those we form in and beyond this group—he shapes their character for our benefit and for his glory. His presence among us is a gift from God. This is especially the case when earthly differences between us are numerous and stark, for God's grace and glory are revealed with particular beauty and clarity when unlikely spiritual friendships form among people who in human terms share very little in common. ✣

# Homework

Each month, remember to read the homework assignment list in its entirety before beginning. This will provide a better sense of what to incorporate into your daily rhythms from the outset of each month. May God bless you as you seek him through these assignments, and may you deeply encounter his grace and presence as you continue this year on the road of spiritual formation.

READING

1. *Life Together*, by Dietrich Bonhoeffer (2009)

    If you are unable to read the entire book this month, read at least chapters 1, 3, and 4. A modern classic written by a martyred German theologian in the years before WWII during the dark days of Nazi rule under Adolf Hitler, *Life Together* explores the rhythms of a life lived in close proximity and relationship to other Christian believers. During the consolidation of Nazi power in the 1930's, Bonhoeffer and the broader community of faithful German brethren stood in costly and courageous opposition to the evils of Nazism and refused to compromise the gospel of Jesus Christ, no matter what the cost. This faithful community came to be referred to as the Confessing Church, and because they stood in opposition to the Nazi regime, its members were, among other things, banned from attending the German seminaries and universities where pastors would normally receive their training. They consequently established a secret seminary and spiritual community of their own in the town of Finkenwalde, and this community of clandestine seminarians formed the context out of which Bonhoeffer ultimately wrote *Life Together*.

    ### AS YOU READ, CONSIDER THE FOLLOWING:

    a. Consider Bonhoeffer's notion of the "wish dream" in regard to your understanding of Christian community. Are there any ways that you have fallen into idealized views of Christian community at the expense of embracing the objective reality of Christ among us? In the weeks ahead, try to notice experiences of the objective reality of Christ's presence in community, no matter how humble and ordinary they might be.

    b. How does solitude contribute to the strength of communal life, and how does communal life contribute to the value and richness of solitude? What do you make of the following quote? "Let him who cannot be alone beware of community. Let him who is not in community beware of being alone."

c. Consider Bonhoeffer's recommendations for weaving various spiritual practices and disciplines into the rhythms of communal life, both in solitary and group contexts. How do solitary encounters with God through practices such as meditation on the Scriptures, prayer, and intercession impact communal life, and vice versa?

d. In chapter 4, Bonhoeffer uses the term "ministry" to describe the simple, concrete, and practical ways we are called to love one another in the context of Christian community. In your own experience of Christian community, what roles do the ministry of holding our tongues, and the ministries of meekness, listening, helpfulness, bearing, proclaiming, and authority play? Which of these ministries is God inviting you to practice in the context of this 12-for-12 group?

e. Consider Bonhoeffer's notion of Christian community as it relates to the cardinal directions of the spiritual life. How did Bonhoeffer envision community members living *upwardly* to God; engaging with God *inwardly* as individuals; living among the people of God in communal, *"one another"* life, devotion, and service; and engaging *outwardly* in love and service to the world?

2. If time permits, look over Chapter 3 and its homework before your next meeting.

THE WORD IMPLANTED

Take time each week to read the following texts *out loud* at least several times. Read the words slowly, varying the intonation each time. It is generally best to stick with one translation for each of the texts, as repeating the same words out loud will help deeply implant them in your mind and heart and will help you commit more and more Scripture to memory.

- Psalm 133
- Romans 12:1–21
- John 13:34–35
- Acts 2:42–47
- I Timothy 1:5

TIP Consider putting reminders on your calendar to help weave these practices into your life rhythms.

OTHER EXERCISES AND PRACTICES

3. Take at least one to two hours to reflect, journal, and act on the "Remembering the Saints" exercise, Practice 2 in Appendix A. Consider devoting some of your regular time with God to this practice. May God meet you and guide your memory as you call to mind the people who have impacted your life with him over the years.

4. Work through the "Prayer of Examen," Practice 3 in Appendix A, several times a week. Try finding a consistent 10–15 minute time slot in your regular daily rhythms and stick with it. The beginning of the day, the drive to or from work, or the end of the workday often works well for many people.

5. Continue to pray for your 12-for-12 group members regularly (at least once a week), lifting them up before the Lord.

6. Practice "Silence and Stillness" in Appendix A. Engage in each of the following practices at least two or three times this month:

   - Five Minutes of Stillness
   - A Quiet Meal with God
   - A Quiet Walk with God

TIP Consider gathering informally with other 12-for-12 members to watch and discuss this film.

RECOMMENDED FILM

Of Gods and Men (2010).

Based on a true story, this winner of the Grand Prize at the Cannes Film Festival tells the story of a community of French Cistercian monks during a time of significant social and religious unrest in Algeria in the 1990's.

AS YOU WATCH, CONSIDER THE FOLLOWING:

1. In what ways do the members of this monastic community both seek out and encounter God (i.e. orient themselves upwardly)? Pay particular attention to the ways the monks are aware of and encounter God in their various "environments" (e.g., physical environment, emotional environment, relational environment, cultural environment, spiritual environment, etc.). Which of these ways are most moving and challenging to you? Why?

2. How do particular monks allow God to work inwardly in them? What does the process look like in different members of this community? What stands out to you?

3. Consider the monks' process of making significant decisions. What most strikes you about their approach? How does God use their relationships with one another to shape them as individuals? How does God use their relationships with one another to sharpen and define their call outward to the world?

4. Recall the scene where the monks sit together in silence, sharing a bottle of fine wine, listening to Tchaikovsky's Swan Lake—a sort of "Last Supper" moment. What about this scene impacts you most deeply? Why?

5. How does this community encounter and participate with God as they interact outwardly with those beyond their walls? How does their relationship with God impact their relationship with the villagers? With the radical Islamist group? With the government and the military?

6. Which monk in this community, or other person in this film, do you most identify with? Why? ✢

NOTES

NOTES

In the Valley of the Elwy

I remember a house where all were good
   To me, God knows, deserving no such thing:
   Comforting smell breathed at very entering,
Fetched fresh, as I suppose, off some sweet wood.
That cordial air made those kind people a hood
   All over, as a bevy of eggs the mothering wing
   Will, or mild nights the new morsels of Spring:
Why, it seemed of course; seemed of right it should.

Lovely the woods, waters, meadows, combes, vales,
All the air things wear that build this world of Wales;
   Only the inmate does not correspond:
God, lover of souls, swaying considerate scales,
Complete thy creature dear O where it fails,
   Being mighty a master, being a father and fond.

GERARD MANLEY HOPKINS

CHAPTER 3

Attentiveness to God

▼

I keep my eyes always on the Lord. With him at my right hand, I will not be shaken.

PSALM 16:8 NIV

▼

The earth is the Lord's and all it contains, the world and those who dwell in it.

PSALM 24:1 NASB

CHAPTER 3

Attentiveness to God

A Life of Actively Noticing God

What we pay attention to and what we actively seek to notice as we go about our everyday affairs comprises much of our spiritual formation. Someone can spend many, many years identifying as a Christian and yet remain largely unchanged, while someone else who may have come to faith only a short time ago can display deep and real transformation in their life. This contrast often exists in significant measure because of differences in how these two persons have oriented themselves in relation to God in the everyday moments that are strung together to make up their respective lives. The larger life decisions we make—the communities we choose to be part of, the people we partner with, the education and career paths we take, the places we live—certainly contribute to our formation. But it is often subtler habits of heart, moment-by-moment ways of being, and imperceptible interior decisions that inform our larger choices and frame the kind of people we ultimately become.

As such, the life-defining habit of attentiveness to God—living with God as our primary reference point at all times—is paramount in the process of our spiritual formation. To what extent do we allow God to mediate and inform every moment of our lives? And to what extent have we made Christ the ever-present hearkening point for every thought, word, feeling, and deed? Much of our spiritual formation rests upon how we answer these questions.

But it is often subtler habits of heart, moment-by-moment ways of being, and imperceptible interior decisions that inform our larger choices and frame the kind of people we ultimately become.

Spirit and Truth

But how can we learn to pay attention to God? Spiritual practices that put us in regular contact with Scripture certainly help, but these habits alone do not turn us godward in the ordinary moments of our lives. Only when we integrate biblical truth and our knowledge of God into habits of heart and the everyday moments of our lives do we experience Scripture's profound and transformational impact. True worship—the turning of ourselves toward God in adoration, and the offering of ourselves to him in sacrificial obedience—is founded on the double helix of Spirit and truth:

> Yet a time is coming and has now come when the true worshipers will worship the Father in the Spirit and in truth, for they are the kind of worshipers the Father seeks. God is spirit, and his worshipers must worship in the Spirit and in truth. (John 4:23–24 NIV)

FOR REFLECTION
How does this idea of praying without ceasing make you more hopeful about cultivating a deeper life of prayer?

We therefore build attentiveness to God into our lives by both engaging with and learning the Bible and by intentionally interacting with God through his Spirit in moment-by-moment ways. This latter is very much what the Apostle Paul means when he instructs us to "pray without ceasing" (1 Thess. 5:17 NASB), for the idea that God intends continual prayer to be a constant stream of intercessions and requests is neither biblical nor feasible. Rather, prayer largely consists of a habit of open and available orientation to God, where we are intentionally aware of and permeable to his presence and the work and leading of the Spirit in real time, even during the most apparently mundane activities of our lives. "Where can I go from Your Spirit? Or where can I flee from Your presence?" the psalmist asks (Ps. 139:7 NASB), not out of a desire to escape from God, but out of the recognition that God actively makes himself available to us in every moment, wherever we may be. We have open access to God and an ever-present invitation to encounter and engage with him at all times and in all places.

The Witness of the Saints

For the saints of old, attentiveness to God was always a foundational part of spiritual life. Abraham pays attention to God's voice when he departs from Haran with his family, not knowing where he is going (Gen. 12:1 ff.). The Hebrew midwives pay attention to God and not Pharoah when they spare the Hebrew boys they deliver. Moses turns aside to the burning bush (Exod. 3:2 ff.), paying attention to this unexpected presence of God, obeying his voice and taking the first step of a lifetime of attentive obedience that would forever characterize him. The prophets pay attention to visions and promptings of God even in evil times. Mary is attentive to God and his messenger when she is called to bear the Messiah in her womb. Jesus notices the evidence and activity of God in the natural world—in the birds of the air and the lilies of the field (Matt. 6:26 ff.)—and invites us to do the same. And in the celebrated "hall of faith" in Hebrews 11, the author speaks of saints who, in the face of great obstacles, are attentive to God in "seeking a country of their own" (Heb. 11:14 NASB).

In the 16th century, Ignatius of Loyola established "finding God in all things" (Warner, p. 16) as the central thrust of both his *Spiritual Exercises* and his overall approach to life and spirituality. In the 17th century, Brother Lawrence of the Resurrection modeled a way of life that his monastic brothers summarized as no more than an "awareness of the presence of God" in the little volume, *The Practice of the Presence of God* (de Beaufort, 1906, p. 50). In the 18th century, the Jesuit mystic Jean-Pierre de Caussade said the aim of the spiritual life is "to keep one's gaze fixed on the master one has chosen and to be constantly listening so as to understand and immediately obey his will" (de Caussade, 1989). The celebrated 19th and 20th century Irish missionary to India, Amy Carmichael, said, "If you refuse to be hurried and pressed, if you stay your soul on God, nothing can keep you from that clearness of spirit which is life and peace (Carmichael 2010)." And Howard Thurman, the celebrated author, theologian, mystic, and civil rights leader, observes that when the core hunger of our soul for God "becomes the core of the individual's consciousness, what was the sporadic act of turning toward God becomes the very climate of the soul" (Howard Thurman, 2003, p. 96). All of these examples share one theme—the priority of *simply paying attention to God*, in both the most ordinary as well as in the most extraordinary circumstances of our lives.

One such extraordinary circumstance occurs in 2 Kings 6. The king of Aram (present-day Syria), enraged at Elisha the prophet, sends his army to surround Elisha and his servant at Dothan. Elisha's servant arises early to find the city surrounded by Aramean horses and chariots:

> "Oh no, my lord! What shall we do?" the servant asked.
> "Don't be afraid," the prophet answered. "Those who are with us are more than those who are with them." And Elisha prayed, "Open his eyes, Lord, so that he may see." Then the Lord opened the servant's eyes, and he looked and saw the hills full of horses and chariots of fire all around Elisha. (2 Kings 6:15b-17 NIV)

In this striking event, while external reality was the same for both Elisha and his servant, only Elisha was initially attuned and attentive to the deliverance that God was bringing. Only when God opened the servant's eyes and, when he was willing to actually look, did he see the activity and provision of God that had been there the whole time. Two people can witness or experience the same situation, and yet only one may be in touch with the presence and activity of God as it unfolds.

Attentiveness in Ordinary Things

An awareness of the presence and activity of God in the extraordinary events of our lives is built upon a foundation of attentiveness to him in the ordinary and routine, and this is a capacity we can actively cultivate in ourselves. The formational exercises and practices that we have already engaged with thus far, as well as those to come this year, have almost all been designed in part to cultivate just such an attentiveness to God in us as a way of life. And as always, it is not the practices or exercises themselves that are the end we are seeking—the end we seek is rather the habits of living and being that these practices help to shape in us in practical ways. "The goal of our instruction," Paul tells Timothy, "is love from a pure heart, a good conscience, and a sincere faith" (1 Tim. 1:5 NASB), and the only hope we have to live such a life is to be ever and always intimately in touch with the God who makes us able to do so.

In the end, it seems, the battle is often won or lost in the small things. The richness of our life with God rises and falls with what we do with our ordinary moments, which taken together make up the minutes and hours, the days, the months, and the years of our lives. May God meet you as you seek his help in living each moment unto him and in inviting him to transform them into a sacred string of pearls offered back as a gift "to him who is able to do immeasurably more than all we ask or imagine, according to his power that is at work within us" (Eph. 3:20 NIV). ✣

Only when God opened the servant's eyes, when he was willing to actually look, did he see the activity and provision of God that had been there the whole time.

Homework

READING

Choose at least one of the following books to read this month:

1. *The Practice of the Presence of God*, by Brother Lawrence (1982)

   This humble collection of the letters, conversations, and reflections of Brother Lawrence of the Resurrection, a 17th century French Carmelite monk, continue after more than three centuries to bear witness to a simple life given over to the pursuit of the presence of God in the most ordinary of everyday circumstances. Spending much of his monastic life in kitchen service and shoe repair, Brother Lawrence never aspired to notoriety or position, but rather simply committed himself to pursuing union with God through abandonment to God, "practicing his presence," and ongoing conversation with God about even the most mundane of things. The abiding value of Brother Lawrence's counsel is to make known to all who live in the world, regardless of status or position, to great and humble alike, the precious and ever-available treasure of the presence of God and the means and motivation to pursue it. This book is widely available online and in libraries for free, as well as in multiple, readily available digital and print editions at low cost.

2. *The Sacrament of the Present Moment*, by Jean-Pierre de Caussade (1989)

   De Caussade's work focuses on what he considers the central duty of the Christian—"to keep one's gaze fixed on the master one has chosen and to be constantly listening so as to understand and hear and immediately obey his will" (p. xiii). This little book assumes that "God speaks to every individual through what happens to them moment by moment" (p. xiii), and therefore teaches us some of what it means to seek and to encounter God in the context of an ordinary day. Originally written in the 18th century, though due to theological conflict in the church not appearing for the first time until 1861 under the title *Self-Abandonment to Divine Providence*, *The Sacrament of the Present Moment* still stands as a wonderful resource for anyone who wants to learn to redeem the sacredness of ordinary moments in an ordinary life.

   The Sacrament of the Present Moment is available for free online, though the HarperCollins edition (translated by Kitty Muggeridge, and with a helpful introduction by Richard Foster) is worth the modest investment.

3. *Beginning To Pray*, by Anthony Bloom (1970)

   Written by an atheist convert to the Christian faith who went on to become a Russian Orthodox priest and bishop, this little volume has come to be viewed as a modern classic on prayer. Original in tone, and with short chapters entitled "The Absence of God," "Knocking at the Door," "Going Inward," "Managing Time," and "Addressing God," as well as a wonderful autobiographical introduction, *Beginning To Pray* leads us in refreshingly simple and practical ways to embrace an increasingly godward life and is very much worth its barely over a hundred pages.

4. If time permits, look over Chapter 4 and its homework before your next meeting.

THE WORD IMPLANTED

Over the next month, take time each week to read one of the following texts out loud several times. Read them slowly, varying the emphasis and intonation if you want, but please choose a version of the Scriptures and stick with that same version for each of the texts. Repeating the same words out loud will really help implant these words in your mind and heart.

- Psalm 24
- Psalm 27
- Psalm 46
- Psalm 104

OTHER EXERCISES AND PRACTICES

5. Take regular times over the course of this month to periodically read the "Breath Prayers," Practice 4 in Appendix A, out loud. Without overthinking, incorporate different ones of these prayers into your daily life as you find yourself drawn to them and as they rise up spontaneously in your prayers.

6. Continue practicing the "Prayer of Examen," Practice 3 in Appendix A, at least a few times a week.

   As you practice the "Prayer of Examen" this month, choose one day each week to write a journal entry about your experience with this practice, for a total of four journal entries over the course of the month. Pay special attention to note in each of your entries when in the day you were most and least aware of and attentive to God. In order to give you a broader sample of the normal rhythms of your life, you might consider choosing a different day of the week for

TIP Try to incorporate the prayer of examen into existing normal rhythms of your life—during your daily commute, or while folding the laundry, walking the dog, etc.

each journal entry, or at least selecting the days you choose from among both weekdays and weekends. Finally, read over the four journal entries you have written, and write a final journal entry in which you note any patterns you notice regarding the times in your normal days when you are most aware of and attentive to God, and the times in your normal days when you are least aware of and attentive to God. Your leader may invite you or some other members of your group to share about what you have noticed, so be prepared to do so at your next group meeting.

7. Continue to pray for the other members of your 12-for-12 group, committing to at least occasionally lifting and holding them up before God.

8. Choose one or more practices you find helpful from the "Silence and Stillness" practice in Appendix A and engage with it this month:

    - Five Minutes of Stillness
    - A Quiet Meal with God
    - A Quiet Walk with God

RECOMMENDED FILM

Tender Mercies (1983)

Watch and reflect on the film, *Tender Mercies*. Robert Duvall won Best Actor honors for his performance in this film, which focuses on the failure and redemption of a country singer in small town Texas and whose title hearkens from language often used in the King James translation of the Psalms. As you watch this film, pay particular attention to the contrast between Mac Sledge and his ex-wife, Dixie, and the ways they do or do not lay hold of and experience the grace of God in the face of difficulty and pain. In what people and circumstances do you most notice God's tender mercies in the life of Mac, his new wife, Rosa Lee, and her son, Sonny? What are some of the specific ways that God reveals his grace and mercy to these three people? What are some of the ways that they or others resist God's grace and mercy? Even as the film ends, and Mac asks searching questions of God, how would you say that God answers those questions? What ways does this film most speak to your own current experience and life circumstances? Where in the ordinary people and circumstances of your life do you most notice the presence and activity of God and his tender mercies toward you?

As a matter of interest, much of the background music in the soundtrack of this film is performed by Robert Duvall himself. ✣

Silence

The silence is thick—
Laden with more than fine snow
falling through fresh morning air,
Than redbud pods trembling against steely skies,
Than salty stains on curbs and cars and tired streets.
She lies heavy and still like smoke above a sleeping city,
Pressing herself softly, as goose down in Egyptian cotton
That lies upon my weary frame.
And she speaks—wordlessly,
Yet more eloquently than orators who,
Though steeped in spoken things,
Cannot compare to the lilt of what flows from her lips.
No, her voice echoes in canyons not of our making,
And reverberates beyond the reach
Of days and hours and the tread of time.
Her speech, unspoken, plumbs deep places
And persuades with more power than heroes or demagogues
In all their wit.
For she makes space for other voices, and truer ones,
Who shun shouting and the bluster of our own intentions,
And invite us into places where we can once again hear
What we ourselves can never speak—
The voice that is not our own.

ANDY SAPERSTEIN

CHAPTER 4

Who Is God?

▼

For since the creation of the world God's invisible qualities—his eternal power and divine nature—have been clearly seen, being understood from what has been made . . .

ROMANS 1:20 NIV

▼

On the glorious splendor of Your majesty and on Your wonderful works, I will meditate.

PSALM 145:5 NASB

CHAPTER 4

Who Is God?

Our Ideas About God

In his 1961 book, *The Knowledge of the Holy*, A.W. Tozer famously states that "what comes into our minds when we think about God is the most important thing about us" (Tozer, 2009, p. 1). Of those things we have some measure of control over, one of the most formational aspects of our lives is our view of God—who we understand God to be and what we understand God to be like. Our ideas about God impact everything about our lives. They impact whether we choose to believe in God at all and whether we choose to relate to God, and if we choose to relate, they impact the character of that relationship. Our ideas about God impact whether we expect God to communicate with us at all, and if so, how we might expect God to communicate. And our ideas about God impact how seriously we take what we believe God to be communicating, if and when God does so.

Our ideas about God also impact the things we choose to prioritize and the things we choose to ignore or avoid. Our ideas about God deeply influence who we choose to build relationships with and the quality and character of the relationships we choose to build. Our ideas about God impact what we do with our money, with our work, with our time, with our bodies, with our words, and with our possessions. Our ideas about God impact our notions of family, community, politics, sexuality, and world events. Whether we recognize it or not, our ideas about God deeply shape our sense of values and ethics in every domain of life and disproportionately influence the kind of people we turn out to be. It is no exaggeration for A.W. Tozer to have said that our ideas about God are the most important thing about us.

But if our ideas about God are so important, how can we ensure that they are the right ideas? What are some of the best ways to shape our ideas about God so that they give us an accurate understanding of God and form us into people who reflect and bear witness to God's character and attributes? Maintaining a deep connection to the Scriptures, a living openness to God through his Spirit, an unyielding focus on Jesus himself, and a rootedness in core spiritual practices such as those outlined in this manual, provide a good place to start.

Peter's Experiences with God in Acts

Approximately 10 percent of the entire Acts narrative is devoted to the Apostle Peter's experience with God in his encounter with the Roman centurion Cornelius and his family. Found in Acts 10 and 11, this account provides a helpful framework for some of the ways we might expect God to shape our ideas about him. There is much to learn by paying close attention to the multiple ways that God reveals himself to Peter over the course of these events and to the ways they impact the emergence of the early church. Peter's ideas of God are dramatically shaped by these central events in Luke's narrative. And Peter's later references to these same events in Acts 15, his ongoing transformation and ministry in their wake, as well as his own letters, 1 and 2 Peter, helped shape others' ideas of God, as well.

God reveals himself to Peter through:

- Open visions on the roof of Simon the Tanner's house
- Speaking directly to Peter by the Holy Spirit
- Concurrently revealing himself to Cornelius in ways that remarkably overlap with what he reveals to Peter
- Peter's own testimony about the death and resurrection of Jesus and what that testimony means for the Gentiles
- Peter witnessing the Holy Spirit dramatically fall on Cornelius and his household upon hearing his testimony
- Peter's retelling before the Jerusalem church of John the Baptist's words about Jesus
- James quoting the Scriptures—both the Pentateuch and the prophets—to help the Jerusalem council interpret the experiences of Peter, Paul, and Barnabas with the Gentiles
- The deliberation of God's people

Through all these means, Peter and the emerging church came to increasingly know who God was, what he was like, and what he was doing in the world. We too can expect our own widely varied encounters with God to shape our understanding of who God is and what he is like.

Our ideas about God impact everything about our lives.

Jesus and the Scriptures

Even in the limited events involving Cornelius and his family, God reveals himself to Peter and others "in many portions and in many ways" (Heb. 1:1 NASB). We learn who God is through the witness of the Scriptures, the natural world, divine revelation, the work of the Holy Spirit, the witness of God's people, and our own lived experience. However, there is simply no fuller revelation of the person of God than Jesus himself, the Christ, the Son of God. He is "the visible image of the invisible God" (Col. 1:15 NLT). He is "the radiance of God's glory and the exact representation of his being..." (Heb. 1:3 NIV).

To the extent that we know Christ, we know both God the Father and God the Spirit. "We proclaim to you," the Apostle John says, "the one who existed from the beginning, whom we have heard and seen. We saw him with our own eyes and touched him with our own hands. He is the Word of life" (1 John 1:1 NLT). Because God reveals himself to us most fully in Christ, we are called to embrace a deeply intentional Christ-centered existence. In order to do that, we focus our attention on the written word of God—the Bible, the Holy Scriptures—where Old Testament prophets paint vivid and poetic pictures of the coming Christ and where Jesus' friends tell us what he said, what he did, and what he was like. We rely on these diverse accounts to testify to our hearts, and "to teach us what is true and to make us realize what is wrong in our lives" (1 Tim. 3:16a NLT). Like the noble-minded Bereans, we eagerly receive the word about Jesus and search the Scriptures to discern what is true about him (Acts 17:11). In the end, to the extent that our knowledge of God diverges from what the Scriptures teach about him, and from the person of Christ himself, our faith will become distorted and anemic, and our entire lives at risk of becoming similarly weak and misshapen. Conversely, to the extent that our knowledge of God is full and rich and touches on the breadth of God's attributes and character as revealed in Christ and in the Scriptures, we will be increasingly open to encountering, responding to, and being shaped by God in ways consistent with his attributes and character.

Knowing God as Whole Persons

In the end, however, it is not merely what and who we pay attention to that matters, or where we look for God, but just as importantly how we look for him, and what parts of ourselves we actually engage as we seek to pay attention to him and know him. Jesus tells us to "love the Lord your God with all your heart and with all your soul and with all your mind and with all your strength" (Mark 12:30 NIV). This means that we engage our bodies, all five of our senses, our minds, our emotions, our capacity to choose—all of who we are—as we seek to know God. The exercises and practices in this and other chapters in this manual will help you engage with God as a whole person—heart, soul, mind, and strength—that you might grow "in every way more and more like Christ" (Eph. 4:15b NLT). May God meet you as you seek to know him better!

Homework

READING

Complete at least *one* of the first two reflective reading assignments below.

TIP Read through the entire list of homework exercises before you begin, and get started as soon as you can. You will benefit far more from the assigned readings and exercises if you consistently engage with them over the course of the month, and not in a more last-minute, concentrated push at the end.

1. *The Knowledge of the Holy*, by A.W. Tozer (1961)

    As you read about the various attributes of God, keep these questions of Tozer's in mind:

    1. WHAT IS GOD LIKE?

    2. WHAT SETS GOD APART FROM ALL ELSE?

    3. HOW MAY WE EXPECT GOD TO ACT TOWARD US?

    AS YOU READ, REFLECT AND JOURNAL ON THE FOLLOWING:

    a. Take some time to sit with and reflect on several of the attributes of God that you find particularly exciting, moving, challenging, or new to you.

    b. Select four of the attributes of God that particularly stood out for you as you read the book. For each one, write a short prayer acknowledging and offering praise and thanks to God for that attribute. You may also choose to meditate on some of the scriptures that Tozer references for each particular attribute, or on other scriptures of your own choosing, or to read aloud the prayers Tozer includes at the beginning of each chapter.

TIP If you have never read the Book of Isaiah or the Gospel of John in their entirety, you might consider this option over *The Knowledge of the Holy*—more than any other book, no matter how good, the Scriptures are our best starting point for learning who God is and what God is like.

2. The Book of Isaiah and the Gospel of John in their entirety

   a. As you read, mark in your Bible everywhere you notice the following:

   1. AN ATTRIBUTE OF GOD

   2. A NAME FOR GOD

   3. ANYTHING ELSE YOU NOTICE ABOUT GOD

   b. After each chapter, jot down (either in the margin of your Bible or in your journal) at least two or three names for God or words that best describe what you noticed and learned about God as you read that chapter.

   c. Then choose four of the attributes of God that particularly stood out for you as you read the books. For each one, write a short prayer acknowledging and offering praise and thanks to God for that attribute. As part of this process, take time to meditate on some of the relevant passages from Isaiah and John.

3. If time permits, look over Chapter 5 and its homework before your next meeting.

REFLECTION AND JOURNALING

Choose *one* of the following exercises to deepen your apprehension of the character and attributes of God:

4. Read Acts 10:1–11:21 and Acts 15:1–31 two times. These texts tell a story of spiritual formation in the life of the Apostle Peter, among Cornelius and his family, in the Jewish church, in the emerging Gentile church, and in all church history, and reveal a great deal about God and about the ways God chooses to reveal himself. They also demonstrate the impact that one transformed life—in this case the life of the Apostle Peter—can have on both Christian community and on the outward progress of God's kingdom in the world.

   AS YOU READ, REFLECT AND JOURNAL ON THE FOLLOWING:

   a. On the roof in Joppa, Peter initially resists the Lord's command to "kill and eat." Yet as the events unfold with Cornelius, Peter not only changes his perspective, but becomes the chief advocate for God's open door to the Gentiles. What do you think most impacted Peter in these events and led to his own transformation and change of perspective? How would you describe Peter's reactions at various stages of this transformational journey?

    b. List all the ways you see God revealing himself through these events, both directly and indirectly. What do you notice about God's attributes, priorities, and character through these events? How does this make you feel?

    c. How would you describe the change that takes place among the Jewish believers when they challenge Peter in both Acts 11 and in Acts 15? How do these changes impact the progress of the Gospel among the Gentiles? What is your response to these ripple effects of Peter's transformation through the church and into Gentile communities? Write a simple prayer of thanks and praise to God that captures some of what you have noticed and felt.

5. Read Matthew 16:13–20 slowly aloud. Read the story aloud again, but this time pause, close your eyes, and imagine that you are in the story as one of Jesus' disciples. Imagine all that you'd sense as you walk the road with Jesus, arriving at the city of Caesarea Philippi. What do you see, hear, smell, touch, taste? As you walk along, imagine Jesus turning to you and asking, "What about you, who do you say that I am?" Pause a moment before you answer Jesus. What do you feel? What are you thinking? Why would Jesus ask you this question? What is your reaction as you hear the other disciples' answers and Peter's answer? A few times over the course of this month, respond again to this question that Jesus asks of you and journal your response to him.

THE WORD IMPLANTED

Over the next month, take time each week to read the following texts out loud several times. Choose one translation and read them slowly, varying the emphasis and intonation in different readings. Repeating the same words out loud will help implant these words in your mind and heart.

- Psalm 103
- Isaiah 40
- Romans 1:18–20
- Colossians 1:15–20
- Hebrews 1:1–4
- 1 John 4:7–16

OTHER EXERCISES AND PRACTICES

6. Work on "Who Is God? Who Are We?," Practice 5 in Appendix A.

    a. Read aloud through the brief "Who Is God?" and "Who Are We?" statements to familiarize yourself with them.

    b. Throughout the month, read the statements aloud again at least twice a week and begin to make them into prayers of your own. For example: "You are the Lord of Hosts, O God, and I worship you!" "You know me, O God, and I open my life up to you." "You love me, O God, and I rest in your love."

    c. Add to both lists as you read the Scriptures and discover further statements about God and yourself and as you continue to reflect on who God is and who God has made you to be.

7. Go through "*Lectio Divina,*" Practice 6 in Appendix A, with at least two of the Word Implanted texts this month.

8. Continue to hold your 12-for-12 companions before God in prayer.

9. Incorporate into your rhythms one or more of the previous months' practices that you have found helpful.

RECOMMENDED FILM

Signs (2002)

This M. Night Shyamalan science fiction film tells the story of Graham Hess, a preacher who has lost his faith after his wife dies in a terrible auto accident. Father Hess, his son, his daughter, and his brother Merrill, who live together in a farmhouse in eastern Pennsylvania, encounter a group of aliens whose presence first becomes known through mysterious crop circles in the surrounding cornfields. The action centers on how the family protects themselves from the aliens and on how these events shape Father Hess's understanding of God.

AS YOU WATCH, CONSIDER THE FOLLOWING:

1. What has Father Hess come to believe about God? What led him to believe this? How do these beliefs about God impact his life overall?

TIP At perhaps the lowest point in the film, Father Hess tells God that he hates him. Have painful experiences in your life ever led you to feel or speak out similar sentiments?

2. In addition to his wife's tragic death, several other challenges—his son's asthma, his daughter's obsession with glasses of water, and Merrill's failure as a professional baseball player—all impact the Hess family home and shape Father Hess's understanding of God. How, at the end of this film, do these very challenges, including his wife's untimely death, impact Father Hess's faith? In what ways are his wife's dying words significant in helping his perspectives to change?

God's Grandeur

The world is charged with the grandeur of God.
    It will flame out, like shining from shook foil;
    It gathers to a greatness, like the ooze of oil
Crushed. Why do men then now not reck his rod?
Generations have trod, have trod, have trod;
    And all is seared with trade; bleared, smeared with toil;
    And wears man's smudge and shares man's smell: the soil
Is bare now, nor can foot feel, being shod.

And for all this, nature is never spent;
    There lives the dearest freshness deep down things;
And though the last lights off the black West went
    Oh, morning, at the brown brink eastward, springs—
Because the Holy Ghost over the bent
    World broods with warm breast and with ah! bright wings.

GERARD MANLEY HOPKINS

CHAPTER 5

Who Am I?: Patterns of Grace

▼

So God created human beings in his own image. In the image of God he created them; male and female he created them.

GENESIS 1:27 NLT

▼

For You formed my inward parts; You wove me in my mother's womb. I will give thanks to You, for I am fearfully and wonderfully made . . .

PSALM 139:13–14A NASB

CHAPTER 5

Who Am I?: Patterns of Grace

Christian Identity is a Cord of Three Strands:

1.
IMAGO DEI

2.
IMAGO HOMINIS

3.
RESTORATION IN CHRIST

In these first months of 12-for-12, as we established the overall framework of the cardinal directions, we turned our attention *upward* to God and to our life with *one another*. It is now time to turn our attention *inward* in order to understand ourselves more fully and to allow God to transform us more completely.

Because we can only rightly do this in relationship to God, we have first considered who God is and renewed our direct connection to him. And because we so often come to know ourselves best in the context of rooted relationship with others—particularly with others who are similarly devoted to the ways of Jesus—we formed this group and spent initial time more intentionally attending to our life with one another. With the reference point of God himself on the one hand, and his people on the other, we are situated to turn our gaze to ourselves.

There are three facets of Christian identity that help us understand ourselves before God. First, in the creation account in Genesis 1, we learn that God created human beings in his image—the *imago dei*. Much theological ink has been spilled exploring the depths of this truly remarkable statement in Genesis, and if we are to press more fully into our own formation in Christ, we too must give it our due attention.

Though it is to be fully realized only in eternity, we must allow the *imago dei* in ourselves to shape every aspect of our lives, here and now, for the inherent beauty and sacredness of human beings, who more than any other aspect of creation reflect the character of their Creator. Thus, we must allow the *imago dei* to inform the way we not only view ourselves, but how we live, or we can never hope to go far in our formation in Christ.

Second, in the account of the Fall in Genesis 3, Adam and Eve depart from the *imago dei* in themselves, which gives rise to the image of man apart from God—*imago hominis*—and to this day the Fall diminishes and distorts the beauty and grace that God placed in us as his appointed image bearers. Both human history and personal experience reveal the many ways we have so profoundly misshapen God's intended design, and the Scriptures similarly bear consistent witness to the impact of sin on every aspect of our lives:

> Then the Lord saw that the wickedness of man was great on the earth, and that every intent of the thoughts of his heart was only evil continually. (Gen. 6:5 NASB)

> The heart is more deceitful than all else and is desperately sick … (Jer. 17:9 NASB)

> There is no one who does good. (Ps. 14: 1, 53: 1 NASB)

> All have sinned and fall short of the glory of God. (Rom. 3:23 NASB)

> When Adam sinned, sin entered the world. Adam's sin brought death, so death spread to everyone, for everyone sinned. (Rom. 5:12 NLT)

Any approach to spiritual formation that fails to address our propensity toward sin and its particular patterns in our lives will significantly miss the mark.

Third, Jesus coming in the flesh, offering himself on the cross for our sake, and rising in power from the grave is the basis of our re-formation. As his broken yet sacred image bearers, two things animate our formation in Christ: the triune God's abiding love for us and his unyielding commitment to restore us and all creation to glory.

Any approach to spiritual formation that fails to address our propensity toward sin and its particular patterns in our lives will significantly miss the mark.

We are created in God's image, distorted by sin, and are able, because of Christ's love, to walk toward full restoration and reformation in him. And because any encounter with his love is as an unearned gift of grace, grasping the depth and breadth of our identity in Christ requires that we learn to notice the particular patterns and gifts of grace he has woven into each of our lives.

FOR REFLECTION
Do you have a particular "lean?" Do you find yourself more likely to focus on your sinfulness—*imago hominis*—or on your own creation in the image of God—the *imago dei*? Why do you think this is?

In different streams of the church, there is sometimes a tendency to focus on only one of the first two strands—*imago dei* or *imago hominis*—at the expense of the other. In more theologically liberal contexts, sin's impact on the *imago de*i is often downplayed. In more theologically conservative circles, the tendency is to focus on human depravity. By squarely facing the cross and resurrection of Christ, however, we also face these two primary facets of our identity: the people God has created us to be and the people we have become due to sin. In that tension we receive a gift of new life that undoes the latter and restores us to the former. As we work out the salvation and new life we have in Christ, we must always factor in both the patterns of grace that come to us by virtue of our original creation and our re-creation in Christ, as well as the residual patterns of sin still resident in us on account of the Fall.

Stewards of Grace

In his first letter to scattered first-century believers, the Apostle Peter charges his readers to employ the gifts of grace given to them "as good stewards of the manifold grace of God" (1 Peter 4:10 NASB). In referring to this "manifold grace," Peter uses the same Greek word used in the Septuagint to describe the coat of many colors—the "varicolored tunic"—that Joseph was given by his father, Jacob. For Peter, God gives grace to each of us in beautifully varied ways—the grace of salvation, the grace of spiritual gifts, and the widely varied graces of relationship, resource, culture, family, education, opportunity, and experience that make up each of our lives.

God invites us to carefully steward this beautiful and unique "varicolored tunic" of grace. This entails learning to identify and develop the particular gifts and graces he has given to us, so that we can do "good works, which God prepared beforehand, that we should walk in them" (Eph. 2:10b RSV). Much of the homework in this chapter is intended to help you do just that and to help you grow as a good steward of the particular graces God has chosen to place in you.

Abiding in the Love of God

The love of God is the starting point for each strand in the cord of self-understanding. To be created in his image is to experience a foundational act of divine love. To sin is to depart from the shelter of God's love. To be restored alongside all creation to the fullness of what we are intended to be is an act of the love of God in Christ. No matter which aspect of our formation in Christ or which of the cardinal directions we attend to, we must first and foremost learn to abide in God's love. How can we do this?

We read throughout the Scriptures of the love of God, and though God's love for his people has always remained faithful, we have often moved in and out from under its shelter. Jesus puts it this way in The Parable of the Vine and the Branches: "Just as the Father has loved me, I have loved you; abide in my love. If you keep my commandments, you will abide in my love" (John 15:9-10, NASB). In this statement, Jesus both affirms God's love for us and links it centrally to our obedience—to the way we conform our lives to Jesus and to his intended plan for us. To disobey God and to reject his intended plan leaves us feeling distant from God and separated from his love. God's love for us has not changed, but we are no longer abiding in it; it is as though there is a warm house with a fire crackling in the fireplace, but we choose to sit on the porch in the cold.

Also, as we have followed Jesus, many of us have at one time or another encountered the love of God through his direct intervention or a strong sense of his presence during a singular life event or experience. But all-in-all, our awareness and experience of the love of God is spotty at best—we often go through most days either vaguely aware or completely unaware of God's active presence and love. The Jesuit poet Gerard Manley Hopkins declared, "I say that we are wound with mercy round and round as if with air." Increasing our awareness of this ever-present mercy and love of God stands as another focus of this and next month's homework. For to fully embrace the reality of both the patterns of grace and the patterns of sin at work in our lives, we must be ever and always rooted in the love of God.

For to fully embrace the reality of both the patterns of grace and the patterns of sin at work in our lives, we must be ever and always rooted in the love of God.

Additional Approaches to Self-Understanding

Beyond traditionally Christian approaches, there are also many frameworks for understanding individual temperament, personality, and behavior, some of which are included in the homework below. Since ancient times, people have observed patterns of behavior that cluster in particular people in particular ways and have organized those patterns into a variety of explanatory frameworks to help make sense of them all. Ancient Greek and Roman medicine referred to four personality types based on the interaction of body fluids and divided people into four groups—phlegmatic, choleric, sanguine, and melancholic—and these ideas have persisted in various forms since. Freudian psychoanalysis continues to deeply influence our perspectives on why we do what we do and how we explain patterns of behavior in individuals and groups. From Myers-Briggs to the Enneagram to DiSC to Clifton StrengthsFinder, it is likely that you have at least heard of one or more of these approaches, taken one or more diagnostic personality tests, and perhaps pursued some of them more deeply at some point.

In 12-for-12, we seek to give primacy to the Scriptures in all we do, including in regard to our own self-understanding, though we still recognize the great value of resources found outside of the Bible, as all truth is God's truth. Beyond the Christian tradition, resources from medicine, social science, clinical counseling, physical and biological science, and the humanities all provide resources useful to our life with Jesus. This said, we engage with all resources in light of Scripture, and we do not ascribe to them the same level of authority as we do God's revealed word. With ongoing reliance on God's word, on wise and healthy Christian counsel and community, and on the living work of the Holy Spirit in our lives, God provides the foundation for all we need to grow "complete in Christ" (Col. 1:28 NIV). As we steadfastly engage with God in these timeless ways and hold in proper balance the tools of self-understanding that may come and go from age to age, we will best ensure our ongoing formation in the way of Jesus.

Homework

READING

1. *The Gift of Being Yourself: The Sacred Call to Self-Discovery*, by David G. Benner (2015)

    Benner asserts that there cannot be deep knowledge of God without deep knowledge of oneself. This book contains a helpful discussion of our calling, our gifting, our sin, and of our being beloved by God, and helps us approach sin not merely as patterns of external behavior, but as ways rooted more deeply within us, and provides some of the beginning ways of grace in helping us overcome them. There are helpful exercises throughout the book, all of which you can complete in under two hours. The exercise at the end of Chapter 5 in *The Gift of Being Yourself* is particularly helpful and is included in the Chapter 6 homework of this book.

2. If time permits, look over Chapter 6 and its homework before your next meeting.

THE WORD IMPLANTED

Practice the repeated oral reading of Scripture again this month using the following Word Implanted texts:

- Psalm 103:8–18
- Lamentations 3:21–26
- John 17:20–26
- 1 Peter 4:10–11
- 1 John 4:16–19

OTHER EXERCISES AND PRACTICES

3. Work through the images and texts in the *visio divina* exercise titled "Encounters with the Love of God" in Appendix B.

4. Set aside some focused time to complete the "Biblical Personality Reflection," Practice 7 in Appendix A, being sure to journal your observations and reflections.

5. Several times this month, pray the "Expanded Jesus Prayer," Practice 8 in Appendix A, out loud as part of your devotional time, when you are driving in the car, working out, on a walk, etc. Consider memorizing this simple prayer and making it your own for use at times when other forms of prayer are harder to engage in.

6. Complete an assessment for at least one of the following more recent approaches to self-understanding. If you are already familiar with these tools and assessments, spend some time further exploring your particular profile in one or more of these frameworks.

    - *Myers-Briggs Type Indicator* (MBTI) Based on Swiss psychiatrist Carl Jung's theory of personality and later developed by Katharine Cook Briggs, Isabel Briggs Myers,

David Keirsey and others, the Myers-Briggs Type Indicator (MBTI) approaches personality according to four primary aspects of personality divided into 16 specific types. *Truity.com* or *16Personalities.com*

- *Enneagram* Of debated origin, the Enneagram has gained traction in Christian circles in recent years, in part due to the writing of Richard Rohr and others. The Enneagram divides people into nine patterned types and multiple subtypes and can help identify and build on patterns of constructive behavior as well as anticipate and avoid patterns of unconstructive behavior. *Truity.com*

- *StrengthsFinder* (Clifton Strengths) A widely used and respected tool in business and industry that helps identify and build on areas of strength, especially as regards work teams and vocation. Based on a detailed test, CliftonStrengths will (for a fee) help you identify and rank your five greatest strengths out of 34 distinct categories, as well as provide input and resources to help you best steward your strengths. *gallup.com/cliftonstrengths/en/254033/strengthsfinder.aspx*

7. Take time each week to practice *lectio divina* with at least one of the five Word Implanted texts above.

8. Continue to incorporate into your rhythms one or more of the previous months' practices that you have found helpful, e.g. Five Minutes of Stillness, A Quiet Meal with God, A Quiet Walk with God, the Prayer of Examen, etc.

RECOMMENDED FILMS

Watch and reflect on *at least one* of the two films below.

1. *Chariots of Fire* (1981)

    This Academy Award-winning film tells the true story of the celebrated British running team in the 1924 Paris Olympics. It focuses on the lives of two members of that team—Eric Liddell, born in China into a devout missionary family and Harold Abrahams, a brilliant secular Jewish man with a background in business and finance. The film has much to say about submission to God and good stewardship of his grace.

AS YOU WATCH, CONSIDER THE FOLLOWING:

    a. Note the differences between Liddell's and Abrahams's approach to running. What motivates each man?

    b. Reflect on Eric Liddell's conversation with his sister, who considers running a trivial pursuit. What do you make of Liddell's famous statement: "When I run, I feel his pleasure"?

    c. In what ways was Liddell's refusal to run on Sunday consistent with both his broader convictions and his reason for running in the first place?

    d. What aspect of this film most impacted you and why?

2. *The Last Emperor* (1987)

   This three-hour Academy Award-winning biographical film focuses on the life of Puyi, the last emperor of China, who was removed from his reign during epic changes in China in the first half of the 20th century. It is an excellent story of how a man wrestles with his own identity in the face of massive upheaval and external change and how he comes to understand himself in the end. While rated PG-13, it is not light fare. Check the IMDb Parent's Guide for a content summary. *imdb.com/title/tt0093389/parentalguide*

   AS YOU WATCH, CONSIDER THE FOLLOWING:

       a. How is Puyi's identity formed during his childhood and early adulthood, and how do his subsequent circumstances and relationships lead him to a very different understanding of himself?

       b. Which characters are particularly influential in Puyi's journey of self-understanding? What are your thoughts about the way these people influence him?

       c. What are Puyi's greatest weaknesses and liabilities? Why?

       d. How does Puyi's path to a better understanding of himself relate to your own self-understanding journey?

NOTES

what can a poem do?

a poem cannot save a life
cannot Luke Cage your skin
fend off a dark alley attack
cannot make you less woman
or less poor
or less Black
and
thus
treated equally

a poem cannot stop a bullet
stop a bomb
stop terror on your doorstep
your step
even with poem in hand
could be your last
a blast would turn the paper poem is written on into dust
particles
   simile up in smoke
metaphors
   just molecules forgotten

a poem cannot turn back time's hand
erase mistakes made
or cut, copy, paste memories
a poem cannot delete history's horrors

but a poem can love
   like hold you and scold you at the same time
a poem can rip away the untruths that have cocooned us
a poem can make you butterfly
   not fly
   you already fly
but a poem can make you float
no need to watch your step

quiet as kept
a poem can introduce you to yourself
help you discover those hidden
   forbidden parts
a poem be like a mirror sometimes
help you see the crust in your eyes
and the plank

on second thought
a poem can save a life
like wise words granddaddy whispered
like the layer of truth just below the scriptures

a poem cannot stop a bullet
but can swallow the hate and spit back
   a sonnet
that sonic booms
a room till
quotes
float like balloons
goblins and goons

soon just nod their heads
snap their fingers
to what's written and said

isn't it ironic

they say the pen is mightier than the sword
but there were few writers on my block
mostly fighters on my block
dropouts that pulled all-nighters on my block
they'd blue and red light us on my block
then indict us on my block
what if there were more writers on my block

on your block
in every barrio and borough
conclave and commonwealth
courtroom and capitol hill
what if they all spilled ink
on pages
allowed the innerworkings of their hearts
to scribble a poem or two

I wonder where we'd be if the masses knew
just what a poem could do.

DARIUS V. DAUGHTRY
Poetry, June 2021 (used by permission of the author)

CHAPTER 6

Who Am I?: Patterns of Sin

▼

Oh, what a miserable person I am! Who will free me from this life that is dominated by sin and death? Thank God! The answer is in Jesus Christ our Lord.

ROM 7:24–25A NLT

▼

Search me, O God, and know my heart; Try me and know my anxious thoughts; And see if there be any hurtful way in me, and lead me in the everlasting

PSALM 39:23–24 NASB

CHAPTER 6

Who Am I?: Patterns of Sin

The Conundrum of Sin

We might prefer to remain focused on the gifts and graces God has given us, both by our creation and through our new life in Christ. And this we must continue to do. But if this is all we do, we fail to deal with reality. If in our quest for self-understanding we focus only on what is good and beautiful and part of God's original intention, we neglect to take into account the ways we distort and deface that good intention. We will live a fantasy life, unable to receive the restored life God makes possible through Christ's death and resurrection.

Likewise, if we flippantly minimize our sin or become despairingly overwhelmed by it, we will similarly miss the mark. To truly walk forward in our lives with Jesus, we must be aware of both the people God has created us to be and the people we actually *are*—we must attend to patterns of grace *and* patterns of sin. Only as we grow more deeply secure in God's abiding love for us are we able to keep both of these realities before us.

Paul encourages us in Romans 12:3 not to think more highly of ourselves than we ought, but to think of ourselves with sober judgment, in accordance with the faith God has distributed to each of us (NIV). Both the overestimation and the underestimation of the patterns of grace and sin in our lives lead us to think more highly of ourselves than we ought and therefore cloud our ability to know and understand ourselves rightly. For both optimistic arrogance and pessimistic despair separate us from the power of God's love and grace and deprive us of our healthy need for both God and others. We either arrogantly believe we have need for neither God nor others or despairingly believe that neither God nor others can offer us any real help. Both attitudes overestimate our own significance and power and underestimate both God's redemptive love and our need for it. We do best when we hold ourselves in a posture of attentive and clearheaded awareness, possessing a holy and humble openness before God regarding both the working of God's grace in our lives as well as our own sin. We should therefore be neither surprised by nor oblivious to our own sin. The sobriety Paul encourages requires a cultivated ability to unflinchingly apprehend and acknowledge our own sin and its impact on others, while at the same time resting in the assurance of God's love and its capacity to transform us. This posture is modeled in several of this month's Word Implanted texts.

The Power of Confession and Repentance

Since its earliest days, the church has regularly set aside times of reflection and self-examination to help us identify our sin and receive the grace and forgiveness of God. The season of Lent is a primary example. Its forty days make up more than a tenth of the entire year, which tells us something about the priority the church has historically placed on this pivotal dimension of our lives with God.

But while a settled awareness and personal acknowledgment of our sin is important, it is only part of the equation. We must also take our sins to God, as David did in Psalm 139:

> Search me God, and know my heart;
>   Test me and know my anxious thoughts.
> See if there is any offensive way in me,
>   And lead me in the way everlasting. (Ps. 139:23-24 NIV)

Confession and repentance are described and modeled elsewhere in Scripture, as well:

- When Isaiah encounters God in his glory (Is. 6)

- When David confesses to sinning against Bathsheba and Uriah (Ps. 51)

- In the posture of the tax collector in Jesus' parable of the Pharisee and the Tax Collector (Luke 18)

- In Paul's instructions for us to put off the old self and put on the new (Col. 3, Rom. 13, etc.)

Here and elsewhere we see that confession—acknowledging our sin to God, and repentance—turning away from sin and back to God, therefore stand as foundational building blocks for spiritual formation. If they are not a regular part of our rhythms, we will make little progress in the way of Jesus.

To truly walk forward in our lives with Jesus, we must be aware of both the people God has created us to be and the people we actually are—we must attend to patterns of grace and patterns of sin.

While this pattern of repentance and confession has its origin in our *upward* life with God and the *inward* contours of our own hearts, it also has important implications for our lives with *one another*. When we sin, we almost always hurt others. Therefore, part of full and clean repentance is to come to grips with that impact and to humbly acknowledge it to those we hurt. Additionally, as David recognizes in Ps. 51:13, it is only after clearly and cleanly confessing and turning away from our sin that we become fully available to God to influence others for his sake and join God in the *outward* progress of his kingdom.

Additionally, it is not only to those we directly injure that we confess and repent of our sins, but we also do so as part of our normal rhythms among the people of God. Though solitary self-examination, confession, and repentance before God are of great benefit, the Scriptures also encourage us to confess our sins to *one another* (James 5:16). The enemy of our souls seeks to isolate us from both God and our community of faith by keeping our sin secret, but there is great power and freedom in taking time to regularly confess our sins to two or three other brothers or sisters. Disclosing our sin both to God and to other faithful friends can neutralize sin's grip on us. To experience God's forgiveness and restoration together, this month's exercises include a simple time of confession and Communion with a few others.

Personal Patterns of Sin

Part of what it means to know ourselves is to understand the patterns of sin particular to our own lives. Just as none of us receive the same gifts and graces, our sin patterns are similarly distinct. Some people's sins are blatantly obvious, while others are hidden, just as some of our virtues are plain for all to see and some are much more subtle (1 Tim. 5:24–25). Regardless of how obvious or subtle, knowing our weaknesses and our particular proclivities to sin allow us to walk in "anticipatory repentance" before God so that we may avoid sin in the first place and break free from the counterfeit ways of being we are naturally inclined toward. This requires a lifelong commitment and resilience that the author of Hebrews understood:

FOR REFLECTION
Does your sin tend to be more blatant and outward or more subtle and hidden? As you consider this, what do you learn about yourself?

When we sin, we almost always hurt others. Therefore, part of full and clean repentance is to come to grips with that impact and to humbly acknowledge it to those we hurt.

> Therefore, since we are surrounded by such a huge crowd of witnesses to the life of faith, let us strip off every weight that slows us down, especially the sin that so easily trips us up. And let us run with endurance the race God has set before us. We do this by keeping our eyes on Jesus, the champion who initiates and perfects our faith. Because of the joy awaiting him, he endured the cross, disregarding its shame. Now he is seated in the place of honor beside God's throne. Think of all the hostility he endured from sinful people; then you won't become weary and give up. After all, you have not yet given your lives in your struggle against sin. And have you forgotten the encouraging words God spoke to you as his children? He said,
>
> "My child, don't make light of the Lord's discipline,
>   and don't give up when he corrects you.
> For the Lord disciplines those he loves,
>   and he punishes each one he accepts as his child."
>
> (Heb. 12:1–6 NLT)

May God meet you this month as you open yourself to him, learn more about your own sin, persevere in his unwavering love, and walk forward in the ways of grace as his beloved child. ✣

 Homework

READING

Choose *one* of the following books to read this month:

1. *Searching for and Maintaining Peace*, by Jacques Philippe (2002)

    This little book, written by a French Catholic priest, is a simple yet profound treatise on peace of heart, and offers gentle, practical ways to encounter and receive from God amid the most ordinary life situations. It is divided into three sections: Part One focuses on the central importance of maintaining a settled, peaceful heart as we walk forward in our life with God; Part Two addresses common internal and external conditions that often cause us to lose our sense of peace and provides practical counsel regarding how to maintain it; and Part Three includes a selection of texts by various authors through the ages who speak to these same themes.

AS YOU READ, REFLECT AND JOURNAL ON THE FOLLOWING:

   a. In Part One, Father Philippe asserts that peace of heart is essential to our own inward transformation, our ability to love others, and our outward fruitfulness in the world, and says that "all the reasons that cause us to lose our sense of peace are bad reasons" (p. 13). He also says that to maintain peace of heart requires great struggle on our part—"combat" in his terms (p. 11 and ff.) and stands as both the means and the end of that struggle. Goodwill, "the habitual determination to always say 'yes' to God" (p. 17) is critical to our ability to maintain peace of heart, he says. Where in your life do you presently find it easiest to say "yes" to God? Why? Where do you find it most difficult? Why?

   b. In Part Two, the author outlines various situations involving our health, our money, our relationships, our fear of suffering, the actions of others, our own sin, the decisions we need to make, etc., that often disrupt our peace of heart. He also suggests ways of maintaining our peace of heart in the face of all these things. As you consider your own life, which of these situations do you presently find most frequently disrupts your own peace of heart? Why do you think that is? Which of Father Philippe's suggestions do you find most helpful?

   c. Which of the excerpts in Part Three do you find most helpful? Why? Both in Part Three and elsewhere in the book, where do you find yourself most resistant? Why?

2. *Interior Freedom*, by Jacques Philippe (2007)

   Jacques Philippe's stated purpose in this little book is this: That "every Christian needs to discover that even in the most unfavorable outward circumstances we possess within ourselves a space of freedom that nobody can take away, because God is its source and guarantee. Without this discovery we will always be restricted in some way . . ." (p. 9). The remainder of the book explores the nature of this "interior freedom" that is available to us all as a gift from God and how in practical terms we can more fully lay hold of it.

   AS YOU READ, REFLECT AND JOURNAL ON THE FOLLOWING:

   a. Pay particular attention to Father Philippe's notion of "consent," which appears throughout Part I of the book and is contrasted with our ideas regarding "choice" and "options." He notes on p. 28 that "Being free also means consenting to what we did not choose." How do you find yourself responding to

TIP Both of these Jacques Philippe books are very much worth reading. If you only have time for one this month, plan to take time later on to read the other.

this idea? What are some examples from your past and present life where you have been asked to consent to a reality that you yourself have not or would not have chosen?

    b. Part II of the book focuses on the centrality of the here and now—"the present moment" (p. 81 ff.)—as we engage with God in our own transformation. "We do not commune with God in the past or the future, but by welcoming each instant as the place where he gives himself to us" (p. 82). Consider and journal briefly on how you can only understand and rightly relate not only to your present, but also to your past and your future, in the context of your here-and-now, real-time relationship with God, and under "God's gaze" (pp. 39–40). Does anything about your actual past or anticipated future stand out to you as you consider these things?

    c. Parts III–V focus on our participation with God through the "theological virtues" of faith, hope, and love. Father Philippe asserts that learning to love means "learning to give and receive freely" (p. 117) and that ultimately "faith will be replaced by sight and hope by possession; only love will never be replaced by anything else ... because it is the goal of all" (p. 104). He also asserts that all three of these virtues are cultivated only in the context of our fundamental "spiritual poverty" and involve not what we have or what we do, but who we are in Christ (p. 121). As you consider your own life, how does your absorption with what you have and with what you do get in the way of who you are—"a poor child who possesses absolutely nothing, who receives everything, infinitely loved and totally free" (p. 124)? How does this make you feel?

3. If time permits, look over Chapter 7 and its homework before your next meeting.

REFLECTION AND JOURNALING

Reflect on the following questions and journal your responses. At the next group meeting, come prepared to share some of what you have written. (The questions are adapted from *The Gift of Being Yourself*, by David Benner, Chapter 5)

4. Ask God to help you see what makes you feel most vulnerable and most like running for cover. It may be conflict, failure, pain, emotional upset, loss of face, or not feeling unique or special. Allow yourself to feel the distress of not avoiding these things. Then, listening to God's invitation to come out of hiding and into his loving presence, step out and allow God to embrace you just as you are.

5. Consider your default self-image. How do tend to think about yourself? What are you most proud of about yourself? Ask God to help you see the ways your self-image defends against feelings of vulnerability. Ask for courage to expose and let go of these false ways of finding security.

6. Ask God to help you see the ways you distract yourself from facing the vulnerabilities and discomforts you noticed above. When you are unable to calm and quiet yourself (Ps. 131:2), and when you feel least available to God and others, what do you find yourself doing? Perhaps you turn to work, substances, food, shopping, social media, or addictive behaviors. At these times, what does your internal and external landscape look like?

7. Write a brief prayer to God acknowledging the "counterfeit" graces and identity you noticed above, and ask for help to embrace the true graces and identity he intends for you.

THE WORD IMPLANTED

- Psalm 51
- Psalm 139
- Isaiah 6:1–8
- Luke 18:9–14
- Hebrews 12:1–6

OTHER EXERCISES AND PRACTICES

8. Once this month, practice "Confession and Communion," Practice 9 in Appendix A, with 2–3 sisters or brothers in your group.

9. At least once each week, choose one of this month's shorter Word Implanted texts to practice *lectio divina*.

10. At least once a week, slowly pray aloud "The Lord's Prayer in Seven Movements," Practice 10 in Appendix A.

11. Continue to incorporate moments of attentive silence and reflection into your daily and weekly rhythms through one or more of the previous months' practices (e.g. five Minutes of Stillness, a quiet meal with God, a quiet walk, the Prayer of Examen, etc.).

RECOMMENDED FILMS

Watch and reflect on *at least one* of the two films below.

1. *The Painted Veil* (2006)

    This film starring Naomi Watts and Edward Norton tells the story of the fracture and ultimate healing of the marriage of Dr. Walter Fane and his wife, Kitty. Based on a novel by W. Somerset Maugham and set in China in the 1920's, it addresses themes of sin and forgiveness, suffering and transformation, life, death, and love, and serves as an excellent story of how we come to know ourselves and others, and how we learn to give and receive love, even as we come face to face with our deepest failures and sins. This movie is rated PG-13 and contains some disturbing images and mature sexual situations—you may want to look over the IMDb listing on the film before you decide to watch it, but it is in the end a beautiful and redemptive film and is worth the time to watch it.

    TIP Consider gathering with some of your 12-for-12 companions this month to watch one, or even both of these films.

    ### AS YOU WATCH, CONSIDER THE FOLLOWING:

    a. Consider the way that Kitty and Walter's relationship begins, and the way that he proposes to her. In what ways do their own character flaws and failures show themselves early on in their relationship? How would you characterize these failures and flaws?

    b. Why would you say that Kitty is susceptible to Charlie's seduction? Where do you first notice her sense of regret, not for getting caught but for having hurt Walter?

    c. How would you describe Walter's attitudes and reactions in the days and weeks after he discovers Kitty's unfaithfulness? When she goes to Charlie and he refuses to divorce his wife and marry her, what does she begin to learn about herself?

    d. When Mr. Waddington later shares his opinions of Charlie to Kitty, what does she begin to realize both about Charlie and herself?

    e. What does Kitty begin to see in her husband when she first visits the convent? How does this begin to change her heart towards him?

    f. What would you say finally leads Walter and Kitty to reconcile? How would you describe the process of their transformation, both as individuals and as a couple? Is it abrupt, gradual, or somewhere in between?

g. Late in the movie, the Mother Superior says to Kitty that "Duty is only washing your hands when they are dirty" and "When love and duty are one, then grace is within you." How does Kitty come to learn the truth of these words as the movie draws to a close?

h. What does the final scene in the movie indicate about the way that Kitty has been transformed by all that has happened?

2. *The Remains of the Day* (1993)

This excellently acted and directed Merchant Ivory film stars Anthony Hopkins and Emma Thompson and centers on the life of James Stevens, a faithful butler to a wealthy, though naïve and tragically misguided English Lord. The story is a tale of regret, of the daunting quest of coming to grips with the truth about oneself and one's sins and failures, and about what it might look like to deal—or not deal—truthfully with what one discovers. It is a quiet, beautiful, slow, thoughtful film, and is worth the time to watch and reflect on.

AS YOU WATCH, CONSIDER THE FOLLOWING:

a. Note particularly the points at which Mr. Stevens has opportunities to press beyond what is comfortable and to do the right thing, and note when he does or does not act upon those opportunities. Also, reflect on the process of him coming to see the truth about himself and about the man he has so faithfully served all his years, as well as the truth about his relationship with Miss Kenton, played by Emma Thompson.

b. Finally, consider what the role and symbolism of "the house" (Mr. Stevens often refers to it as "this house") might be. Be sure to pay particular attention to the final scene of the movie in this regard, and consider what this scene says about Mr. Stevens and his relationship to the truth and to the central relationships of his life.

c. What do you learn from this movie regarding your own life with Jesus and regarding the truth about your own sins and failures as He gives you opportunity and makes you able to see them and bring them to Him?

The Agony

Philosophers have measured mountains,
Fathomed the depths of seas, of states and kings;
Walked with a staff to heav'n, and tracèd fountains:

But there are two vast, spacious things,
The which to measure it doth more behove;
Yet few there are that sound them—Sin and Love.

Who would know Sin, let him repair
Unto Mount Olivet; there shall he see
A Man so wrung with pains, that all His hair,
His skin, His garments bloody be.
Sin is that press and vice, which forceth pain
To hunt his cruel food through ev'ry vein.

Who knows not Love, let him assay
And taste that juice which, on the cross, a pike
Did set again abroach; then let him say
If ever he did taste the like,
Love is that liquor sweet and most divine,
Which my God feels as blood, but I as wine.

GEORGE HERBERT

CHAPTER 7

Authentic Community: Confession and Hospitality

> *Above all, keep fervent in your love for one another, because love covers a multitude of sins. Be hospitable to one another without complaint.*
>
> **1 PETER 4:8-9** NASB

> *Therefore confess your sins to each other and pray for each other so that you may be healed. The prayer of a righteous person is powerful and effective.*
>
> **JAMES 5:16** NIV

CHAPTER 7

Authentic Community: Confession and Hospitality

Two Cords Entwined as One

It may seem odd to pair something as personal and vulnerable as confession with something as communal and outward as hospitality. However, these pivotal parts of our life with Jesus are the very best of friends—two cords entwined as one.

Opening ourselves to God and others in confession is akin to openly sharing with others the welcome we receive from God. For in all things, including confession and hospitality, the posture we seek toward God and others is one of non-defensive openness. This permeability and availability, in contrast to a more fearful and self-protective posture, transforms us in two ways:

1.
WE LET DOWN OUR DEFENSES
and allow God and others to know us as we are.

2.
WE RELEASE OUR GRIP
on what we view as ours in order to give freely of ourselves, both to God and other people.

In both cases, God invites us to embrace risk and vulnerability. Confession and hospitality dare to ask: What will happen if we let God and others truly know us and access what we view as ours? Will we experience shame and loss, or will we receive God's love and offer ourselves as vessels of his love to others?

The Power of Vulnerability and Transparency

Honestly and specifically confessing our sins to another person can leave us feeling anxious and exposed. It is the rare person who intentionally makes space in their life to confess sins to someone else. However, John tells us that to say that we have no sin is an act of deception that separates us from the truth, whereas to confess our sins opens the way to God's forgiveness and our own cleansing and restoration (1 John 1:8–9).

Some faith traditions involve at least occasional confession to a priest or other clergy member. While confessing our sins to a priest or pastor may help us overcome some of the resistance we feel to the prospect of confessing our sins, to confess our sins to sisters and brothers we have ongoing relationship with is another matter entirely. Likewise, the thought of inviting people into our personal space, or of stepping out of our personal space into contexts and communities where we feel less secure and more exposed, is similarly daunting. Not many people readily offer hospitality to those beyond their most intimate family and friend circles. Even fewer step out of those circles into contexts where they have little familiarity or control.

Thus, the vulnerability and transparency which we must embrace in confession is not unlike what we embrace in living availably and hospitably toward others. To draw near to God and to others, and to foster environments where people are most able and willing to do the same, is often bound to our own willingness to be open, exposed, and known. To the extent that we resist these things for ourselves, we contribute to an atmosphere of unreality and isolation. Love requires vulnerability; intimacy entails transparency.

Who We Actually Are

Who we actually are—not who we once were, wish we were, or imagine ourselves to be—must always stand as our point of engagement with God and others. When we hide from reality or present a fictional or sanitized image of ourselves, we make it impossible to build genuine relationship, which is the foundation of both community and mission. It also takes great energy to project and sustain these false impressions—much of social media is given precisely to this. Is it any wonder that ours is an age of increased isolation and fragmentation?

To draw near to God and to others, and to foster environments where people are most able and willing to do the same, is often bound to our own willingness to be open, exposed, and known.

When we are not real before God and others, and when we are not truly known, we have no confidence that we are loved. We render ourselves unable to fully love others, as well. The effort we expend in projecting a mirage is much better invested in building something true and real.

Truth and authenticity move us toward a settled place of peace in the way we view ourselves and others before God. To get there, we must:

1.
KNOW AND ACKNOWLEDGE what is true about ourselves.

2.
PUT OFF POSTURING aimed at making ourselves appear better than we are.

3.
RIGHTLY UNDERSTAND both the value and limits of the resources God has put under our control.

In doing these things, we become free to make ourselves and our resources genuinely available to God and others. We release any compulsion to prove ourselves. We worry less about our deficiencies, even our sins. Though we do not become complacent about them, we do not add to our sins the power of shame, which keeps us from sincere and vulnerable engagement. Similarly, we find freedom from perfectionism, which keeps us from offering the good that we do have simply because it does not meet a standard of perfection that we wrongly hold ourselves to and can never attain.

Giving What We Have

We need not be wealthy, or skilled entertainers, in order to practice hospitality. As I reflect on my own experiences of hospitality, it is not the most lavish occasions that made me feel most welcome. Rather, my most powerful experiences of hospitality were extended to me by the poorest people I have known—neighbors in inner city Columbus, Ohio; Afghan refugees at camps and makeshift settlements in Pakistan; friends in the Central Asian city where we lived for many years.

In all these situations, the hospitality was genuine because it was perfectly rooted in imperfect reality. People shared from what they actually had, not from some unattainable or unsustainable ideal. With a warm posture of genuine welcome, I have been served everything from a few scrambled eggs, toast with sweetened condensed milk, a cup of tea and a piece of bread, to

FOR REFLECTION
Do any particularly meaningful experiences of hospitality immediately come to mind for you? What especially stands out for you about these experiences?

a humble futon to spend the night on. My hosts expressed joy at the honor of having me in their home; they were unashamed and confident about what they had to offer me, serving me even the simplest of fare with expressions of warmth and honor.

And as I consider better-resourced friends, those who extend hospitality with the same relaxed, generous warmth of my poorer friends have made me feel the most welcome. What is important is not so much *what* we offer but *how* we offer it—joyfully and generously, with a focus on the guest, and not on what we ourselves might have or lack.

The Word Became Flesh

Jesus himself, the Word who became flesh and who offered himself in the supreme act of divine hospitality, models the way of authentic vulnerability in all he does. Though God himself, he chose to lay aside all divine power and privilege to welcome us into his household (Phil. 2:6-7). And though he himself knew no sin, he was made to be sin on our behalf (2 Cor. 5:21), opening the way for us to confess and turn away from our own sin and to be freed from its power over us.

We often experience these realities in the sacraments, some of which are part of this chapter's homework. During the Communion meal, we hear "the body of Christ, given for you," and "the blood of Christ, shed for you." In communal confession we enter into fellowship with Jesus and one another as we confess our sins and receive his life in us. And as we enter into these realities, we are renewed and refreshed and made better able to join God in extending his welcome to the world.

What is important is not so much what *we offer but* how *we offer it—joyfully and generously, with a focus on the guest, and not on what we ourselves might have or lack.*

Homework

This month's homework invites us into the practices of confession and Communion in community with God's people, as well as the outward expression of divine hospitality to others, both within and beyond the church.

READING

FOR REFLECTION
How long has it been since you read a novel? Do you find yourself excited about or resistant to reading this novel? Why?

1. Read at least Parts I and II of *Watership Down*, by Richard Adams.

   This celebrated novel began as stories told to the author's two young daughters. At their insistence, Adams eventually put it into novel form. Following the epic adventures of a band of rabbits in the English countryside, this unusual book may seem an unlikely selection for a spiritual formation group. However, it contains much wisdom and substance for fruitful reflection and application in our lives and relationships.

   ### AS YOU READ, REFLECT AND JOURNAL ON THE FOLLOWING:

   a. Observe Hazel as a leader. How does he interact with his companions? How does he bring the best out of each of them and create an atmosphere in which every one of them plays a valuable role in the success of their community? What are his greatest faults?

   b. Contrast the communities Hazel and his band encounter in their travels. What is wholly lacking in Cowslip's warren? In what ways is the society in that warren unhealthy and enslaved? What is wholly lacking in Efrafa, General Woundwort's warren? In what ways is the society in that warren unhealthy and enslaved?

   c. Consider those who left the warren at the beginning of the novel: Hazel, Fiver, Bigwig, Blackberry, Dandelion, Silver, and Pipkin. How does each character contribute in crucial ways to the success of their mission? What are each one's strengths and gifts, weaknesses and faults? In what ways are they limited as individuals and yet empowered as a cooperative community to accomplish far more than any of them could by themselves? How do they adapt to unforeseen circumstances and deal with loss and setbacks?

   d. How does this group interact with outsiders and with later members, e.g. Kehaar, Blackavar, Holly, etc? How do they learn even from those whose approach to life they reject?

e. What lessons on leadership, team, community, and mission does this novel offer? What else captures your attention and stirs your imagination?

2. The Book of Ruth

    Ruth is among the most beautiful narratives in all of Scripture. It covers a range of human experience—from promising beginnings to tragedy to companionship to destitution to restorative kindness. As you read, consider the ways Naomi, Ruth, and Boaz participate with God in his unfolding plan through their acts of kindness and hospitality to one another. What does this speak to you about acts of kindness and hospitality in your own life?

3. If time permits, look over Chapter 8 and its homework before your next meeting.

REFLECTION AND JOURNALING

4. Complete "Hospitality to Strangers," Practice 11 in Appendix A. Reflect and journal on the two prompts. Then follow through on the rest of the exercise by inviting and connecting with someone you have never extended hospitality to in the past.

5. Using "Imaginative Reading of Scripture," Practice 12 in Appendix A, as a guide, spend some extended time reading, reflecting, and journaling on one or more of the texts listed below, and on the participants in the events they describe—Abraham, Sarah, and the angelic visitors; Ruth, Naomi, and Boaz; Elijah, the widow of Zarephath, and her son; and Jesus as he serves breakfast to Peter and the disciples after his resurrection. Pay particular attention to the way the participants in these events do or do not make themselves sensitive, vulnerable, and open—*permeable*—to God and others, and also to the way they do or do not make themselves *available*—placed at the disposal of God and others. How do these postures and attitudes help advance or get in the way of God's purposes and plans in the world and in the lives of the participants?

    - Genesis 18:1–15
    - The Book of Ruth
    - 1 Kings 17:1–16
    - John 21:1–17

THE WORD IMPLANTED

Regularly read the following texts aloud over the course of this month.

- Genesis 18:1–15
- 1 Kings 17:1–16
- John 21:1–17
- Ephesians 2:11–22
- James 5:16–18
- 1 Peter 4:7–9

TIP Contemplative prayer bears the most fruit when practiced regularly over time, so commit to persevering in the practice even if you don't feel its impact right away.

OTHER EXERCISES AND PRACTICES

6. Practice "Confession and Communion" following the guidelines in Appendix A. Your group leader will assign you to a group of 2–3 others of the same sex for this practice. Then, once this month, meet with your group to engage in these practices together.

7. Pray aloud at least once per week using "The Lord's Prayer in Seven Movements," Practice 10 in Appendix A, as a guide.

8. Early this month, engage in Contemplative Prayer for at least 5 minutes per day for a week straight. Over the following weeks, try increasing the time to 10–20 minutes, even if you only engage in the practice more occasionally.

9. Review practices from the past several months and incorporate into your rhythms one or more you have found helpful.

RECOMMENDED FILMS

Watch and reflect on *at least one* of the films below.

1. *A Raisin in the Sun* (1961)

    This celebrated and brilliantly acted Sidney Poitier film tells the story of an extended Black family in Chicago caught in the throes of grief and conflict. As they seek to resolve their differences, the family experiences failure, forgiveness, racial bias, and personal transformation, while its main character, Walter, comes to a deeper and more settled understanding of himself.

    ### AS YOU WATCH, CONSIDER THE FOLLOWING:

    a. Notice the hopes and aspirations of the central characters in this film: Walter Lee Younger; Ruth Younger, his wife; Lena Younger

(Mama), his mother; Beneatha (Bennie) Younger, his sister; and Travis Younger, his son. How does each family member wrestle with these hopes and aspirations individually, within their family relationships, and in their broader community context?

b. This film addresses a wide range of broader issues: race, housing discrimination, gender roles, abortion, questions of faith and of God himself, economic opportunity, etc. Consider at least one of these broader issues more deeply as you watch and reflect on this film.

c. Lena (Mama) plays a central role in helping each family member discover their own identity and purpose and remain unified as they do. In what ways does Mama most help or hinder that process? How does her approach to faith, compassion, trust, love, and forgiveness factor into the outcomes for each family member?

d. Notice quotes throughout the film that stand out for you and impact you most deeply. Consider jotting some down and reflecting on them afterwards.

e. What are the most important ways Walter is formed during this film by his own and others' words, attitudes, and actions? What can you take away from this film regarding your own formation and that of those you have influence over in your own life?

2. *Seabiscuit* (2003)

This film, based on true events, tells the Great-Depression-era story of individuals who unite with long-shot aspirations for an undersized and injured racehorse named Seabiscuit. It is a tale of how hurt and broken people can help each other grow, change, and step back into the identity and purpose each person was originally designed for.

AS YOU WATCH, CONSIDER THE FOLLOWING:

a. Pay particular attention to the main characters in the film: Charles Howard, Seabiscuit's owner; Tom Smith, Seabiscuit's trainer; and Red Pollard (Johnny), Seabiscuit's jockey. Each man experienced significant loss and pain. In what ways had both things done to them and things they had done obscured the people they were made to be?

b. A number of lines serve as refrains and reference points in the film. Reflect on the following and how they might apply to a life of spiritual formation:

- When they first meet (41:00), Charles Howard asks Tom Smith, "So why are you fixing him?" Tom replies, "Because I can. Every horse is good for something... And he's still nice to look at. You don't throw a whole life away just because he's banged up a little."

- Later, when beginning to train Seabiscuit (51:30), Tom says, "He's so beat up it's hard to tell what he's like. I just can't help feelin' like they got him so screwed up runnin' in a circle, he's forgotten what he was born to do. He just needs to learn how to be a horse again."

- As Seabiscuit and Red Pollard recover from their leg injuries (1:53:00), Red says, "I know. I know. I'm in a hurry too, Pops. But you know what Hadrian said about Rome: 'Brick by brick, my citizens; brick by brick.'"

c. Notice the role rest plays in both Red's and Seabiscuit's healing and recovery. What are some of the most important components of this rest? In your own life, how is Sabbath rest central to growth and flourishing in the way of Jesus?

d. How do the characters, including Charles Howard's second wife, Marcela, challenge and support each other so each one may grow and flourish? Reflect on the quote near the end of the film with an eye toward our own formation in the way of Jesus: "He fixed us, every one of us. And I guess in a way, we kinda fixed each other, too."

NOTES

A Thanksgiving to God, for his House

Lord, Thou hast given me a cell
    Wherein to dwell,
A little house, whose humble roof
    Is weather-proof:
Under the spars of which I lie
    Both soft, and dry;
Where Thou my chamber for to ward
    Hast set a guard
Of harmless thoughts, to watch and keep
    Me, while I sleep.
Low is my porch, as is my fate,
    Both void of state;
And yet the threshold of my door
    Is worn by th' poor,
Who thither come and freely get
    Good words, or meat.
Like as my parlour, so my hall
    And kitchen's small;
A little buttery[1], and therein
    A little bin,
Which keeps my little loaf of bread
    Unchipp'd, unflead;
Some brittle sticks of thorn or briar
    Make me a fire,

---

[1] pantry, larder

Close by whose living coal I sit,
    And glow like it.

Lord, I confess too, when I dine,
    The pulse[2] is Thine,

And all those other bits, that be
    There plac'd by Thee;

The worts[3], the purslain[3], and the mess
    Of water-cress[3],

Which of Thy kindness Thou hast sent;
    And my content[4]

Makes those, and my beloved beet,
    To be more sweet.

'Tis Thou that crown'st my glittering hearth
    With guiltless mirth;

And giv'st me wassail-bowls to drink,
    Spic'd to the brink.

Lord, 'tis Thy plenty-dropping hand
    That soils[5] my land;

And giv'st me, for my bushel sown,
    Twice ten for one[6];

Thou mak'st my teeming hen to lay
    Her egg each day;

Besides my healthful ewes to bear
    Me twins each year;

---

[2] peas, beans, lentils, or other legumes
[3] various kinds of herbs and greens
[4] i.e., contentment
[5] creates soil on
[6] i.e., a twentyfold harvest

The while the conduits[7] of my kine[8]
    Run cream, for wine.

All these, and better, Thou dost send
    Me, to this end,

That I should render, for my part,
    A thankful heart,

Which, fir'd with incense, I resign,
    As wholly Thine;

But the acceptance, that must be,
    My Christ, by Thee.

ROBERT HERRICK

---

[7] i.e., udders
[8] milk cows

CHAPTER 8

Wisdom and Discernment

The fear of the LORD is the beginning of wisdom, and the knowledge of the Holy One is understanding.

PROVERBS 9:10 NASB

But the wisdom from above is first pure, then peaceable, gentle, reasonable, full of mercy and good fruits, unwavering, without hypocrisy.

JAMES 3:17 NASB

CHAPTER 8

Wisdom and Discernment

The Pursuit of Wisdom

There are many things we might say about our own day and time, but few of us would be tempted to call it an age of renewed wisdom. In this, the words of *qoheleth*, the Preacher of Ecclesiastes, ring especially true:

> What has been will be again, what has been done will be done again; there is nothing new under the sun. (Ecc. 1:9 NIV)

For since ancient times, the cry of the wise has often been one of searching and lament, akin to the words of Job 28, where in what is likely the oldest book in the Bible, Job, after enumerating some of the great feats of human endeavor in his own time as well as some of the great riches of the earth, asks:

> But where can wisdom be found? And where is the place of understanding?
> (Job 28:12 NASB)

Job goes on in this same discourse to eliminate possibilities—wisdom is not to be found among the living or among the dead, in the deepest sea, or among any earthly treasures. As the wisdom literature and entire arc of Scripture affirm, wisdom is found in God and God alone. "God understands its way," Job says, "and he knows its place" (Job 28:23 NAU). If we are to find wisdom, we must find God. If we are to seek after wisdom, we must first seek after God.

Throughout both the Old and New Testaments we encounter the intertwined thread of the pursuit of both God and of the wisdom that is found in him alone. We discover that neither the pursuit of God nor the pursuit of wisdom are casual affairs, but as God's people throughout the ages have also discovered, they require all that we are and all that we have. In Proverbs we read:

> Make your ear attentive to wisdom, incline your heart to understanding; for if you cry for discernment, lift your voice for understanding; if you seek her as silver and search for her as for hidden treasures; then you will discern the fear of the LORD and discover the knowledge of God. (Prov. 2:2–5 NASB)

In the New Testament, Jesus is shown to be the heart of all wisdom. To the Corinthian church, the Apostle Paul speaks of the crucified Christ as both "the power of God and the wisdom of God" (1 Cor. 1:24b NASB). To the Colossian church, he affirms that in Christ alone "are hidden all the treasures of wisdom and knowledge" (Col. 2:3 NASB). And to the Philippian church he therefore testifies:

> I count all things to be loss in view of the surpassing value of knowing Christ Jesus my Lord, for whom I have suffered the loss of all things, and count them but rubbish so that I may gain Christ... (Phil. 3:8 NASB)

Jesus himself points to the source of wisdom when he challenges us to "seek first his kingdom and his righteousness" (Matt. 6:33 NAU), and he says that "if anyone comes to Me, and does not hate... even his own life, he cannot be My disciple" (Luke 14:26 NASB). Both the heroes of the faith and the Lord himself challenge us to lay aside all other pursuits and to make God himself, and the wisdom to be found in him, the chief aim of our lives.

The Beginning of Wisdom

But how do we get started in the pursuit of wisdom? The aims of this group—deeper connection with God, increased conformity to Christ, and the bearing of outward fruit in the world—can reasonably be summed up as the pursuit of wisdom. To take our first step in that journey, we must know where to begin. Job answers the question like this:

> "And to man He said, 'Behold, the fear of the Lord, that is wisdom; And to depart from evil is understanding.'" (Job 28:28 NASB)

The Book of Proverbs echoes this same assertion:

> The fear of the Lord is the beginning of wisdom, and the knowledge of the Holy One is understanding. (Prov. 9:10 NASB)

> The fear of the Lord is the beginning of knowledge; fools despise wisdom and instruction. (Prov. 1:7 NASB)

If we are to find wisdom, we must find God.
If we are to seek after wisdom, we must first seek after God.

FOR REFLECTION

What kinds of thoughts or feelings does the idea of the fear of the Lord stir in you?

The fear of the Lord stands as both the definition of and starting point for both wisdom—our ability to act rightly and well in all circumstances, and knowledge—our ability to know what is real and true in the world. Therefore, no matter how challenging it is to attain, it is of utmost importance to have a clear sense of just what the fear of the Lord consists.

Whenever Scripture references the fear of the Lord, many modern Christians squirm. One common approach is simply to avoid talking or thinking about it at all, which given the centrality of its place in the Bible we are plainly not at liberty to do. Another approach is to overemphasize the "fire and brimstone" aspect of the fear of God, which reduces the fear of the Lord to something far less than what the authors of Scripture intend and communicate. Yet another approach, perhaps closer to the mark, essentially replaces the word "fear" with "reverence," understanding the fear of the Lord to be a general sense of awe that we are to bring to our life with God. None of these approaches, however, perfectly captures the fullness of what the Scriptures teach about the fear of the Lord or of what will set us on the right course in our pursuit of wisdom.

The fear of the Lord consists of our posture in relation to God, ourselves, other persons, and all of creation at all times and in every situation. The fear of the Lord involves how we steward our bodies, attention, resources, thoughts, emotions, relationships, and actions. Moment by moment, the fear of the Lord is in touch with the fact that "the earth is the Lord's and all it contains, the world and those who dwell in it" (Ps. 24:1 NASB).

It is important here to draw a distinction between the fear of the Lord and all other objects of our fear. The fear of the Lord is intended to draw us *toward* God, whereas the fear of other things drives us reflexively *away* from them. As we come to know God in not only his infinite power and authority but also in his breathtaking beauty and expansive love, we find that the shape the fear of God takes in us is neither a desire to flee nor a posture of anxious subservience. Rather, as we come to know God by faith, we join David in saying that the one thing we seek from him is to dwell in his house for all our days, to behold his beauty, and to meditate in his temple (Ps. 27:4).

The fear of the Lord is intended to draw us toward God, whereas the fear of other things drives us reflexively away from them.

And we do well to consider the words of the great Christmas hymn, "What Child Is This," regarding the babe, Jesus, in the manger: "Good Christian, fear, for sinners here the silent Word is pleading." Alongside the shepherds and the Magi of old, we are drawn to Jesus in the fear of the Lord as we behold such tremendous tenderness and power uniquely cohabiting together in our Lord.

To live out this fear of the Lord requires us to walk in the world "with our shoes off," like Moses at the burning bush. We must embody an acknowledgment of the legitimate authority, power, beauty, and love of God at all times. For because all that exists was created by and belongs to God and because God is ever present, we always "walk on holy ground." Fear of the Lord considers the inherent sacredness of all times, places, and persons simply because they are created by and belong to God. To walk in the fear of the Lord, then, means that we humbly yield our whole selves to God at all times, in all places, and with all people. Every aspect of our lives ought to be impacted by the fear of the Lord. It is no wonder the authors of Scripture refer to it as the beginning of wisdom.

Discernment: Wisdom Made Practical

Because the fear of the Lord touches on every aspect of our lives, the wisdom it leads us to is not abstract and amorphous, but is pithy, concrete, and practical. Wisdom has much to say about everyday matters like money, sex, power, politics, words, work, relationships, thoughts, emotions, food, drink, health, rest, education—literally every sphere of human experience and activity. Faithful pursuit of wisdom will lead to transformation in all areas of life.

As we seek wisdom and cultivate the fear of the Lord in ourselves, we will encounter practical implications at every turn. In the context of concrete life situations and practical decision-making we are called upon to practice *spiritual discernment*, relying on God's word, God's Spirit, and good counsel to "discern righteousness and justice and equity and every good course" (Prov. 2:9 NASB).

The pursuit of wisdom and the practice of spiritual discernment integrate each of the cardinal directions and invite us to grow in all four. It leads us to look upward to God at all times and in all situations; it invites us to humbly yield to God as he affects inward change in us; it impacts our relationships with one another, whether in the church, in our families, or beyond; and it shapes the outward thrust of our lives as we seek God's kingdom in our separate callings and vocations and in our shared mission in the world for Jesus' sake.

The reading and homework assignments below will help you become more intentional and focused in your pursuit of wisdom, spiritual discernment, and the fear of the Lord. In doing this work, a potential temptation is that of the Pharisees, who with a desire to leave no ambiguity in any situation or decision, constructed a rigid labyrinth of law instead of cultivating a tender and responsive heart toward God. In the Book of James, however, which one might rightly view as New Testament wisdom literature, we are not so much told the elaborate details of what wisdom looks like but are rather urged to ask God for wisdom, with an unwavering commitment to act on what he reveals to us. James also provides a helpful glimpse into the character of God's wisdom, as opposed to other so-called "wisdoms" we might encounter in the world. He says:

> But the wisdom from above is first pure, then peaceable, gentle, reasonable, full of mercy and good fruits, unwavering, without hypocrisy. And the seed whose fruit is righteousness is sown in peace by those who make peace. (James 3:17–18 NASB)

TIP This passage from James serves as a real-time "litmus test" when we find ourselves unsure of the posture of our own hearts and minds. Consider committing it to memory and to slowly reflecting on it when you are agitated or confused or seeking God for wisdom.

As we embrace these words of James, along with the wisdom found in the rest of Scripture, we develop an increasingly rooted and intuitive sense of the "wisdom from above"—we develop a "nose" for wisdom, as well as a sense of what is not wisdom. And with the help of the Holy Spirit, we can, like Jesus, discern the Father's voice and increase "in wisdom and stature, and in favor with God and men" (Luke 2:52 NASB).

Homework

READING

1. Read the following biblical books and chapters, marking as you go anything that stands out regarding wisdom, discernment, and the fear of the Lord. Spend more focused time reflecting and journaling on any specific areas of wisdom that stand out for you (e.g., money, sex, power, words, thoughts and emotions, relationships, work, rest, learning, food and drink, etc.).

    - Job
    - Proverbs
    - Ecclesiastes
    - James
    - 1 Corinthians 1–2

2. Finish reading *Watership Down*, by Richard Adams, and reflect on the questions in the Chapter 7 homework.

3. If time permits, look over Chapter 9 and its homework before your next meeting.

REFLECTION AND JOURNALING

Choose a present decision or challenging situation in your life that requires wisdom and discernment. Reflect on that decision and journal according to the prompts below.

4. Describe in one or two sentences the situation you are facing. Try to distill it into one straightforward question to God

5. In light of what you already know, as well as what you have learned this month about wisdom, write a few sentences applying this knowledge to the situation.

6. Examine your emotions. How do you feel about this situation? Are you settled and at peace? Are you anxious and confused? Are you frustrated and angry? Joyful and excited? Describe your feelings to God in a few sentences.

7. Read James 3:13–18 aloud at least twice and spend a few minutes reflecting on it in the presence of God. Then spend a few minutes reflecting again on your responses to the above prompts.

8. If you had to make a decision right now, what would you do? Why? Write a few sentences outlining what you have chosen to do, and why, with particular reference to the passage in James. How do you sense God answering the question you framed above?

9. Finally, reread your responses to these prompts and write a brief prayer to God in which you thank him for the wisdom he has given, and ask him for the wisdom you still need.

THE WORD IMPLANTED

Several times this month, read the following texts aloud:

- Job 28
- Psalm 90
- Proverbs 2:1–15
- Matthew 12:33–37
- James 1:2–8; 3:13–18

OTHER EXERCISES AND PRACTICES

10. Choose one week this month to practice "Contemplative Prayer" for at least ten minutes per day. See Appendix A for details.

11. At least once per week this month, practice the "Examen of Words" outlined in Appendix A.

12. Continue to incorporate into your rhythms one or more of the previous months' practices that you have found helpful.

RECOMMENDED FILMS

Watch *one* of the following films in light of the prompts provided.

1. *12 Angry Men* (1957)

    This film focuses on the jury deliberations in a murder trial in Chicago and takes place almost entirely in the locked room where the jury is deciding the fate of the accused man, an 18-year-old immigrant man accused of murdering his father. Through their sometimes-heated conversations, the 12 jurors come to better understand themselves and their own biases and ultimately arrive at a verdict that is both different, and wiser, than they had first expected. There is much to learn in this film about the power of attentive conversation to shape us, as well as about courage, conscience, bias, and the profound impact of our simply paying attention on our ability to discern the truth.

    ### AS YOU WATCH, CONSIDER THE FOLLOWING:

    a. Even before they begin their deliberations, the personalities, biases, priorities, and points of distraction of each of the jurors begins to emerge. What do you notice about different jurors, both as they get settled in the room and throughout their deliberations?

    b. After the first secret ballot, only one juror dissents. After some objection, someone asks, "What do we do now?" "I guess we talk," he replies, setting the stage for the remainder of this film, which is nothing more than an extended conversation. As you watch this film, consider who among the jurors influences the group toward constructive, transforming conversation and who does not. What qualities modeled in this film most contribute to or get in the way of constructive conversation?

    c. Much of the conversation in this film reveals the unexamined grids and assumptions that each of the jurors brings to their understanding of the truth—in this case the truth about a murder. What most stands out to you about how we can best hope to see and understand what is true in the world and how that connects with what we both cultivate inwardly in ourselves and choose to notice outwardly in others?

NOTE Notice how the close-up camerawork in this film helps draw attention to the emotions, distractions, wisdom, and biases of the different jurors.

d. The oldest juror at the table plays a particularly important role in helping the other jurors notice things they would not otherwise have seen. The two jurors raised in the slums, one of whom is an immigrant watchmaker, bring a unique perspective to the conversations, as well. How do the voices of these three men, who in many contexts are ignored, influence the outcome of their deliberations?

e. While God is not mentioned in this film, there is much that the Scriptures have to say about the words and behaviors of both the wise and the foolish among these 12 jurors. As you reflect biblically on this film, what are some texts and narratives, particularly from the wisdom literature, that come to mind?

2. *Inside Out* (2015)

This animated film focuses on the emotions—joy, fear, anger, disgust, and sadness—in the life of a young girl experiencing a major family move, and it sheds helpful light on how the ways we identify and navigate these emotions in our own lives contributes to our ability to make good choices and to live wisely and well.

AS YOU WATCH, CONSIDER THE FOLLOWING:

a. Which of the five emotions—joy, sadness, fear, anger, and disgust—stand out most for you as you watch this film? Why?

b. When properly attended to, each of these emotions contributes to our ability to live wisely and well. What are some examples of this from your own life? How has your emotional life contributed to your own spiritual formation over the years?

c. When unnoticed, overprioritized, or avoided, how can each of these emotions lead to distorted ways of being in our lives? What are some examples of this from your own life?

d. Consider your own emotional life and ask God to reveal areas where you either avoid or overindulge these five basic emotions. Spend some time journaling and describing to God what you notice, thanking him for areas of grace, and inviting him into areas of needed growth.

NOTES

Sophia

When wisdom comes we seldom know her,
Looking as we do for someone well-dressed, in finer form.
But she is weak and worn, and whispers when she stands before us, bleeding,
Pleading in her often wordless ways that we would see something more
Than what our eyes so often see, or want to,
Reading as we do our own hoped-for glories into things,
And wishing that it would be easier than it is.

But she waits, content to gently suffer our bewildered ways
Until the days when we finally lay aside our wearied wantings
And let her speak,
And let her lie as lifeless in our arms, and in her softness and silence
Utter words unfathomably deep,
That more than waves that swell,
Wash over us, and seep into our long-forgotten cellars.

For she, unwearied, knows that nard,
Poured out for as yet uninflicted wounds
And for unseen scars that mar a future still obscured,
Will in due course fill the house with its sweet scent;
So too her perfume will work its fragrant ways and fill our house too,
Giving us through her pain the hope by which we gain
The life we thought we'd lost.

ANDY SAPERSTEIN

CHAPTER 9

Calling and Vocation

▼

May the favor of the Lord our God rest on us; establish the work of our hands for us—yes, establish the work of our hands.

PSALM 90:17 NIV

▼

Whatever you do, do your work heartily, as for the Lord and not for people, knowing that it is from the Lord that you will receive the reward of the inheritance. It is the Lord Christ whom you serve.

COLOSSIANS 3:23–24 NASB

CHAPTER 9

Calling and Vocation

The "Varicolored Tunic" of Calling and Vocation

Human beings are created in God's image and commissioned to join him in the creative enterprise of stewarding and cultivating creation. Though sin introduced futility and corruption into the work God entrusted to humanity, many fruitful, image-bearing expressions of work remain and have even multiplied through the centuries.

Scripture depicts an extraordinary array of vocations, professions, giftings, and skills among the people it describes. Most are useful, admirable, and established by God. Likewise, the work that followers of Jesus do today reveals a beautifully "varicolored tunic" of calling and vocation at work in the world.

Those who wrote the books of the Bible were drawn from a wide array of vocations—kings, prophets, judges, warriors, farmers, shepherds, tax collectors, fishermen, physicians, government officials, poets, and musicians. Inspired by God, these authors in turn wrote about an incredibly diverse array of workers—midwives, prophetesses, artists and artisans, laborers and slaves, farmers and shepherds, city planners, seamstresses, soldiers, prostitutes, cupbearers, builders, tax collectors, queens, nursemaids, priests, homemakers, pastors, teachers, tentmakers, tanners, scribes, religious scholars, and household servants. The story of God's work in history is intertwined with our work. In our vocations, professions, avocations, knowledge, and skills, God is at work in the world.

God is pleased to work through people of immensely varied callings and background. This is part of God's intended plan—part of how he brings glory to himself in the world. In his poem, "Pied Beauty," Gerard Manley Hopkins points to the "dappled" variation on display in the world, including "all trades, their gear and tackle and trim." This diversity of work points to the multi-faceted beauty of the one who created all things. "He fathers forth whose beauty is past change," Hopkins says. "Praise Him." Our varied vocations and callings are intended, as is all of creation, to bring glory to God.

Diligence, Competence, and Calling

In light of this, it is therefore fitting to give focused attention to our work. Part of spiritual formation involves a growing understanding of God's view of work in general and the unique ways he has created and equipped each of us to create and labor with him in the redemptive work of his kingdom for his glory.

We encounter and reveal our Creator through our work, and as we offer our work back to him as a gift, and as we labor "godwardly," we learn contentment and diligence in the face of even mundane tasks. And as we attune to the particulars of our individual competencies and callings, we find ourselves more joyfully consecrated to God in all things.

The inherent value and dignity of labor is foundational to our ability to glorify God through our work. God labored for six days and rested on the seventh. Likewise, as image-bearers of God, much of our own time is given to productive work. While Sabbath rest is an essential part of a life well lived, much of our life consists of work—to participating with God in stewarding and cultivating the corner of creation appointed for us, no matter how humble that corner might be. Through work we act upon the world to improve it, develop it, and steward it according to God's revealed intentions.

The Scriptures illuminate the value of *diligence* in our work. Proverbs gives us the example of the industrious ant and contrasts it with the idle fool (Prov. 6:6, ff., etc.). In his parables, Jesus tells of people undertaking their work with diligence and attentiveness—the Faithful Steward (Luke 12:35 ff.), the Good Shepherd (John 10:11 ff.), and the Parable of the Talents (Matt. 25:14 ff.) are good examples. The opposite of diligence is *sloth*, which describes not only indolence and laziness, but also excursions into vain and futile substitutes for the work God calls us to. These substitutes keep us busy and fill our attention, but also nibble away at our central purpose and calling.

FOR REFLECTION

Think of jobs you have had that have neither paid handsomely nor been of high status. What has God taught you through these jobs?

Through work we act upon the world to improve it, develop it, and steward it according to God's revealed intentions.

The Scriptures similarly praise *competent* work. Examples include Bezalel and Oholiab, Spirit-filled Tabernacle craftsmen (Ex. 31, etc.); Nehemiah, cupbearer and rebuilder of Jerusalem; Deborah, prophetess, warrior, and judge (Jdg. 4:4, ff.); and Tabitha (Dorcas), devoted disciple and maker of garments (Acts 9:36 ff.). Even in unwanted circumstances, diverse Biblical characters do their work with diligence and competence. Daniel and his companions, taken against their will to Babylon as exiles, received gifting and favor from God, faithfully stewarded those gifts, and therefore rose to positions of prominence and influence for God's sake in a land not their own and in circumstances not of their choosing. Joseph's life in Egypt is another case in point.

Finally, the biblical notion of *calling* comes into play. Without calling, there is no vocation, which beyond being a mere synonym for our employment, often refers to work that God has specifically fitted us for and appointed us to undertake. The word "vocation," derived from the Latin *vocare*, "to call," invites us to seek God's voice as we discern the particulars of our calling both in community over time and through direct summons from God. When we say yes to God's call, we embrace his customized and tailor-made work for us, and follow in the footsteps of biblical figures as diverse in identity and situation as Moses, Esther, Joseph, Daniel, Jeremiah, Mary, and the Apostle Paul. All heard from God through some combination of his direct word to them, the testimony of the Scriptures, the circumstances of their lives, the counsel and direction of others, and the leading of the Holy Spirit, and all worked diligently and competently to fulfill work that God had specifically called them to do.

Calling often relates to our most evident spiritual gifts. In some cases, however, calling goes far beyond previously-identified abilities, gifts, or graces. Moses resists his calling by drawing attention to his lack of eloquence (Ex. 4:10 ff.). Peter denies the Lord, and later, when he is slow to acknowledge and embrace the gifts and calling Jesus has for him, the Lord commissions him to tend and feed his sheep (John 21:15 ff.). Calling includes yet transcends our existing, identified gifts and abilities and ultimately depends on God's initiative and bringing to fruition, not our own (1 Thess. 5:24).

No matter the work he calls us to, we are assured that God makes himself present to us, offers contentment, and affords us dignity.

Practical, Personal, and Prophetic Dimensions of Work

Apart from the particulars of God-given graces, giftings, and calling, there are also profoundly practical dimensions to work. Paul encourages Thessalonian believers "to make it your ambition to lead a quiet life and attend to your own business and work with your hands … so that you will behave properly toward outsiders and not be in any need" (1 Thess. 4:11–12). To the Ephesian church, Paul instructs former thieves (and all of us, by implication) to "work, doing something useful with their own hands, that they may have something to share with those in need" (Eph. 4:2 NIV). And Paul practiced what he preached. Along with his ministry partners Priscilla and Aquila, he paid his way in Corinth by working as a tentmaker (Acts 18:1–4). Humble work, often in the form of manual labor, is part of how God provides for us, preserves the reputation of the church, and creates surplus resource for those in need.

The privilege and affluence of modern life in the minority world is different from the world Paul lived in. Historically and geographically, most people have had far fewer vocational opportunities and less access to resources than we do. So how do we heed Paul's words in our present world of excess, complexity, and choice?

FOR REFLECTION
Where have you noticed God in your most ordinary and humble experiences of paid or unpaid work?

While an increase in vocational options makes us able to improve our economic lot, there is a downside—discontent often grows in proportion to the options available to us. Whether we are affluent or not, God desires that we work joyfully and contentedly unto him. No matter the work he calls us to, we are assured that God makes himself present to us, offers contentment, and affords us dignity. A Pakistani bicycle mechanic, a Cambodian seamstress, and a Venezuelan farmer are invited into sacred vocation as followers of Jesus just as white collar and professional sisters and brothers in their own or other lands are. Those whose work consists of caregiving and running a household enjoy the same dignity and invitation to sacred vocation as those who work outside the home and are paid handsomely for it.

In the end, God meets us in our work, whether it is paid or unpaid, of high or low status, provides for us in practical ways, and issues sacred callings that supersede the social and economic place our vocation holds. All of us are called to resist being lovers of money—wealth itself poses distinct challenges to faith (1 Tim. 6:10, etc.); all are called to be content with what we have (Heb. 3:5–6), for contentment itself is a great gain (1 Tim. 6:6–7); all, especially the wealthiest, are called to generosity (1 Tim. 6:17 ff., Matt. 10:8, etc.), that all may share equally in the blessings God gives (2 Cor. 8); and all are called to work unto God, aligning what we do with the graces and gifts he places in each of us (Col. 3:23–24, Eph. 1:18, 2 Thess. 1:11, etc.). By heeding these admonitions, we embody the prophetic dimensions of vocation, glorify God, and preserve the reputation of the church.

Finding Our Calling in God

Discerning and embodying our calling and vocation is not a self-centered pursuit, but one oriented toward the other three cardinal directions. We work unto God for the sake of others, and in service of God's outward purposes in the world. We offer our gifts and resources in service to the church and to the world. We do not demand of God that he fulfill our every ambition and inclination, but rather cultivate a humble posture of stewardship with all he's given us, seeking increasingly to offer ourselves as "a living and holy sacrifice" to God (Rom. 12:1).

A biblical notion of calling is never anxious and turned in on itself, angry at what God has not provided, but is rather outward and open-handed, eager to acknowledge gifts and graces and multiply them for good in the lives of others in the church and in the world, with the end purpose of our calling and formation being love itself (1 Tim. 1:5). The homework below is intended to help you reflect on and pursue the particulars of your own calling so that you might walk in the good works God has prepared for you (Eph. 2:10), and that you might grow, along with all of God's people, in the ways of God's love. ✢

Homework

READING

1. Read the following selected scriptures in their entirety. Consider reading at least some portions of these texts aloud:

    - Genesis 37–50 (The life and calling of Joseph, son of Israel)

    - 1 Samuel 1–3 (The calling of Samuel)

    - Daniel 1–6 (Daniel, Shadrach, Meshach, and Abednego)

    - The Book of Esther (Queen of Persia and deliverer of the Jewish people, "for such a time as this")

2. Choose *at least one* of the following books to help you reflect more deeply on calling and vocation:

   a. *The Way of Discernment: Spiritual Pracrtices for Decision Making,* by Elizabeth Liebert

   We all make decisions constantly—some with careful reflection, some without much thought. But what if we understood these decisions, minor as well as major, as matters of faithful Christian living? In this helpful and encouraging book, Elizabeth Liebert outlines several complementary approaches to discernment and decision making along with prompts and practices to help you engage with each.

   b. *Markings*, by Dag Hammarskjöld

   This modern classic contains the posthumously published journals of the celebrated Swedish economist, diplomat, and Secretary General of the United Nations between 1953 and his death in a plane crash in 1961. Hammarskjöld, a public man of deep private faith, offers years of personal reflections, poetry, and spiritual wrestling. His writing is of great value to anyone desiring to incorporate Christian faith into a more public calling.

   c. *Every Good Endeavor*, by Timothy Keller

   This excellent 2012 work by bestselling author and former pastor of New York's Redeemer Presbyterian Church provides a biblical theology of work and calling and offers much practical wisdom in the pursuit of God in the context of career.

   d. Choose a biography of someone whose vocation is significant and inspiring to you and reflect on it in light of God's view of work and calling, and the particulars of your own life of faith.

3. If time permits, look over Chapter 10 and its homework before your next meeting.

REFLECTION AND JOURNALING

4. Work through "Core Books," Practice 15 in Appendix A. Journal in response to this exercise as you further consider your own calling and vocation.

5. Read through "Core Calling," Practice 16 in Appendix A. Spend at least an hour or two further reflecting on your own calling and vocation through the life of one of these characters in the Scriptures.

THE WORD IMPLANTED

Practice the repeated oral reading of Scripture again this month using the following Word Implanted texts:

- Proverbs 6:6–11, 10:4–5, 16:3, 31:1–31
- Luke 2:39–52
- Luke 6:12–16
- 1 Corinthians 12 and 13
- 1 Thessalonians 4:9–12

OTHER EXERCISES AND PRACTICES

6. Read "Giving Gifts," Practice 17 in Appendix A.

7. Create a gift for God (and perhaps for someone else) in response to the prompts in this exercise. At the next meeting, come prepared to take 10 minutes or so to share your gift with the group.

8. Continue to incorporate into your rhythms one or more of the previous months' practices that you have found helpful.

RECOMMENDED FILMS

Watch and reflect on at least one of the films below, each of which focuses on a person faithfully practicing their vocation with integrity, many with a sense of calling from God.

1. *A Man for All Seasons* (1966)

   Winner of six Academy Awards, including Best Picture, Best Actor, and Best Director, this film tells the story of Sir Thomas More, celebrated English author, statesman, philosopher, and ultimately Lord Chancellor of England under Henry VIII. More's unyielding integrity in undertaking his public post cost him his life in 1535 when he was beheaded by the king for refusing to support him in his self-proclaimed supremacy over the English church and the right to annul his marriage with Catherine of Aragorn, the first of Henry's eight wives. This film stands as an excellent study in maintaining personal integrity in the context of a public calling and political career.

2. *Concussion* (2015)

    Based on actual events, this film starring Will Smith tells the story of Nigerian American forensic pathologist Dr. Bennett Omalu, who first discovered and published findings linking repeated head trauma among NFL players with chronic traumatic encephalopathy, a destructive and sometimes fatal neurodegenerative disease. Against the opposition of NFL leadership, Omalu persists in researching and publishing his findings, and his story is a helpful glimpse into a career yielded to God and committed to integrity and truth.

3. *Something the Lord Made* (2004)

    Also based on actual events, this film starring Mos Def and Alan Rickman tells the story of skilled African American carpenter Vivien Thomas, who becomes the unlikely partner to the celebrated Dr. Alfred Blalock in the development of bypass surgery in the care of so-called "blue babies." Without medical training, but with remarkable gifting and intuitions in the work of surgery, Thomas rose from the position of janitor to lab technician to Instructor of Surgery at the Johns Hopkins School of Medicine, and worked for 34 years with Blalock, who initially received disproportionate credit for their achievements. This film stands as a helpful example of a humble man of faith who employs his God-given abilities on an unexpected path for the public good.

4. *Arrival* (2016)

    Nominated for Best Picture, this science fiction film tells the story of linguistics professor Louise Banks, played by Amy Adams, as she leads a team seeking to understand the written language of extraterrestrial visitors in the quest to communicate with them and avoid potential war. Focused on a committed professional faithfully practicing her craft in a high-stakes context, this film provides much to reflect on regarding the use of vocation to bring good into the world.

NOTES

As Kingfishers Catch Fire

As kingfishers catch fire, dragonflies draw flame;
As tumbled over rim in roundy wells
Stones ring; like each tucked string tells, each hung bell's
Bow swung finds tongue to fling out broad its name;
Each mortal thing does one thing and the same:
Deals out that being indoors each one dwells;
Selves—goes itself; *myself* it speaks and spells,
Crying *What I do is me: for that I came.*

I say more: the just man justices;
Keeps grace: that keeps all his goings graces;
Acts in God's eye what in God's eye he is—
Christ—for Christ plays in ten thousand places,
Lovely in limbs, and lovely in eyes not his
To the Father through the features of men's faces.

GERARD MANLEY HOPKINS

CHAPTER 10

Living Missionally

> You are the light of the world . . . let your light shine before others, that they may see your good deeds and glorify your Father in heaven.
>
> MATTHEW 5:14, 16 NIV

> You will receive power when the Holy Spirit comes on you; and you will be my witnesses in Jerusalem, and in all Judea and Samaria, and to the ends of the earth.
>
> ACTS 1:8 NIV

CHAPTER 10

Living Missionally

A Sent People

Taught by Jesus himself, Christians through the ages pray, "Your kingdom come. Your will be done, on earth as it is in heaven" (Matt. 6:10 NASB) and seek to "make disciples of all the nations" (Matt. 28:19a NASB). In Luke 9, the Lord calls the 12 together, gives them power and authority over demons and disease and sends them out to heal the sick and proclaim the kingdom (Luke 9:1 ff). They are overjoyed to see God work through them as they obey and go. In the following chapter, Jesus appoints 70 more followers to do the same (Luke 10:1-10).

In the Nicene Creed, Christians proclaim belief in "one, holy, catholic, and apostolic church." The church, "the assembly of God's firstborn children, whose names are written in heaven" (Heb. 12:23a NLT), alongside the great cloud of witnesses (Heb. 12:1 NIV), comprises believers from every tribe and tongue and people and nation who have been purchased for God by the blood of Jesus (Rev. 5:9), and it is this church that is called to be both catholic and apostolic. To be "catholic" here means to be universal—the followers of Jesus of any time or place or denomination or tradition belong to the Lord because of his finished work on the cross. And to be "apostolic" means not only to be part of the church first established by the Apostles, but also to be like them: to be *sent* by the Lord into the world to bring his kingdom to bear in new places and among new communities of people.

Every one of us is therefore a *sent* person, and the church is a sent people. As such, we are all called by God to participate in the apostolic mission of the church in the world and to seek God for the particular ways he positions and equips us to do so.

Those fully formed in Christ work for mercy and justice,

proclaim the coming kingdom of God, preach the Gospel, heal

the sick, feed the poor, and establish new kingdom communities.

Mission and Formation

Given this apostolic identity of the church, our formation in Christ is incomplete if it does not lead to participation in the broader mission of God and outward expressions of his love in the world. Those fully formed in Christ work together for mercy and justice, proclaim the coming kingdom of God, preach the Gospel, heal the sick, feed the poor, and establish new kingdom communities.

A Christian turned in on himself and enclosed within the *"one another"* of his own community may have some *upward* connection to God and *inward* growth in grace. But without committed participation in the *outward* progress of God's kingdom in the world, he is like a windmill missing a blade, a bird with one wing, a bicycle with one pedal.

In the book *The Church of Mercy*, Pope Francis speaks of this outward, missional expression of God's love as an essential part of the Lord's heartbeat in us, the "systolic" outward pulsing of God's love for the world following the "diastolic" infilling of his love as we abide in Christ. This rhythm of God's heartbeat leads us to proclaim the Gospel boldly and joyfully; gives us courage to share God's love with people near and far; and constrains us to live humbly, vulnerably, and availably in service to God and others for his good purposes in the world.

A Diversity of Missional Callings

By gifting and disposition, calling and opportunity, each of us is assigned to a *particular* dimension of God's kingdom mission. Alongside our individual calling, we also experience the *fullness* of God's kingdom mission, often in prayer and in giving. The petitionary prayers of "your kingdom come, your will be done on earth as it is in heaven" and asking God to send more workers into the harvest are just two ways to engage in broad kingdom mission.

Whether for a particular dimension or the full expression of it, as we give of our time, money, talents, and other resources to further God's missional purpose in the world, we align ourselves more deeply with God himself, our hearts grow in love for others, and God more fully forms his heart within us; for where our treasure is, there our hearts will be also (Matt. 6:21). The homework in this chapter invites you to explore and engage in the particulars of God's missional calling on your own life. May God meet you, form you, and give you good courage as you follow him "to the outskirts" and even to the ends of the earth (Acts 1:8) on mission with him.

Homework

READING

1. Selected books of Scripture

    As you read, note the ways God transforms his messengers and removes obstacles that keep people from experiencing the fullness of his kingdom.

    - Exodus 1–18

        This archetypal deliverance narrative is an invitation to experience God's salvation and invite and assist others to do the same.

    - Jonah

        God uses this reluctant prophet to save lives. Jonah has much to teach us about pressing beyond prejudices and preferences to join God in the mission of his kingdom.

    - Acts

        Written by Luke, the beloved physician, this remarkable account of the progress of the infant church captures God's relentless commitment to gather all the nations back to himself as one beloved people. Central themes of Acts include the coming of the Holy Spirit and the welcoming of the Gentiles into the emerging church, a seismic shift that still informs our participation in God's mission in the world today.

2. Recommended book

    The Church of Mercy: A Vision for the Church, by Pope Francis

    A collection of essays, homilies, and other excerpts taken from the first year of Pope Francis' papacy beginning in 2013. As both the first Jesuit pope and the first pope from South America, Francis seeks a church whose people have personal union with Christ and who are engaged with the world in Christ's mission. As you read, pay particular attention to Chapter 5, "Being with Christ," as it is a helpful summary of the overall themes of the book.

3. Other optional books

   a. *Cry the Beloved Country*, by Alan Paton (1948)

      Written by a white South African author during the horrors of apartheid, this modern classic tells the fictional story of two fathers whose lives intersect when the son of one, a Black pastor, murders the son of the other, a white landowner and farmer. The story of grace and reconciliation unfolds in the face of great pain, systemic racism, poverty, and loss. As you read, notice the role of Reverend Theophilus Msimangu in bringing grace and redemption to bear in the different communities he touches.

   b. *How the Irish Saved Civilization*, by Thomas Cahill (1995)

      This book tells the remarkable story of St. Patrick's 5th century call to return to his Irish enslavers and how the ensuing Irish missional and monastic movement emerged in the following centuries, winning many to faith, promoting education and justice among the poor and marginalized of Europe, and preserving Classical Greek and Latin texts along the way.

   c. *Death Comes for the Archbishop*, by Willa Cather (1927)

      Among Cather's most celebrated novels, this tells the story of a devoted Catholic missionary priest in the 19th century American Southwest. Without sentimentality or idealism, this simple story illuminates qualities of perseverance, resourcefulness, and grace in a cross-cultural missional context.

   d. *The Art of Neighboring*, by Jay Pathak and Dave Runyon (2012)

      In The Art of Neighboring, Pathak, a local pastor and National DIrector of Vineyard USA, provides a winsome and practical approach to connecting in the way of Jesus with the people in our own neighborhoods. Living missionally, according to Pathak, best begins when we pay attention and make ourselves available to the people we see every day in our own neighborhoods.

   e. Choose a book of your own. Read and reflect on the biography of a Christian leader engaged in the outward expression of God's kingdom in the world—a Christian missionary, a leader in social justice, medical care, service to the poor, etc., in keeping with your own sense of missional calling in the world.

4. If time permits, look over Chapter 11 and its homework before your next meeting.

REFLECTION AND JOURNALING

5. Set aside approximately one hour this month to do the following four-step journaling exercise:

    a. Ask God to guide your time and to reveal his heart and mind to you. Ask God to draw your attention to people and situations that are part of your own missional calling.

    b. Consider your life in light of Acts 1:8. Begin with your family, friends, workplace, and neighborhood. Move on to your state and nation. End with nations and people beyond your own national boundaries. At each level, ask God to draw particular people and situations to mind, and jot them down in your journal. Pay particular attention to people and situations who are on "the outskirts" of your life and who by geography or economics, culture or education, language or politics, are distant from you, yet for whom you sense God's love.

    c. Once you have a few people and places listed, begin to pray over them. Use the fourth movement of the Lord's Prayer—"Your kingdom come, your will be done, on earth as it is in heaven"—as you pray over each person, place, or situation. Note in your journal anything or anyone that particularly stands out for you as you pray.

    d. Review your notes and prayers before God and write a personal prayer a few sentences in length that summarizes what you sense God leading you to pray and do for the people he has led you to consider.

THE WORD IMPLANTED

Practice the repeated oral reading of Scripture again this month using the following Word Implanted texts:

- Genesis 12:1–3
- Psalm 67
- Isaiah 58:6–12
- Matthew 28:18–20
- Revelation 5:9–10, 7:9–12

TIP Music is another good way to learn about and develop God's heart for people of widely varied cultures and backgrounds. Take time to listen to some music from a cultural or social group different from your own through one of the many online sources.

OTHER EXERCISES AND PRACTICES

6. Read "The Lord's Prayer in Seven Movements" in Appendix A and use this guide for your own prayers at least once a week this month.

7. Revisit your "Hospitality to Strangers" journal entries from the Chapter 7 homework. Invite and connect with another person who you have never extended hospitality to in the past.

8. As a follow-up to the "Reflection and Journaling" prompts in the preceding list, choose one person, place, or situation to intentionally learn more about and engage with this month.

    a. If it is a person, you might simply make them the one you extend hospitality to this month.

    b. If it is a nation or people group, you might read an article or watch a documentary to help better understand and love them, or simply visit a local restaurant, grocery store, or social context where you can cultivate God's heart for them.

    c. If there is an opportunity to serve with a ministry or organization in your church or community, take a first step toward doing so.

9. Continue to pray for your 12-for-12 companions.

RECOMMENDED FILMS

Watch and reflect on at least one of the films below, each of which focuses on a person faithfully practicing their vocation with integrity, many with a sense of calling from God.

1. *The Mission* (1986)

    Nominated for seven Academy Awards and winner of Best Cinematography, this 1986 film starring Robert DeNiro and Jeremy Irons focuses on the establishment of a Jesuit mission in the heart of the Amazon in the late 18th century and its protection of the indigenous population from pro-slavery Portuguese colonial powers. This film raises important questions about the complex relationship between Christian mission, evangelism, justice, culture, power, and money.

    AS YOU WATCH, CONSIDER THE FOLLOWING:

    a. The symbol of the waterfall

    b. The symbol of Rodrigo's bundle of armor

c. The development of conscience in Father Gabriel, Rodrigo, and His Eminence Altamirano

   d. The recurring appearance of the young Guarani boy as a witness, and as a participant in the events

   e. Father Gabriel's question to Altamirano regarding what he will do with the Jesuit missions. He replies, "As my conscience dictates—what else?"

   f. The different ways Father Gabriel, Rodrigo, and Altamirano respond to Portuguese colonial aggression and their responsibility to God, one another, and the indigenous communities they live among. Reflect on your own experiences practicing your faith in the midst of complex moral choices in the real world.

   g. The last words in the film: "You had no alternative, Your Eminence. We must work in the world. The world is thus." "No, Señor Hontar. Thus, have we made the world. Thus, have I made it."

2. *Cry the Beloved Country* (1995)

   Based on Alan Paton's novel of the same name, *Cry the Beloved Country* tells a moving story of death, loss, justice, mercy, and redemption in the face of horrific racial injustice under South African apartheid. As you watch, notice how Reverend Theophilus Msimangu's words and actions model missional living in the way of Jesus and bring about an unlikely reconciliation.

3. *Just Mercy* (2019)

   This 2019 film tells the true story of Bryan Stevenson, Harvard-educated attorney and founder of the Equal Justice Initiative, who rather than pursuing lucrative opportunities, moves to Alabama to defend wrongly convicted prisoners. This film focuses on the defense and ultimate exoneration of Alabama death row prisoner, Walter McMillian. Stevenson's celebrated social justice work is deeply influenced by his Christian faith and early formation in the African Methodist Episcopal Church.

To the True Nurse

GOD's own true nurse is she who knows
"By constant watching wise"
Just where the scalding current flows
That, hid from casual eyes,
Make life an arid wilderness;
Then does the true nurse bless.

For she, without the noise of words
Most lovingly will do,
Till, like the song of happy birds,
The joy of ease pours through
That which was arid wilderness—
So does the true nurse bless.

And when the spirit drifts afraid
To strange and unknown lands,
Then does the true nurse, undismayed
(Her dear love understands),
Follow and comfort and caress—
So does the true nurse bless.

O nurse, God-given, your ministry
Is something all divine;
With all you do, in all you be,
His love will intertwine
The gold threads of His gentleness—
So will His true nurse bless.

AMY CARMICHAEL
Source: *https://dohnavurfellowship.org/ Used by permission*

CHAPTER 11

Establishing Rhythms of Grace

▼

Unless the Lord builds the house, They labor in vain who build it; Unless the Lord guards the city, The watchman keeps awake in vain

MATTHEW 5:14, 16 NIV

▼

… blessed is the one who trusts in the Lord … They will be like a tree planted by the water … its leaves are always green. And it never fails to bear fruit."

JEREMIAH 17:7–8 NIV (PORTIONS)

CHAPTER 11

Establishing Rhythms of Grace

A Seamless Tunic

At this point in our 12-for-12 journey, it is time to weave the year's patterns, practices, habits, and ways of being into a garment to be worn for many years to come. This "spiritual tunic" is suitable when days are radiant and warm and when they are not. Like the seamless tunic Jesus wore when arrested (John 19:23), this garment is to be a unified fabric, free of unnecessary stitches and sections, simple, durable, and adaptable to all situations. Also, like the Lord's tunic, we want to weave ours "from top to bottom" (literally "from above," "from the top," or "from the beginning" in Greek) (John 19:23b, NIV)—with an unobstructed gaze upward to God as we weave.

Like Jesus, we will wear this tunic as an undergarment, often covered by outer garments according to the occasion but always closest to our skin—closest to the person God has made us to be. No matter the season, setting, or occasion, the fabric maintains its integrity: we are who God has made us to be in all the various contexts and communities we inhabit. Part of formational work involves taking inventory: to identify and curate the fluid, flexible, and timeless habits that best root us in God and make us available to him and to others. This is therefore a month of review and reflection, a chance to take stock of our lives and make space to seek God for ways of living and being that help us flourish in all the cardinal directions in every season of our lives.

Rules and Rhythms

Since at least the sixth century, Christian communities have woven their own seamless tunics—a "rule of life"—a pattern of recurring habits and practices to wear "close to their skin." While Christians and other religious communities before this time certainly sought to establish similar patterns of living (the Jewish Law is a case in point), St. Benedict of Nursia (480–547 C.E.) was among the earliest to articulate these patterns for an intentional Christian monastic community. The Rule of St. Benedict, while more involved than most modern lay Christians will find practical, is a framework for all who seek holistic intentionality and order in their life with Jesus.

We may chafe at the notion of establishing a "rule" for our own lives. The notion of "rule" may evoke a sense of legalism that impedes rather than promotes our ability to embrace the way of life God offers to us. "Rhythms" perhaps lands more gently than "rules," as a rhythm speaks more of a repeated cadence than it does of a legal code. Or perhaps the metaphor of a "seamless tunic" is more appealing. By whatever name or metaphor, spiritual patterns of engagement and abstinence are part of the saints' lives from the beginning and are abundantly supported in Scripture.

Jesus is the best example of an embodied and intentional rule and rhythm of life. On many occasions in the Gospels:

- Jesus went off alone to pray (Matt. 14:23, Luke 9:18, John 6:15, etc.).

- Jesus went to the synagogue to teach, pray, heal the sick, and cast out demons (Matt. 4:23, 9:35; Mark 1:39; Luke 4:44; John 18:20, etc.).

- Jesus compassionately engaged the poor, the foreigner, the outcast, and the sinful (Matt. 9:9-13, Mark 5:21 ff., Luke 8:43 ff., John 4:7 ff, etc.).

- Jesus taught and modeled prayer (Matt. 6:9-13, Mark 14:36, Luke 11:1-13, John 17, etc.), fasting (Matt. 4:1-11, Matt. 6:16 ff., etc.), and feasting (Mark 2:15 ff., John 2:1-12, etc.).

The Old Testament Scriptures—the Pentateuch, Histories, Psalms, Wisdom Literature, and Prophets—also offer lessons on the habits we ought to adopt and those we ought to avoid. The Epistles contain regular instruction and admonition regarding habits for a flourishing life that blesses others and glorifies God. Paul's letters, for example:

- Instruct Timothy to pay close attention to himself and his teaching (1 Tim. 4:16).

- Instruct the Ephesian church to be careful how they live, walking wisely and not unwisely, making the most of their time (Eph. 5:15-16).

- Describe his own approach to life as intentional, not aimless, disciplined, not careless (1 Cor. 9:26-27).

The arc of Scripture encourages us to live focused, disciplined, and intentional lives infused by God's grace, full of the Holy Spirit, and a witness to the world.

Part of formational work involves taking inventory: to identify and curate the fluid, flexible, and timeless habits that best root us in God and make us available to him and to others.

Living Within the Boundaries of Grace

Earlier this year we considered the Apostle Paul's admonition not to think more highly of ourselves than we ought but to use sound judgment instead, according to the faith God has given (Rom. 12:3). Once during a season of burnout, a wise friend encouraged my wife and me not to go "beyond grace," by which he meant to live within the limits of God's provision. To live as though we had no limits was to think more highly of ourselves than we ought and to misunderstand God's manifold provision.

FOR REFLECTION
What are some of the particular graces God has provided for you to help you walk out your calling?

God's grace is the entire range of resources that enable us to walk in our callings. Grace takes the form of food, drink, rest, money, partnership, friendship, intellect, creativity, time, spiritual gifts, fruit of the spirit, etc.—any physical, spiritual, emotional, relational, or other provision Old Testament authors refer to as our "portion" or "boundary line"—the finite provision given from God's infinite resource (cf., Ps. 16:5–6, Prov. 30:8, Ecc. 11:2, etc.) to support us in our life with God.

To overestimate our limits is to go "beyond grace." A rule and rhythm of life makes us increasingly aware of and content to live within the limits God places on each one of us—to live "within the boundaries of grace."

This requires an honest assessment of the portion God gives us, for good stewardship begins with an accurate understanding of the resources at hand. Neither the prodigal son nor the servant who buried his talents served as a good steward; one squandered resources and the other fearfully failed to invest them. Upon coming to faith, and even throughout the journey, the Lord calls us to "calculate the cost" and to assess our enemy's power (Luke 14:26–33).

Our starting point is a willingness to bear our own cross—to pay whatever cost the Lord may ask of us as we yield our life to him day by day. And yet the actual cost of discipleship varies from person to person in proportion to the provision given and the circumstances of our individual lives and callings. The Lord asks for everything but may not require it of us, and he both provides for us through our "daily bread" (Matt. 6:11) in small portions of grace along the way and leads us in stewarding that grace day by day in ways unique to each of us.

Our ability to assess and steward the grace God gives us is greatest when we live attentively to God, to his provision, and to his calling on our lives, and when we regularly reassess the boundaries of grace he has set for us. This requires focused attention and rooted connection with God. Jesus, at both the beginning and the end of his earthly ministry, in counting both the cost and the grace given him, said yes to the Father, resisted the devil, and for the joy set before him (Heb. 12:2), gave himself unto death for our sake. We are to follow in his steps (1 Pet. 2:21).

The Ultimate Limit

Mortality is our ultimate limit. Every year on Ash Wednesday we acknowledge this truth when we say to one another: "Remember that you are dust and to dust you shall return" (Gen. 3:19b). This is not a place many like to dwell—in thoughts of our own death. But dwell at times we must. To live wisely and within the boundaries of grace requires us to regularly pause and behold the reality of our own death.

Ecclesiastes declares it better to go to a house of mourning than to a house of feasting, for that is the end of every person, and it is in mourning that we are best able to take this to heart (Ecc. 7:2). The central prayer of Psalm 90 is "Teach us to number our days, that we may gain a heart of wisdom" (Ps. 90:12 NIV), because only when we acknowledge our mortality before God can we pray the psalm's closing prayer: "Establish the work of our hands for us—yes, establish the work of our hands" (Ps. 90:17 NIV). Embracing mortality allows us to establish a realistic rule and rhythm of life and moves our gaze back to God in the hope of eternal life.

Being mindful of our mortality allows us to offer our lives to God as a moment-by-moment, living and holy sacrifice (Rom. 12:1), never intoxicated by our own resources or power but wholly dependent on the presence and mercy of God to bear good fruit in and through us all our days. We desire long life and along with our Orthodox brethren pray "God grant you many years" over one another, and yet we rest in the psalmist's gentle reminder that God extends his expansive love to us in light of the fact that "he knows how weak we are, he remembers we are only dust" (Ps. 103:14 NLT). Part of our work this month will be to learn, consider, and rest in the reality of our own mortality.

The Lost Gift of Sabbath

God's fourth commandment, the Sabbath mandate (Ex. 20:8–11), is a weekly commemoration of our limits and God's sufficiency. We "cease striving and know that [he is] God" (Ps. 46:10a NASB), acknowledging that unless God builds the house, our labors are in vain; unless God guards the city, we guard it in vain (Ps. 127:1). It is a step of deep faith and humility to cease productivity in order to rest in the fact that God, with no help from us, "upholds all things by the word of his power" (Heb. 1:3b NASB). Sabbath is a weekly rhythm of slowing down, delighting in God and his gifts, acknowledging our limits, and resting like a weaned child on its mother (Ps. 131:2), content to lie still in the arms of God and be renewed for another week of fruitful labor.

To live wisely and within the boundaries of grace requires us to regularly pause and behold the reality of our own death.

Sabbath does not come easily. As members of an extroverted, active, productivity-driven society, we often find ourselves resistant or unwilling to slow down or stop. We readily expend all our energy all the time, and even when not productively working, we are prone to distract ourselves with things that disconnect us from God, ourselves, other people, and our own physical surroundings. And in all this frenzy and distraction, we often not only justify our behaviors but even label them as good. In contrast, Sabbath rest is a revolutionary, countercultural act.

The Practice of Sabbath

How can we make the grace and gift of Sabbath part of life's healthy rhythms? Here are a few suggestions:

BE INTENTIONAL

Just as you would any meeting or important task, schedule your Sabbath. Add it to your calendar. Aim for roughly the same 24-hour time period every week, but if you need to break the time into a few smaller pieces, that is much better than not setting aside any time at all.

Mark the beginning and end of your Sabbath time by lighting a candle, reading a Psalm, saying a prayer, etc. Schedule an out-of-office email message for this time period.

INVENTORY WHAT "COUNTS" AS SABBATH

Silence, solitude, worship, rest and sleep, time in prayer and Scripture reading, meals and playtime with friends and family, leisure reading, creative activities, hobbies, time in nature, celebration, and other refreshing activities fit well with a time of Sabbath. And of course, children, other dependents, and pets will need your care. Most other aspects of domestic labor, however, such as laundry, gardening, cooking, cleaning, grocery shopping, home projects, etc. are harder to categorize. Ask yourself:

- Does this task turn me toward God in a settled and relaxed way?
- Does it help me delight in my surroundings and those in it?
- Does it provide refreshment and renewal?

As members of an extroverted, active, productivity-driven society, we often find ourselves resistant or unwilling to slow down or stop.

Be honest. If we sense bubbling anxiety, a striving, or loss of peace as we consider an activity, we would probably do well to skip it. Some weeks, a grocery errand, yard work, or a minor home project may leave us rested, renewed, and turned godward. Other weeks, the same activities may inflict the opposite. That said, limiting technology use on the Sabbath is almost always beneficial. Set your phone to "Do Not Disturb," refrain from checking email, turn off the TV, don't scroll social media, etc. Consider limiting or completely avoiding commercial activity and shopping—online or otherwise. Whatever the particulars, one's Sabbath must center on delight and rest. Even all-powerful, all-knowing God, who never grows weary or tired, ceased from his labor and "was refreshed" on the seventh day (Ex. 31:17, Is. 40:28). This same posture is how we are to observe Sabbath.

BE FLEXIBLE. BE GENTLE. START SMALL.

If you are not presently observing Sabbath, start small. Do what you can, not what you can't. For example, begin with two or three hours of Sabbath, adding an hour or two per week to gradually work up to a 24-hour period. If you get caught up in work or less refreshing activities, be gentle with yourself. Simply pause, acknowledge where you are, and gently return yourself, both inwardly and outwardly, to a posture of godward rest and delight.

TIP If you live in a family or other household community, take time to discuss what Sabbath might look like for others in your household, and consider ways you might support each other in it.

Living Sabbatically

A weekly Sabbath anchors an entire life lived in "sabbatical" rhythms. Its refreshment flows into the channels of our everyday life, helping us live not out of our own striving but out of the strength and grace only God can provide. We can weave small portions of stillness, delight, reflection, rest, and gratitude into each day.

Living "sabbatically" regularly acknowledges the limits of our own strength, knowledge, wisdom, power, influence, resources, and hours in a day. It is a way to revere the Lord and yield to his rightful claim on our lives. It helps us delight in others and in creation. It brings intentionality and shalom to our lives—a posture steeped in the peace of the Lord.

This month's homework, in preparation for our final meeting, will help you consider your own life, establish rhythms for the "long game," and become like the tree that Jeremiah speaks of:

> They will be like a tree planted by the water
>   that sends out its roots by the stream.
> It does not fear when heat comes;
>   its leaves are always green.
> It has no worries in a year of drought
>   and never fails to bear fruit. (Jer. 17:8 NIV)

Homework

READING

Early this month, carefully read through this entire section before starting any assignments. You will find the "Building for Life" assignment easier to do if you first complete the preparatory work.

1. *Neighbor Rosicky*, by Willa Cather

    First published in *Woman's Home Companion* in 1930, this gentle short story tells the story of Czech immigrant Anton Rosicky and his family on their humble farm in Nebraska. Told from the perspective of the local country doctor and containing flashbacks of Anton Rosicky's days in London as a poor immigrant, "Neighbor Rosicky" considers the life of a man and a family given to relationship and simple domestic graces rather than ambitious pursuit of profit.

    > **TIP** This story can be found online or in various short story or Willa Cather anthologies.

2. Choose one of the following books:

    a. *The Sabbath: Its Meaning for Modern Man*, by Abraham Joshua Heschel

        This modern classic by a celebrated Jewish scholar, mystic, activist, and theologian uses metaphor, imagery, narrative, and verse to frame Sabbath as a "palace in time" where we reconnect with eternity and with God himself.

    b. *Sabbath Keeping: Finding Freedom in the Rhythms of Rest*, by Lynne M. Baab

        By addressing Sabbath resistance and sharing testimonies from her congregation, this book by Presbyterian minister Lynne Baab stands as a practical guide to embracing Sabbath.

3. If time permits, look over Chapter 12 before your next meeting.

REFLECTION AND JOURNALING

Complete these two reflections before moving on to "Building for Life" in the "Other exercises and practices" section.

3. Looking Back

    Prayerfully review the previous chapters, homework assignments, and appendices alongside your own journal entries over the year. Notice themes, practices, and scriptures that most impacted you.

Remember the monthly gatherings with your 12-for-12 companions: meals you ate together, moments of listening, moments of speaking, etc.

4. Mortality Reflection

   a. Ask for God's guidance as you consider your mortality.

   b. Read aloud passages like Psalm 39, Psalm 90, Psalm 103:13–18, Ecclesiastes 12:1–7, Matthew 10:28–31, Galatians 2:20, Philippians 1:19–26, Colossians 3:1–4, and Revelation 21:1–7.

   c. Allow feelings to surface as you read. Keep yourself in the presence of God, open and receptive to him. Without despair, face the reality of your limits and your numbered days. You may sense weightiness, an almost physical ache, and this is okay. Stay aware of God's loving gaze as you face these realities.

   d. Read Psalm 103:13–18 again, which captures our paradoxical reality: Our lives are fleeting and fragile; God's love and mercy is everlasting. If recollections of people loved and lost surface, let them. But don't press beyond God-given capacity. Journal a short prayer to acknowledge your mortality to God, consecrate your life to him, and seek his grace for a heart of wisdom. Read it aloud to God a time or two, and keep it as a resource for the future.

THE WORD IMPLANTED

Practice the repeated oral reading of Scripture again this month using the following texts:

- Exodus 20:8–11
- Psalm 127
- Ecclesiastes 3
- Isaiah 58
- Matthew 7:24–27
- Ephesians 5:15–16

OTHER EXERCISES AND PRACTICES

Engage the three practices below before doing "Building for Life," Practice 20 in Appendix A. They foster a yielded attentiveness to God, which is helpful for considering life in more holistic terms. For instructions on exercises 2–5, see Appendix A.

Practice "Postures of Prayer", Practice 18 in Appendix A, daily for the first week of the month. Ease into "Practicing Sabbath" and "Selective Abstaining," Practice 19 in Appendix A, during the first week and beyond.

5. Practicing Sabbath

   Begin (or continue) the practice of weekly Sabbath, and maintain it beyond this group's conclusion. Use "The Lost Gift of Sabbath" and "The Practice of Sabbath" sections above as a guide. Early in the month, set aside several hours to a full 24-hour day each week to savor God's presence, cultivate contentment and delight, and rest in solitude or community before God. Along the way, take time to consider what "counts" as Sabbath, recognizing it may vary from week to week or season to season.

6. Postures of Prayer, Practice 18

   Engage in this spiritual and physical practice for several days in a row to help express the posture you want to embrace in your overall life with God.

7. Selective Abstaining, Practice 19

   Gradually incorporate this practice early in the month to help "unclutter" your life as you seek God for more intentional rhythms of grace.

8. Building for Life, Practice 20

   Do this exercise after completing the "Reflection and journaling" homework, and after engaging with the three preceding practices. Next month, come to your gathering prepared to share some of what you sense God leading you into, especially regarding the "life mission statement," as well as some aspects of your "foundation," "framing," and "finishing."

9. Continue to practice helpful exercises from previous months.

10. As you move toward your last meeting together, regularly hold your fellow 12-for-12 companions in prayer.

RECOMMENDED FILMS

Watch and reflect on at least one of the previously assigned films you have not yet viewed. ✥

The Negro Speaks of Rivers

I've known rivers:
I've known rivers ancient as the world and older than the
    flow of human blood in human veins.

My soul has grown deep like the rivers.

I bathed in the Euphrates when dawns were young.
I built my hut near the Congo and it lulled me to sleep.
I looked upon the Nile and raised the pyramids above it.
I heard the singing of the Mississippi when Abe Lincoln
    went down to New Orleans, and I've seen its muddy
    bosom turn all golden in the sunset.

I've known rivers:
Ancient, dusky rivers.

My soul has grown deep like the rivers.

LANGSTON HUGHES

https://en.wikisource.org/wiki/The_negro_speaks_of_rivers

*This poem was written by celebrated Black poet Langston Hughes when he was just seventeen years old and marks the beginning of his long literary career. It still stands as among his most famous and defining works.

CHAPTER 12

Summing Up and Pressing On

▼

One thing I do: forgetting what lies behind and reaching forward to what lies ahead, I press on toward the goal for the prize of the upward call of God in Christ Jesus.

PHIL. 3:13B–14 NASB

▼

Now may . . . God . . . equip you with everything good for doing his will, and may he work in us what is pleasing to him, through Jesus Christ, to whom be glory for ever and ever. Amen.

HEB. 13:20, 21 NIV

CHAPTER

12

Summing Up and Pressing On

Moving Forward in the Cardinal Directions

An ending is also a beginning. Consider a commencement address that focuses on the graduates' future, with wistful reflection playing only a supporting role. The emphasis is on what is about to *commence*, not on what has just ended. As we end our 12-for-12 year together, we too both wistfully remember our year together and expectantly embrace the season about to begin.

The cardinal directions of the spiritual life have accompanied us throughout the year—may they continue to guide us going forward as we pursue them with grace and intentionality. Like blades on a windmill facing upward to lay hold of the wind's power, we turn ourselves godward, that God's Spirit and truth might power our ongoing inward transformation, animate the "one anotherness" of spiritual community, and lead us outwardly to bear fruit in the world. May God keep us ever upwardly engaged, that we might continue to grow, change, labor, and love for his sake for all our days. "Unless the Lord builds the house," the Psalmist says, "they labor in vain who build it" (Ps. 127:1, NASB); so too our own flourishing and fruitfulness depends not on our willpower and striving but on the mercy of God (Rom. 9:16).

Like blades on a windmill facing upward to lay hold of the wind's power, we turn ourselves godward, that his Spirit and truth might power our ongoing inward transformation, animate the "one anotherness" of spiritual community, and lead us outwardly to bear fruit in the world.

Practicing the Way of Shalom

We have also increased our attentiveness this year to patterns of grace and patterns of sin in our lives. Avoiding the extremes of both hubris and despair, we abandon ourselves to the currents of God's grace that we might both willingly embrace our weakness and ever seek his all-sufficient strength. "We have this treasure in jars of clay," the Apostle Paul tells us, "to show that this all-surpassing power is from God and not from us" (2 Cor. 4:7 NIV).

Yet strikingly, God gives us genuine agency in stewarding the graces he gives us. He entrusts to us the sacred responsibility of imparting to others the graces he has first imparted to us. *We* get to choose some of the particular ways God's grace is given to the world—what a remarkable responsibility and privilege!

We best discern how to do this in community with others who are seeking to do the same. In the vulnerability of hospitality and confession, we come to know one another as we truly are and share with others what we actually have, as much or as little as that may be. Together we passionately pursue "wisdom from above" (James 3:17), which God is pleased to grant us if we are similarly pleased to act on what he reveals. As we do so, our calling, vocation, and mission in the world takes shape, usually as patterns of small, repeated graces that over time become a fuller and clearer picture of the life God intends for us.

Thus, life is not one of multiple discrete parts but rather a life full and whole—a life of *shalom*, in which God's grace, goodness, and abundance suffuse every corner and overflow beyond personal and communal borders. Here, joy is birthed, not from the absence of trials and suffering but from God's presence in their midst, in hope for the day that God will dry every tear, abolish death, and make all things new (Rev. 21:3-5).

Paying Attention and Living Reflectively

To experience this shalom, we seek to live attentively and reflectively, committed to seeking God and noticing where we are and where we've been, in both everyday moments *and* through rituals of reflective pause. French philosopher Gabriel Marcel called the latter "secondary reflection"—an exercise distinct from moment-by-moment "primary reflection," which tends to be immediate and pragmatic (see *The Mystery of Being, Vol. 1: Reflection and Mystery*, Chapter V). "Secondary reflection" is intentional, helps us regain and refresh our connection with God, and reorients us in God's larger story, as well as to the specifics of our own calling and vocation within it.

This year's readings, practices, films, journaling prompts, and other assignments encourage a reflective approach to our lives. They engage our minds, emotions, bodies, and senses in our pursuit of God. In Exodus 6, rather than advocating for a legalistic approach to obeying the Ten Commandments, Moses promotes a holistic, everyday way of remembering and engaging with God:

> These commandments that I give you today are to be on your hearts. Impress them on your children. Talk about them when you sit at home and when you walk along the road, when you lie down and when you get up. Tie them as symbols on your hands and bind them on your foreheads. (Ex. 6:6–8 NIV)

God uses rhythms of reflection to form us, not in fragmentary ways but as whole people—heart, soul, mind, and strength. We embody the Beatitudes (Matt. 5:3-10). God fills our hearts with his treasure, and in both word and deed, we share it with the world (Matt. 12:33-37).

Passing the Mantle

Recall Paul's words to Timothy regarding the chief aim of learning and formation:

> But the goal of our instruction is love from a pure heart and a good conscience and a sincere faith. (1 Tim. 1:5 NASB)

Formation in Christ transforms us from closed, self-absorbed people into open, available people living in service to God and others.

One of our initial group commitments was to give away what we gain from our year together. As we draw to a close, prayerfully consider the gains you can impart and to whom. "Pass the mantle," as Elijah did with Elisha after having been gently refreshed and renewed by God on Mt. Sinai (1 Kings 19).

Formation in Christ transforms us from closed, self-absorbed people into open, available people living in service to God and others.

Offering Prayers of Consecration and Blessing

Finally, we close our year by consecrating ourselves to God and praying blessing over one another. The following prayers can be recited privately, or together in your group if there is time in your last meeting. Throughout this month, recite the prayer of consecration on your own, and then, using the prayer of blessing, pray for each of your 12-for-12 companions by name.

A PRAYER OF CONSECRATION

O God—Father, Son, and Holy Spirit—I come to you and offer my life to you once again. I offer my physical body, my waking and sleeping, my strength and my weakness, and all five of my senses. I offer my heart, my emotions, my affections, my time, and my attention. I offer my mind, my thoughts, my memory, all that I know, my opinions, my reflections, my learning. I offer my will, my choices, my inclinations, my volition, my very freedom. I offer my words, my deeds, my career, my vocation, my work, my leisure, and all that I am.

I entrust to you my relationships with family, friends, colleagues, neighbors, and all whose paths I cross. I offer my wealth—my money, my home, my car, and even the humblest of my possessions. All that I have and all that I am is yours, O Lord, and I offer it back to you, O Faithful One, lover of my soul. Bind me to you, O God, that I might be truly free.

TIP You can edit and adapt this prayer for use in other non-12-for-12 communities and contexts.

Thank you, Lord, for the faithful companions who have walked with me this year and for the good work you have done in me during our time together. As this group draws to a close, seal and establish the qualities of life and character that you have shaped in me. Give me grace, O Father, to rest in your love and share it with others. Make me, O Jesus, more like you in word and deed. Fill me, Holy Spirit—make me responsive and attentive to you and quick to yield to your promptings. Give me faith, O Lord, to know and see what is of lasting value and to always choose it. Give me courage, O God, to pursue you no matter the cost and grace to repent cleanly and quickly when I fail. Establish rhythms of grace and ways of obedience in me for all my days, O Lord. Protect me from the evil one, and lead me in your everlasting way. I am yours, O Lord, you are mine, and I consecrate my life to you, O Father, O Son, O Holy Spirit. Amen and amen.

A PRAYER OF BLESSING

I thank you, O God, for my sister/brother _____ and for the gift of her/his/their life, and I thank you for the opportunity to have been in this group together. As we end our time together, I hold her/him/them before you and commit her/him/them to your care.

O Lord, take the graces and gifts you have placed in _____ and weave them into a fabric of your making. Remove threads that are not from you, keep her/him/them rooted in your love, and fill her/him/them with wisdom from above. Give her/him/them grace in relationships, favor in her/his/their work, and make her/him/them healthy and whole—heart, soul, mind, and strength. Lead her/him/them, O Holy Spirit, and fill her/him/them. Surround her/him/them with your love and give her/him/them a joyful heart.

And now _____, I bless you in the name of the Father and the Son and the Holy Spirit. May your heart always be soft toward God and your life always shaped by him. May you know courage, peace, and joy all your days, and may the Lord's name always be on your lips. May God give you favor in your family and community and bear good fruit in and through you in the world. May you always sense his loving gaze, and may your eye always be kind toward others. I bless you, _____, in all things for all your days, in the name of the Father, and the Son, and the Holy Spirit.
Amen and Amen.

A CLOSING BENEDICTION

Now to him who is able to keep you from stumbling, and to make you stand in the presence of his glory blameless with great joy, to the only God our Savior, through Jesus Christ our Lord, be glory, majesty, dominion and authority, before all time and now and forever! Amen. (Jude 24–25 NASB)

The Glassblower

The glassblower leaves signs for those who see, and who know his craft,
And who by seams and striations,
Marks of mold, form, and feature,
Can discern intent and purpose shaped in molten glass.
Through blowpipe, breath, fire, and forge,
He shapes a vessel with an eye to what it will hold, and pour, and for whom,
And by elemental tincture chooses a hue suited to the solution to be decanted,
and for how long a time.
In cruet or carboy, jar, jug, demijohn, or bottle indelibly embossed,
Though stone may shatter, sunlight shift the shade,
Minerals bleach and stain, and earth swallow into its dark womb,
He sculpts in viscous sand a shape that remains,
That tells a story of why, of art and industry past,
Fragile, translucent, and that even chipped and cracked allows the light to pass;
And that bears hints, though distant, of form and beauty and function,
Whether fine or familiar, left by the annealer,
Who by heat and cold has tempered
What now may be mere fragments.
O give us to see your craft in us,
And allow, even in glints and gleams,
Your light to pierce the shards we are,
And to be bent, in the end, into beams from the fire of your forge.

ANDY SAPERSTEIN

APPENDIX A

Practices

TABLE OF CONTENTS

PRACTICE

1

Silence and Stillness

A6

PRACTICE

2

Remembering the Saints

A8

PRACTICE

3

Prayer of Examen

A9

PRACTICE

4

Breath Prayers

A11

PRACTICE

5

Who Is God? Who Are We?

A13

PRACTICE

6

Lectio Divina

A16

PRACTICE

7

Biblical Personality Reflection

A18

PRACTICE

8

Expanded Jesus Prayer

A20

PRACTICE

9

Confession and Communion

A21

PRACTICE

10

The Lord's Prayer in Seven Movements

A24

PRACTICE

11

Hospitality to Strangers

A28

PRACTICE

12

Imaginative Reading of Scripture

A29

PRACTICE
13
Contemplative Prayer
A30

PRACTICE
14
Examen of Words
A32

PRACTICE
15
Core Books
A33

PRACTICE
16
Core Calling
A34

PRACTICE
17
Giving Gifts
A36

PRACTICE
18
Postures of Prayer
A37

PRACTICE
19
Selective Abstaining
A39

PRACTICE
20
Building for Life
A41

PRACTICE

1
Silence and Stillness

Be still, and know that I am God . . . (Ps. 46:10a NIV)

Among the most important steps we can take as we start this year of spiritual formation is to slow down, quiet down, eliminate distraction, and pay attention. The three practices below provide opportunities to establish these life habits right where they need to be—in the context of our daily lives. Small, simple practices like these, when made part of our everyday lives—when waking up, sitting at home, taking a walk, eating lunch, going to bed—form the foundation of a life lived attentively to God, to others, and to the world where he has placed us. Though not necessarily bound to waking up or going to bed, you might consider making one or more of them, or practices like them, among the first things you do in the morning or the last things you do before bed—even before checking your phone or turning on the radio. When beginning and ending your day, and woven into the ordinary moments of your day, habits of silence and stillness will stand as times to renew and refresh your connection with God, without which none of us will make true progress in our life with him.

A Quiet Walk with God

At the giving of the Law, Moses charged the people of Israel to carry the Law in their hearts and to speak of it when they rose up, when they lay down, when they sat at home with their children, and when they walked in the way. The point of this was simply that the Law of God, and God himself, was to be the ever-present thought and companion of his people in all times and places. The practice of a quiet walk with God stands as a simple way to redeem the most basic activity—taking a walk—and make it into a time of connection with God.

To do this, simply choose a time and place—in your own neighborhood to start or end the day or in a park during your lunch break—and then take a quiet walk with God. Try to make it a regular routine—once a week at the same time, weekday mornings, etc.—but at least once a week will make it easier to make it a habit. As you walk with God, pay attention to the sights, sounds, and smells along the way, and the feel of the air as you walk. Leave your cell phone off or at home, don't hurry as you go, and gently turn your attention to God as you walk, enjoying both his presence and the world around you. If you meet someone on the way who you want to connect with, simply do so, and then return to your walk, savoring the silence and the presence of God.

Five Minutes of Stillness

From Beginning to Pray, *by Anthony Bloom, (1970) pp. 85–86.*

Born in Switzerland in 1914 to Russian parents, trained as a medical doctor, and sojourning in places ranging from Persia to Paris to London during his remarkable life, Anthony Bloom was drawn to Christ from an atheist background while in his twenties. He went on to hold positions in the Russian Orthodox Church ranging from priest to monastic to Archbishop.

Bloom's faith was earthy and concrete. Throughout his many writings he advocates for a rooted, experiential faith that communes with God in the ordinary moments of our lives and in ordinary places and times. Silence and stillness stand as two of the basic building blocks of a spirituality committed to a moment-by-moment attentiveness and connection to God. He describes the practice as follows:

"Sit down and say, "I am seated, I am doing nothing, and I am doing nothing for five minutes," and then relax, and then continually throughout this time (one or two minutes is the most you will be able to endure to begin with) realize, "I am here in the presence of God, in my own presence, and in the presence of all the furniture that is around me, just still, moving nowhere." There is, of course, one more thing you must do: you must decide that within these two minutes, five minutes, which you have assigned to learning that the present exists, you will not be pulled out of it by the telephone, by a knock on the door, or by a sudden upsurge of energy that prompts you to do at once what you have left undone for the last ten years. So you settle down and say "Here I am," and you are. If you learn to do this at lost moments of your life when you have learned not to fidget inwardly, but to be completely calm and happy, stable and serene, then extend the few minutes to a longer time and then to a longer while still."

A Quiet Meal with God

An average person eats more than a thousand meals a year, and if we set aside even an occasional meal to spend alone with God, we will have made a most ordinary part of our day into a time of connection with him. For parents of young children, or for particularly busy households, this may be harder to arrange, but even with others near at hand, we can spend an occasional meal with God as our primary companion, and as we enjoy him and the food he has given us, we will better learn to participate in the sacred reality of every moment lived in the presence of God.

To make this practice part of your life, choose at least a few times over the next month to remove the usual distractions in order to enjoy a meal with a more conscious awareness of God's presence. Do not to listen to, watch, or read anything while you eat. Silence all digital devices and place them in another room. Then, simply sit down in a quiet place alone to eat your meal slowly and silently in the presence of God. Savor the taste and texture of your food, the physical environment around you, and your experience of God's presence with you as you eat. As you enjoy your meal, silently express gratitude to God for your food and for his presence, and then rest in the quiet simplicity of this very ordinary but also truly sacred time. In the traditional Jewish Passover seder meal, a place is set for Elijah as the invisible guest. While you don't need to set a place for God as you share a quiet meal with him (though you can if you want to), do enjoy him as your invisible but ever-present guest as you eat.

PRACTICE 2

Remembering the Saints

Remember those who led you, who spoke the word of God to you... (Heb. 13:7a NASB)

...since we are surrounded by such a great cloud of witnesses... (Heb. 12:1a NIV)

Whether you have been a follower of Jesus for a long or a short time, if you take some time to consider it, you should be able to call to mind a number of people—perhaps a large number—who have impacted your life with Jesus and who have contributed to your spiritual formation. This "Remembering the Saints" exercise is an act of recollection and gratitude to help you call to mind and create a list of those sisters and brothers who have impacted your life over the years. Consider this list a living document that you can add to in the seasons ahead.

To begin, list the various Christian communities you have been part of since you came to faith. If you were raised in the church, include the spiritual communities you grew up in, as well as your own family of origin. Next, list the people from those communities who have had the biggest impact on your spiritual life—noteworthy family members, leaders, pastors, mentors, and other spiritual friends who have shaped your life in significant ways.

With this initial list of people who have most deeply shaped your life with Jesus, slowly review the names and call to mind specific ways each person impacted you. Ask God to help you connect particular words, themes, milestones, breakthroughs, or events to each person on your list. Jot down a few notes regarding what comes to mind. Give thanks to God for those you have remembered and for the ways they have impacted your life.

Next, choose one person from your list who you have not spoken to for some time or who God particularly calls to your attention. Write and send a letter or email to them expressing your appreciation for the ways they have blessed and formed you in your walk with Jesus. Mention specific memories and specific ways they have impacted you. The more specific the letter, the more impactful it will be. The person you have written will be encouraged and blessed to read it, and you will be encouraged and blessed by writing them.

Remember to periodically return to and add to your "Remembering the Saints" list, expanding it with both newcomers to your life and those from your past who you didn't list before. As you invite God into your times of remembering and adding to your list, you will be surprised by the people he brings to mind and the resurfacing of memories you have not considered for many years. Even casual acquaintances God has used just once to bless you with small graces may appear on your list. Consider making it a regular practice to reach out to some of these sisters and brothers to let them know that you remember and give thanks to God for how he has used them in your life.

PRACTICE

3
Prayer of Examen

The Prayer of Examen is a short, focused, and intentional time spent with God to help us:

- Review the events of a day or other period of time.

- Review our emotions, attitudes, and actions in the midst of those events.

- Pay attention to God's activity in those events and our awareness or unawareness of it.

Dennis Hamm, SJ helpfully refers to this way of praying as "rummaging for God" as we pray backwards through our day. (*Rummaging for God: Praying Backwards through Your Day—IgnatianSpirituality.com*)

First instituted in 16th century Spain by Ignatius of Loyola, the founder of the Jesuit order, the Prayer of Examen has been embraced by Christians of many traditions over the centuries. In keeping with the overall focus of his *Spiritual Exercises*, the Prayer of Examen helps us to "find God in all things" and is of great benefit as we seek to live a life of unbroken attentiveness to God. It takes only a few minutes and can be practiced anywhere—during a break at work; lying in bed before you go to sleep; when your kids are napping; while driving, taking a walk, or riding a bike, etc. By regularly practicing the Prayer of Examen, you will become more aware of God's presence and activity in your daily life, of your own inner life and outward actions, and of the degree to which you notice God's activity in everyday events and interactions, moment by moment. This increasing awareness of God and ourselves bears fruit in each cardinal direction of the spiritual life: upward, inward, one another, and outward.

Two Ignatian concepts—*consolation* and *desolation*—help frame the practice of the Prayer of Examen. *Consolation*, literally "accompanied by comfort or solace," characterizes a posture of active openness and receptiveness to God, an upward permeability where we position ourselves to notice and receive from God, even in difficult or painful experiences. *Desolation*, on the other hand, literally means "out of aloneness or isolation," and characterizes an unawareness of God and his activity. It is marked by a posture of self-absorption, alienation, and aloneness, and can occur even in the face of superficial pleasure and exhilaration. As such, consolation and desolation are not necessarily indicative of whether an experience is painful or pleasurable in itself but rather suggest whether we experience it in an isolated and individualistic way or in a posture of open receptivity to God. Practicing the Prayer of Examen cultivates in us an increased awareness of patterns of consolation and desolation in our own lives, and with God's help, we should over time find ourselves growing into patterns of increasing consolation and diminishing desolation, regardless of the situations we find ourselves in.

The Prayer of Examen in Practical Terms

The prayer is traditionally separated into two distinct parts. One part, the *examen of consciousness*, focuses on the extent to which we were *aware of God*. The other part, *the examen of conscience*, focuses on the extent to which we were *obedient to* God. Both our awareness of God and our obedience to him—a yielding to his desires and direction in our lives—become clearer to us as we make the Prayer of Examen part of our regular spiritual practice. As we review before God the most recent events of our lives—a sort of "rearview mirror" glance at the road immediately behind us—and as we pay specific attention to both our awareness of and yieldedness to God in those events, we cultivate in ourselves an increased awareness of God in real time, moment by moment, that impacts not only what we notice about the past, but how we live in the present.

The Prayer of Examen appears in many forms. One common, simple version is found below. No matter how it is structured, however, this prayer helps us discern whether the flow of our life has been toward or away from God today and helps us to answer how, when, and why it has been that way. Examen therefore helps us answer three basic questions:

What happened today?

What happened in me today?

How aware of God and how obedient to him was I in these things?

✠

GENERAL EXAMEN

Search me, O God, and know my heart; try me and know my anxious thoughts; and see if there be any hurtful way in me. And lead me in the everlasting way (Ps. 139:23–24 NASB).

1.
Enter God's presence, receive his love, and give thanks to him.

2.
Ask God to help you review your day and notice both his presence and your own attitudes and actions.

3.
Review the events and interactions of your day, paying special attention to your thoughts, words, feelings, and actions at various points, as well as your awareness of and responsiveness to God's loving presence and leading. Note any patterns of consolation and desolation.

4.
Thank God for his gifts, ask his forgiveness where needed, express sorrow for your sin, and receive his forgiveness.

5.
Ask God for grace to change and to more fully live out of a rootedness in his love.

6.
Rest briefly in God's presence, savoring his love for you, and return to your day.

PRACTICE

4

Breath Prayers

Breath prayers provide simple words to help you connect with God in any given moment, especially when you find yourself less able to articulate "wordier" prayers, and help establish an internal, ongoing rhythm of prayer. Consider periodically reading this list of prayers out loud, repeating those that stand out to you and shortening or modifying the prayers as you see fit.

Over time, these simple prayers will become part of your internal prayer "repertoire," and as you continue to pray and read the Scriptures, you will undoubtedly come up with new breath prayers of your own—the Psalms are especially rich with possibilities. Whatever the source of your breath prayers, you will find it helpful to choose a prayer that seems right and to "camp on it" for a few days, making it one of the anchors in your practice of moment-by-moment turning toward God in the midst of your ordinary days—when you are driving to work, sitting at your computer, fixing a meal, changing a diaper, doing the dishes, etc. In the end, breath prayer is often a helpful way to ever-so-gently incline yourself to God when internal or external distractions make it hard to do so.

The first breath prayer listed below is the widely known "Jesus Prayer," which is foundational within the Eastern Orthodox tradition and echoes the tax collector's prayer in Luke 18. If you can't decide which breath prayer to choose, this is a good place to start.

- Lord Jesus Christ, Son of God, have mercy on me, a sinner. (The Orthodox "Jesus Prayer")

- Jesus!

- O Lord!

- Arise, O Lord; save me, O my God! (Ps. 3:7a NASB)

- Be merciful to me, Lord! (Ps. 6:2a NIV)

- O God, come to my assistance; O Lord, make haste to help me. (Ps. 69:2 Douay-Rheims)

- O Lord, heal me! (Ps. 6:2b NIV)

- Return, O Lord, and rescue me! (Ps. 6:4 NLT)

- Save me because of your unfailing love. (Ps. 6:4b NLT)

- Do not forsake me, O Lord! (Ps. 38:21a NASB)

- My God, do not be far from me! (Ps. 38:21b NASB)

- Make haste to help me, O Lord! (Ps. 38:22a NASB)

- O Lord my savior! (Ps. 38:22b NLT)

- Hear my prayer, O Lord! (Ps. 39:12a NLT)

- O God, have mercy on me! (Ps. 56:1a NLT)

- Come quickly to me, O God! (Ps. 70:5a NIV)
- O Lord, do not delay. (Ps. 70:5b NIV)
- Rescue me, O my God! (Ps. 71:4a NASB)
- Lord, help! (Ps. 107:6, 13, 19, 28 NLT)
- Keep me from deceitful ways, [Lord.] (Ps. 119:29a NIV)
- Save me, for I am yours! (Ps. 119:94a NIV)
- Heal me, Lord, and I will be healed; Save me and I will be saved, for you are the one I praise. (Jer. 17:14 NIV)
- O Lord, listen! O Lord, forgive! O Lord, hear and act! (Dan. 9:19a NIV)
- Our Father in heaven . . . (Matt. 6:9b NIV)
- Hallowed be your name . . . (Matt. 6:9c NIV)
- Your kingdom come. Your will be done (on earth as it is in heaven) . . . (Matt. 6:10 NIV)
- Give us today our daily bread . . . (Matt. 6:11 NIV)
- And forgive us our trespasses (as we forgive those who trespass against us). (Matt. 6:12, The Book of Common Prayer)
- Lead us not into temptation . . . (Matt. 6:13a NIV)
- Deliver us from evil . . . (Matt. 6:13b NASB)
- Have mercy on me, Lord, Son of David! (Matt. 15:22a NASB)
- Lord, help me! (Matt. 15.25 NASB)
- Lord, [you are] with [me] always, even to the end of the age. (Matt. 28:20 NLT)
- God, have mercy on me, a sinner! (Luke 18:13b NIV)
- Jesus, you have loved me to the end. (John 13:1)
- Come, Lord! (Maranatha!) (1 Cor. 16:22b NIV)
- Come, Holy Spirit! (The "Vineyard Prayer," often attributed to John Wimber)
- More, Lord! (Another common prayer in the Vineyard tradition)
- You will never desert me, Lord! (Heb. 13:5b NASB)
- You will never forsake me, Lord! (Heb. 13:5b NASB)
- Fill me with your Spirit, Lord!
- Fill me with your Spirit, Lord, that I might be transformed.
- Fill me with your Spirit, Lord, that I might walk in your ways.
- Fill me with your Spirit, Lord, that I might love as you do.
- Fill me with your Spirit, Lord, that I might join you in bringing your kingdom to the world.
- Help me, Father, to rest in your love.
- I rest in your love, Lord. I rest in your love.
- Jesus, lover of my soul! (from "*Jesus, Lover of My Soul*," by Charles Wesley)
- O, mighty Master! O, fond Father! (from "*In the Valley of the Elwy*," by Gerard Manley Hopkins)
- Thank you, Lord!
- Praise you, Lord!
- Lord, have mercy! Lord, have mercy! Lord, have mercy! (Kyrie eleison! Kyrie eleison! Kyrie eleison!) ✣

PRACTICE 5

Who Is God? Who Are We?

This practice is designed to help call to mind simple biblical statements about who God is and who we are. It is intended as a prompt for prayer, preferably aloud, where each reference stands as a statement to be woven into your own prayers of adoration, worship, thanksgiving, confession, and grateful acknowledgment to God. Speak each statement back to God in the second person, (e.g. "You are Creator of heaven and earth! You are Lord!," etc.), pausing to savor its significance, adding more statements of your own to the list as you notice them in the Scriptures, and taking time as you are able to read the broader Scriptural contexts of the references listed. Then speak each "Who Am I?" statement back to God in the first person (e.g., "I am created in your image; I am precious and honored in your sight," etc.), resting in and savoring the truth of who you are in Christ.

Note: Most translations below are taken from the New American Standard Bible (NASB, 1995).

Who is God?

- Creator of heaven and earth (Gen. 14:22)
- Father, Son, and Holy Spirit (Matt. 28:19, Eph. 2, etc.)
- Lord (Ex. 15:3, Deut. 6:4, Hos. 12:5)
- The Lord of Hosts (Neh. 9:6, Ps. 84:1, Ps. 148:2, Is. 47:4, etc.)
- The shepherd of Israel (Ps. 80:1)
- The God and Father of our Lord Jesus Christ (2 Cor. 1:3a)
- The Father of mercies and God of all comfort (2 Cor. 1:3b)
- Immanuel, God with us (Is. 7:14, Matt. 1:23)
- Wonderful Counselor (Is. 9:6)
- Mighty God (Is. 9:6)
- Eternal Father (Is. 9:6)
- Prince of Peace (Is. 9:6)
- A man of sorrows, and acquainted with grief (Is. 53:3)
- The true God, the living God, and the everlasting King (Jer. 10:10)
- The Maker of all (Jer. 10:16)
- Son of Man (Ez. 6:2, John 5:27)
- Master (Matt. 10:24, Luke 12:47)
- Like a hen gathering its chicks (Matt. 23:37)

- Father of lights (James 1:17)
- The Son of the Most High (Mark 5:7)
- The Helper, the Holy Spirit (John 14:26)
- The Lamb of God who takes away the sin of the world (John 1:29)
- The Lord of Sabaoth (James 5:4, Rom. 9:29)
- The Lord Jesus Christ (Gal. 1:3)
- The Father of Glory (Eph. 1:17)
- The Lord of the Sabbath (Matt. 12:1–8, Mark 2:23–28, Luke 6:1–5)
- Rich in mercy (Eph. 2:4)
- A merciful and faithful high priest (Heb. 2:17)
- A priest forever according to the order of Melchizedek (Heb. 5:6)
- Jesus, the mediator of a new covenant (Heb. 9:15)
- Jesus, the author and perfecter of faith (Heb. 12:2)
- Our helper (Heb. 13:6)
- The bread of life (John 6:35, 41, 48, 51)
- The light of the world (John 8:12)
- The door of the sheep (John 10:7, 9)
- The good shepherd (John 10:11, 14)
- The resurrection and the life (John 11:25)
- The way, the truth, and the life (John 14:6)
- The true vine (John 15:1, 5)
- A consuming fire (Heb. 12:29)
- Love (1 John 4:8)
- The Lawgiver and Judge (James 4:12)
- Abba, Father (Mark 14:36)
- The Alpha and the Omega, the first and the last, the beginning and the end (Rev. 1:8, 22:13)
- The one who gives to all people generously and without finding fault (James 1:5)
- The one who is able to save and to destroy (James 4:12)
- A faithful Creator (1 Pet. 4:19)
- Jesus Christ (1 John 4:15)
- The Holy Spirit (Matt. 28:19)
- Our Father (2 Cor. 1:3)
- The Son of God (Matt. 14:33, Acts 9:20)
- Jehovah Jireh (The God who provides) (Gen. 22:14)
- Jehovah Rapha (The God who heals) (Ps. 147:3, etc.)
- Jehovah Nissi (The Lord is my banner) (Gen. 22:14)
- Omniscient (Job 37:16, Ps. 147:5, 1 John 3:19–20)
- Omnipresent (Jer. 23:23–24, Prov. 15:3)
- Omnipotent (Matt. 19:26, Luke 1:37)
- King of kings (1 Tim. 6:15)
- Lord of lords (1 Tim. 6:15)

Who Are We?

- Created in God's image (Gen. 1:26-27)
- Precious and honored in God's sight (Is. 43:4)
- Deceitful and desperately sick of heart (Jer. 17:9)
- Forgiven by God (Matt. 26:28, Eph. 4:32, Ps. 86:5)
- Branches in the vine (John 15:5)
- Lost and straying sheep (Ps. 119:176, Is. 53:6, Jer. 50:6, Luke 15:1-7)
- Beloved by God (John 15:13, 1 John 4:11, Is. 43:4)
- Receivers of mercy (Rom. 11:32, Jude 1:21, Neh. 9:31)
- Descendants of Abraham (Gal. 3:7-9)
- God's workmanship (Eph. 2:10)
- God's dwelling place (1 Cor. 6:19)
- Known by God (1 Cor. 8:3)
- Members of the body of Christ (1 Cor. 12:27)
- Jars of clay (2 Cor. 4:7)
- Fearfully and wonderfully made (Ps. 139:14)
- Like a lonely bird on a housetop (Ps. 102:7)
- Adopted by God (Gal. 4:4-5, Eph. 1:5)
- Chosen by God (Eph. 1:11)
- Once dead, but now alive (Eph. 2:1-6)
- Formerly without hope and separated from God (Eph. 2:12, Job 7:6)
- Brought near by the blood of Christ (Eph. 2:13)
- Fellow citizens with God's people and members of God's household (Eph. 2:13)
- Sharers in the heavenly calling (Heb. 3:1)
- Sharers in Christ (Heb. 3:14)
- First fruits of all he created (James 1:18)
- Members of a chosen race, a royal priesthood, a holy nation, once no people, but now God's people, proclaiming God's marvelous light (1 Pet. 2:9)
- Choice and precious living stones in God's house (1 Pet. 2:4-5)
- Like a weaned child resting against its mother (Ps. 131:2) ✣

PRACTICE 6

Lectio Divina

Named after the Latin phrase for "divine reading," *lectio divina* is an ancient approach to reading Scripture. In more modern terms, it is helpful to think of *lectio divina* as a "reflective reading," a "meditative reading," or a "spiritual reading" of the Scriptures. It is primarily for the purpose of our own spiritual formation and not necessarily for the gaining of more general biblical and theological knowledge. Simply put, *lectio divina* is more formational than informational.

The meditative reading of Scripture is found in both the Old and New Testaments (cf. Ps. 119: 11, 15, 23, 48; 1 Cor. 2:8–13, Col. 3:16a, etc.) and has been part of the life of the church since its earliest days. Practiced and passed on by Church Fathers including Origen, Ambrose, and Augustine, *lectio divina* was further codified and established within the Benedictine monastic tradition. It has found proponents within the Catholic tradition since that time and has enjoyed support among Protestants beginning with Calvin and within Anglican and other traditions up to the present day, including its emphasis in the excellent book by Eugene Peterson *Eat this Book* (2006).

Complementary to more inductive, historical, and analytical approaches to Scripture reading, which clearly play a foundational role in our understanding and interpretation of the word of God overall, *lectio divina* draws us to a place where we read the Scriptures in an intentionally personal way, with our hearts open to the work and the whispers of the Holy Spirit, making ourselves able to hear God speaking to us through particular texts at particular times. You may practice *lectio divina* using a Bible passage on one occasion only to have a completely different encounter with God when practicing with the same text at another time. The practice of *lectio divina*, therefore, stands as an opportunity for us to invite the direct, timely, and personal work of the Holy Spirit in us through the words of Scripture.

There are four long-established key steps to *lectio divina*:

- Reading (*lectio* in Latin)
- Reflection (*meditatio* in Latin, literally "meditation")
- Response (*oratio* in Latin, literally "speaking," in this case, in responsive prayer)
- Rest (*contemplatio* in Latin, literally "contemplation," a posture of quiet waiting before God)

Following Robert Bello's book *Prayer as a Place* (2009) and Steve Summerell's Vineyard Institute course, "Spiritual Formation," an initial step of preparation, "Ready," and a final step, "Return," have been added. These make entering into and exiting from the practice back into daily life separate steps in their own right. Here is a summary of the "six R's" of *lectio divina*:

READY (1–3 minutes)

Find a place where you can be quiet and undisturbed. Choose a brief passage of Scripture, typically no more than ten verses in length. Quiet your heart, sit in silence, and ask God to meet you during this time of reflective reading. Invite the Holy Spirit, who inspired the word of God, to open its message to you in particular ways during this time.

READ (3–5 minutes)

Read the passage slowly, either silently or out loud, letting your attention rest on each word. Read the passage again slowly and out loud, especially if you have chosen to read it silently the first time. If you are practicing *lectio divina* in a group, consider having two different people read the text out loud in the same translation—hearing the word in different voices can help us notice things we might otherwise miss and contributes to the communal dimensions of this practice.

As you read or listen to the text, be aware of any words or phrases that particularly stand out for you. Don't force something to happen here—if God is not drawing to your attention anything in particular, then relax and let him speak to you through the passage in more general ways. If something does stand out for you, make a note of it. If you are practicing *lectio divina* in a group, you might invite group members simply to speak out the words or phrases that impact them, though without offering an explanation as to why.

REFLECT (5–10 minutes)

Meditate and reflect on the words or phrases that caught your attention. Imagine these words as smooth pebbles you gently turn over in your hand, noticing how they feel, and what stands out for you as you pay even closer attention. If nothing in particular stands out to you, then simply let the overall words and rhythms of this passage wash over you. As you reflect, listen and allow God to speak to you. Pay attention to the thoughts, emotions, images, or memories that rise to the surface as you reflect on the text. Do not hurry, but allow time for God to speak so that you may fully take in what he is showing you or speaking to you.

RESPOND (3–5 minutes)

Respond in prayer to the word or phrase, if any, that God has brought to your attention. Ask God why these particular things caught your attention. What do you sense God saying to you in response? Dialogue with God about what you are sensing or feeling, and about what he is showing you. Ask God a question or offer God a request for yourself or someone else. Listen for what God is asking you to do. Consider journaling some of what you have noticed, what he is saying to you, and the ways you are responding to him.

REST (3–5 minutes)

Rest quietly in God's loving presence, savoring the time you have just spent with him in his word, letting it settle more deeply into your heart. This quiet rest in the presence of God is often referred to as "contemplation." It helps to better seal and set apart both the words of the passage and your encounter with God.

RETURN (1 minute)

Finally, return to the rhythms and responsibilities of your normal day. Ask God to imprint on you in the hours ahead the things he has brought to your attention during this time of *lectio divina*. As you go through your day, keep calling to mind the passage you reflected on, and particularly the specific words or phrases God called to your attention. Are there specific ways God is leading you to act upon what you have noticed and what he has shown you? Are there specific ways to incorporate these things into your life, beginning today?

PRACTICE 7

Biblical Personality Reflection

Quiet yourself before God, pray, and consider the list of biblical figures below. As you survey this list of people, take note of those you most identify with and why. Who most reflects the patterns of both grace and sin you notice in yourself? If a number of people stand out, choose the one or two whose lives you sense God inviting you to reflect on in greater depth. If you identify with a biblical figure not listed, feel free to select that person instead.

Next, visit Scripture passages where the individuals you have chosen are described or revealed in greater detail. For some people, like Moses and David, there is a great deal of Scripture to consider; for others, there is much less. Read through some or all of the sections where the person is described, sit with God, and reflect on what you notice.

Now take some time to journal on what caught your attention. Why did you choose these particular people? What personality traits and gifting, as well as patterns of sin and brokenness, do you notice in both yourself and in these persons? What are you most surprised by and why? What are you most challenged or embarrassed by and why? To finish this time of reflection, jot a brief prayer of response to God.

Note: For many people listed below, Scripture references are only representative, and there are often other helpful references to consider beyond the ones listed here. A comprehensive list of references for the people below, or any other figure in the Bible, can be found in any standard Bible program or concordance, as well as in other reference works.

Old Testament

- Abraham, father of many nations (Gen. 12–25, etc.)
- Sarah, Abraham's wife (Gen. 17–23, etc.)
- Hagar, Sarah's handmaid and mother of Ishmael (Gen. 16, 21, etc.)
- Isaac, promised son of Abraham (Gen. 17–25, etc.)
- Ishmael, son of Abraham and Hagar (Gen. 16, 17, 25, etc.)
- Rebekah, wife of Isaac (Gen. 24–28)
- Jacob, son of Isaac and father of the 12 tribes of Israel (Gen. 25, 27–37, 42, 45-50, etc.)
- Esau, son of Isaac and brother of Jacob (Gen. 25–28, 32–33, 35–36, etc.)
- Rachel, first wife of Jacob (Gen. 29–31)
- Leah, second wife of Jacob (Gen. 29:16–33)
- Joseph, son of Jacob (Gen. 39–50, etc.)
- Moses, receiver of the Law and leader of Israel (Ex., Lev., Num., Deut., etc.)

- Bezalel and Oholiab, chief artists and builders of the tabernacle (Ex. 31–38)
- Joshua, successor of Moses (Deut. 31:23 ff., Book of Joshua, etc.)
- Deborah, warrior and judge (Judg. 4–5)
- Ruth, daughter-in-law of Naomi; wife of Boaz (Book of Ruth)
- Samuel, prophet and kingmaker in Israel (1 Sam., etc.)
- David, shepherd, poet, warrior, king, and man after God's own heart (1 Sam. 16–1 Kings 2, Book of Psalms, etc.)
- Elijah, mighty prophet of Israel (1 Kings 17–19, 21; 2 Kings 1–2)
- Elisha, successor to Elijah the prophet (1 Kings 19:19–2 Kings 13:21)
- Nehemiah, rebuilder of the walls of Jerusalem (Book of Nehemiah)
- Esther, Queen of Persia and deliverer of Israel (Book of Esther)
- Solomon, king of Israel, son of David and Bathsheba (1 Kings 1–11, Prov., Ecc., etc.)
- Isaiah, the greatest writing prophet of Israel (Book of Isaiah)
- Jeremiah, the weeping prophet (Book of Jeremiah)
- Daniel, prophet, exile, and adviser to foreign kings (Book of Daniel)

New Testament

- Joseph, husband of Mary and stepfather of Jesus (Matt. 1–2, etc.)
- John the Baptist, forerunner of Jesus and prophet in the way of Elijah (Matt. 3, 11, 14; Luke 3, 7, etc.)
- Peter, impetuous apostle (throughout all four Gospels, 1 and 2 Peter, etc.)
- James, brother of the Apostle John (throughout all four Gospels, etc.)
- John, the beloved Apostle, brother of James (throughout all four Gospels; 1, 2, and 3 John; Book of Rev., etc.)
- Matthew, tax collector and apostle (Matt. 9, Mark 2, Luke 5, etc.)
- Luke, beloved physician, companion of Paul, writer of Luke and Acts (Acts 16:10–17, 20:5–15, 21:1–18, 27:1–37, 28:1–16, Luke 1, Col. 4:14, etc.)
- Timothy, beloved colleague and co-laborer of the Apostle Paul (throughout Book of Acts, 1 and 2 Timothy, multiple references in other Pauline Epistles, etc.)
- Tabitha (Dorcas) beloved sister in the church in Joppa (Acts 9:36–42)
- Mary, mother of Jesus (Luke 1–2, Matt. 1–2, etc.)
- Mary, sister of Lazarus, sister of Martha, friend of Jesus (Luke 10, John 11., etc.)
- Martha, sister of Lazarus, sister of Mary, friend of Jesus (Luke 10, John 11., etc.)
- James, half-brother of Jesus, leader of the Jerusalem church, author of Epistle of James (Epistle of James, Acts 15, etc.)
- Nicodemus, Pharisee believer in Jesus (John 3:1–9, 7:50, 19:39)
- Paul, Apostle to the Gentiles (Book of Acts, Pauline Epistles, etc.)
- Barnabas, encourager of the saints and co-worker with the Apostle Paul (Acts 11:22–15:35)
- Apollos, eloquent co-worker with the Apostle Paul (Acts 18:18–19:1, etc.)
- Mary Magdalene, follower of Jesus and witness to the resurrection (Matt. 27–28; Mark 15–16; Luke 8, 24; John 19–20; etc.)
- Priscilla, colleague and co-laborer with the Apostle Paul (Acts 18) ✣

PRACTICE

8

Expanded Jesus Prayer

The Orthodox Jesus Prayer, "Lord Jesus Christ, Son of God, have mercy on me, a sinner," is based on the tax collector's prayer in the Parable of the Pharisee and the Tax Collector in Luke 15. As one of the foundations of Orthodox spirituality, this simple breath prayer (see "Breath Prayers," Practice 4) can turn us godward when expansive or extemporaneous prayers feel inaccessible or beyond grace. Sometimes, however, we may sense an invitation from God to press beyond the minimalism and simplicity of the Jesus Prayer and yet still engage with it as a springboard to help us pray a bit more expansively.

The "Expanded Jesus Prayer" below is longer than the Jesus Prayer, intentionally Trinitarian, and oriented toward the cardinal directions of the spiritual life. While more expansive than the Jesus Prayer alone, it is still short enough to easily memorize. Each phrase can stand as a breath prayer in its own right. Taken together, they orient us to God—Father, Son, and Holy Spirit—and invite God to help us engage with him in the transformation of our own lives, our churches and communities, and the broader world. It's a simple way to recall, receive, and recommit to the broad purposes and priorities God calls us to and to rest in his abiding love as we do so.

To practice the "Expanded Jesus Prayer," recite it out loud several days in a row, perhaps at the same time every day. Prayed frequently and aloud, it will be easier to memorize, internalize, and make a prayer of your own.

Lord Jesus Christ, Son of God, have mercy on me, a sinner.

Lord Jesus Christ, Son of God, have mercy on me, your child.

Fill me with your Spirit, Lord, that I might be transformed.

Fill me with your Spirit, Lord, that I might walk in your ways.

Fill me with your Spirit, Lord, that I might love as you do.

Fill me with your Spirit, Lord, that I might join you
in bringing your kingdom to the world.

And as I walk, faithful Father, help me to rest in your love.

I rest in your love, Lord; I rest in your love.

PRACTICE

9

Confession and Communion

If we claim to be without sin, we deceive ourselves and the truth is not in us. If we confess our sins, he is faithful and just and will forgive us our sins and purify us from all unrighteousness. If we claim we have not sinned, we make him out to be a liar and his word is not in us. (1 John 1:8–10 NIV)

Confession is a simple, historic practice where we openly admit our sins to God in the presence of one or more brothers and sisters in Christ, receive forgiveness from God, and turn from our sin. It ought to be a normative practice undertaken out of simple obedience to Christ. Taking Communion immediately following confession is helpful, as this simple sacrament both reminds us of Christ's body and blood given for the forgiveness of our sins and serves as a concrete means of God's presence and grace. It is no accident that in many Christian traditions, confession is encouraged or required before Communion is received.

Biblical Basis for Confession

The practice of confession is rooted in Scripture. John says this:

> If we claim to be without sin, we deceive ourselves and the truth is not in us. If we confess our sins, he is faithful and just and will forgive us our sins and purify us from all unrighteousness. If we claim we have not sinned, we make him out to be a liar and his word is not in us. (1 John 1:8–10 NIV)

And James writes:

> Therefore confess your sins to each other and pray for each other so that you may be healed. The prayer of a righteous person is powerful and effective. (James 5:16 NIV)

Finally, in The Parable of the Pharisee and the Tax Collector (Luke 18:9–14), it is the latter who, unable to lift his eyes to heaven out of shame, beats his breast and simply prays, "God, have mercy on me, a sinner" (Luke 18:13 NIV). In admitting his sin to God and asking for mercy, the tax collector goes home justified, while in blinding himself to his own sin and judging others for theirs, the Pharisee does not.

By confessing our sins to one another and praying for one another, we find freedom not only from the trappings of sin itself, but also from our experience of condemnation, which arises from both our own hearts and from the enemy of our souls, "the accuser of our brethren" (Rev. 12:10 NASB). Confession is a gentle invitation from God to renew the life of freedom he has already granted us in his Son, Jesus Christ.

When Offering a Confession

Few of us relish the thought of disclosing our sins and shortcomings to God, much less to others. But there is much consolation and spiritual benefit in resisting fear and shame's attempts to keep us from confessing our sins. The more we open ourselves to God and others in confession, the easier it becomes to do so.

As you prepare to confess your sins, commit to being honest and specific. Without going into unnecessary detail, name particular instances of sin, not mere generalities. When you confess a specific sin, turn from a specific sin, and receive forgiveness for that specific sin, the shame and accusation you experienced beforehand will dissipate, and you will be better able to walk in joy and freedom.

When Receiving a Confession

Recognize that you are entering a tender and sacred time. Get in touch with the magnitude of your own sin and your own need for forgiveness. Deeply and fully rely on God's mercy alone for your standing before him. This positions you to gently and mercifully receive a sister or brother's confession.

As others confess, assume a posture of warm, prayerful attentiveness. Your primary role is not to judge, counsel, comment, or inquire after more details. Nor is it to pray at length over the person confessing. Rather, attentively listen, humbly bear witness to the confession and the forgiveness God offers, and pray a brief blessing over your sister or brother. While in some cases a brief word of counsel or encouragement is in order, it is generally best to be quiet and let God be the one who speaks a word of response. Finally, hold your sister or brother's confession in confidence.*

Confession and Communion Order of Service

Duration:
Approximately one hour

Participants:
Two to four brothers or sisters of the same sex. Three seems ideal, as it offers the right balance of accountability, support, and confidentiality.

Before meeting:
- Select a meeting place that is private and free from interruptions—often someone's home is best.
- Gather Communion elements and have this order of service on hand.

Step 1: General Confession

Read out loud together the following prayer, adapted from *The Book of Common Prayer*:

> *Most merciful God,*
> *we confess that we have sinned against you*
> *in thought, word, and deed,*
> *by what we have done,*
> *and by what we have left undone.*
> *We have followed the plans and desires*
> *of our own hearts, and we have rejected*
> *your holy commands.*
> *We have not loved you with our whole hearts;*
> *and we have not loved our neighbors as*
> *ourselves.*
> *We are lost, and sick, and have no hope or*
> *health apart from you.*
> *We are truly sorry and we humbly repent.*
>
> *But you, O Lord, are merciful.*
> *Restore us and free us according to your*
> *promises in Jesus our Lord.*
> *Fill us with your Holy Spirit.*
> *Have mercy on us and forgive us,*
> *that we may delight in your will,*

*and walk in your ways,
to the glory of your name.*

Amen.

*And as we prepare to confess our sins,
O Lord, we pray:
Search me and know my heart; test me and know my anxious thoughts.
Show me God, where there have been hurtful ways in me; show me where I have failed to obey you, where I have left undone what I should have done, and where I have turned myself away from you in any way.*

Lead us, Lord, and be with us as we confess our sins to one another.

Amen.

Step 2: Silent Reflection

Take 2–3 minutes to reflect on the general confession and discern what you are to confess.

Step 3: Confession

One person at a time, go through the following steps. This should take about 10–15 minutes per person for all the remaining steps.

1. Begin your confession with:
   I confess to the Lord and to you . . .

2. End your confession with:
   This is my confession.

Step 4: Prayer of Absolution

Next, another group member prays the following over the person confessing.

Lord, you say in your word that if we confess our sins, you are faithful and just and will forgive us our sins and purify us from all unrighteousness (1 John 1:9 NIV). *[Person's name], we therefore declare that by the blood of Jesus your sins are forgiven, and that God will purify you from all unrighteousness. We ask, O God, that you give [person's name] true repentance and your Holy Spirit, so that she/he will find freedom from this sin. Give her/him/them peace, cleanse her/him/them from within, and allow her/him/them to serve you in joy and freedom. We pray in the name of your son Jesus, whose precious blood cleanses us from all sin. Amen.*

Step 5: Communion

Serve Communion to the person who has just confessed.

- Taking the bread, say, *"The Lord Jesus, on the night he was betrayed, took bread, and when he had given thanks, he broke it and said, 'This is my body, which is for you; do this in remembrance of me.'"*

- Offer the bread, saying: *"The body of Christ, given for you."*

- Taking the cup, say, *"In the same way after supper he took the cup saying, 'This cup is the new covenant in my blood, which is poured out for many for the forgiveness of sins.'"*

- Offer the cup saying, *"The blood of Christ, shed for you."*

Step 6: Silence and Closing Blessing

After a few seconds of silence, close with a prayer of blessing.

Lord, we commit [person's name] to your loving care, and [person's name], we bless you in the name of the Father, and the Son, and the Holy Spirit.

Amen.

✣

* Note: If the confession is one of violent crime, crime against a minor, or of sin committed from a place of church leadership or privilege that brought harm to someone in a more vulnerable position, report the confession to appropriate authorities and/or church leadership.

PRACTICE 10
The Lord's Prayer in Seven Movements

And when you pray, go into your inner room, and when you have shut your door, pray to your Father who is in secret, and your Father who sees in secret will repay you ... Pray, then, in this way ... (Matt. 6:6, 9a NASB)

In the Sermon on the Mount, Jesus provides some basic instructions regarding prayer (Matt. 6:5–8) and then gives to the church what we now call the Lord's Prayer as a template for how to make those instructions real in our actual practices of prayer (Matt. 6:9b–13). Today, virtually every Christian tradition prays the Lord's Prayer as part of its normal practice, recognizing its words as one of God's greatest gifts to the church, and making it probably the most widely memorized text of Scripture in history.

But such familiarity is not without risk. For to recite even the best prayer unreflectively may follow more from reflexive memory than from personal engagement with God. The Lord's preamable to his prayer is central: We must forsake both the vain, repetitive prayers of the Gentiles as well as the showy public prayers of the Jewish leaders. There is indeed great benefit to reciting the Lord's Prayer, but if that is the only way we ever engage with it, we may miss the fullness of its gift to us and even risk returning to the very ways of praying that it was meant to replace. The Lord's Prayer is also a springboard and a pattern, an invitation to seek God, ideally in a quiet place—an "inner room." Inner rooms are found most anywhere—in our car on the morning commute, in the middle of a busy day, or any time or place we turn ourselves toward God according to the pattern he has provided.

"The Lord's Prayer in Seven Movements" follows this pattern: worship and adoration of God, intercession for people and nations, humble requests for our own needs, confession, forgiveness, and the pursuit of protection from the evil that dwells both within and outside of ourselves. Two things you will notice about this prayer:

1. It is collective in nature and focuses on the "we" and "us" of Christian community. We are not isolated individuals but are bound up with the people of God, the church.

2. Each movement ends with a "response." Here you are invited to pray personally, specifically, and extemporaneously as the Spirit leads you.

As you pray, consider changing your posture in some way: stand, bow, kneel, raise your hands or hold them open, lift your eyes to God, bow your head, or cover your heart with your hands. See "Postures of Prayer," Practice 18. Once the prayer's movements become familiar, you can adapt them in other ways as you sense God leading you. Consider praying aloud.

And so we pray ...

OUR FATHER . . .

O Lord, we remember your abiding, fatherly love for us. Apart from your love, we are nothing—we are wholly and completely lost. Your love is the source of our very life and the cause of our joy. You look upon us with a kind eye; your words to us are tender, and you discipline us only and always out of your abiding love and only and always for our good. When we are far from you, O God, you pursue us and you run after us; you put your ring on our finger and your cloak over our shoulders; you kill the fattened calf and celebrate on our behalf when we return to you. Your heart is warm and welcoming; you delight in us as your beloved children; you take pleasure in us, and you enjoy us. You provide for all our needs, and you give us good gifts that far exceed mere necessity. You are extravagant in your love, O God, and we choose to receive and to rest in your love as the foundation of our very lives.

> **Response:** *Speak to the Lord of your experience of his love. Give thanks for your every enjoyment of his love, no matter how small.*

WHO IS IN HEAVEN . . .

O God, you are the creator and sustainer of the heavens and the earth; you uphold all things. You are the Alpha and the Omega, the beginning and the end. You are the Everlasting Father, the Prince of Peace, the King of Kings, and the Lord of Lords. All power and wisdom and knowledge are yours, and nothing is too difficult for you. You are far above rule and authority, power and dominion, and every name that is named in this age and the one to come. Nothing is impossible for you—you know all things, and you hold the entire universe in your hands. To you, a thousand years are as a day and a day as a thousand years—you are outside of all time. You are eternal and infinite in being. You are above all things, and all things belong to you. You are our great and mighty God, the Lord Almighty, and we worship you.

> **Response:** *Proclaim the reality and fullness of God's power, wisdom, knowledge, and authority.*

HALLOWED BE YOUR NAME . . .

O God, you are holy. Your ways are not our ways, and your thoughts are not our thoughts. Every virtue has its origin and fullest expression in you, and no evil is to be found in you. You are perfectly good, righteous, true, just, faithful, beautiful, and pure. You are light and life, free and perfect, set apart from all creation, and yet you embrace us and reveal yourself to us. You are the one true and holy God; we worship and adore you. You are worthy of our praise and of our very lives; we offer both our praise and our lives to you.

> **Response:** *Speak back to God his virtues and excellencies. Worship and praise him for his holiness.*

YOUR KINGDOM COME, YOUR WILL BE DONE, ON EARTH AS IT IS IN HEAVEN ...

We welcome your rule and your reign over all things. We joyfully welcome your triumphal entry into every corner of creation, and we commit ourselves to joining you in bringing your kingdom to the world. We bring before you our families and our communities, our cities and towns and neighborhoods, our own nations and the nations of the world, our own people, as well as all other tribes, tongues, nations, and people. Bring your just and righteous rule to all these places and peoples, bring peace and justice, healing and health, salvation and beauty to all places and all people. Use us as your partners and agents for your good purposes and for the sake of your glorious kingdom.

> **Response:** *Intercede for your family, your community, and for the world.*

GIVE US THIS DAY OUR DAILY BREAD ...

We are but dust. We are women and men of flesh, weak and full of need. Because we know you, we are unashamed to come before you with even the smallest of our daily needs—food and drink, wisdom in our families and in our work, practical direction in our finances, in our homes and in our households, and in the ordinary worries and burdens of our lives. Help us call to mind without shame our daily needs and to bring them before you, O lover of our souls and provider of our every need.

> **Response:** *Bring your personal needs to God.*

AND FORGIVE US OUR TRESPASSES, AS WE FORGIVE THOSE WHO TRESPASS AGAINST US ...

Not only are we needy, Lord, but we are sinners. Even our most righteous works are tainted by sin and imperfection. We fail in word and deed, in thought and feeling, in purpose and intention, and we need your help in even knowing and bringing our sins before you. Help us call to mind and bring our sins before you, confident that as we confess our sins, you are faithful and just to forgive and cleanse us from all that is unclean in us. We rejoice that you so graciously and completely forgive us, Lord, and we come before you boldly and without shame to receive your mercy and offer our thanksgiving.

> **Response:** *Confess your sins to God, ask forgiveness, and offer gratitude to God for his mercy and love.*

And as forgiven people, O Lord, we give ourselves to being gracious and merciful toward people who have wronged us, even as you are so gracious and merciful to us. Help us identify the places where we have been wronged, and who has wronged us, and also where our hearts are still hard and unforgiving. Do a work of grace in us—give us desire to forgive where we have none, and power to forgive where all we have in us is judgment and bitterness. Make us like you, O God—make us able to love our enemies and pray for those who persecute us, even when they are bone of our own bone and flesh of our own flesh. We choose to forgive others as you have forgiven us, O Lord, and we ask your help as we do so.

> **Response:** *Seek God to show you people who you still view with bitterness and unforgiveness in your heart. Bring them before God, pray for help to forgive them, and pray for God's favor and blessing upon them.*

AND LEAD US NOT INTO TEMPTATION, BUT DELIVER US FROM EVIL ...

We are aware of the evils that we have allowed to dwell in our hearts as well as of those that crouch at the door of our lives through no fault of our own. Our battle is not with flesh and blood but with the powers and principalities of hell. O God, therefore give us victory over our evil inclinations, keep us from temptations that turn us away from you, and give us courage and strength to resist evil when it comes and from wherever it comes. Root out our evil thoughts and behaviors. Protect us from evil that comes upon us from others and from unknown forces. Keep us from the evil one and from those who serve him. Keep us from fire and flood, earthquake and storm, violence and injustice, accident and injury, sickness and despair, and from all that would hurt us and harm your good purposes in and through us. Apart from you, O Lord, we are at the mercy of our own hearts and of the evil that surrounds us in the world. Lord have mercy, Lord have mercy, Lord have mercy!

> **Response:** *Seek God to reveal your heart's evil inclinations, the things that regularly tempt you, and the evil around us in the world. Seek the Lord's protection and help to overcome these things.*

FOR YOURS IS THE KINGDOM AND THE POWER AND THE GLORY FOREVER.

Amen and amen.

PRACTICE

11
Hospitality to Strangers

The Scriptures hold hospitality in high regard. In their old age, Abraham and Sarah extend hospitality to the three strangers who foretell the miraculous birth of their son Isaac. Boaz extends hospitality to Ruth and Naomi as they endure displacement and famine. Jesus feeds the 5,000 and then, after his resurrection, extends hospitality to his disciples by cooking them breakfast on the beach.

The New Testament letters encourage cheerful hospitality to stranger and friend alike and make it a qualification for leadership in the church. Even the promise of Revelation 3:20 is one of mutual hospitality—we share food and fellowship with Jesus as we open our lives to him.

The following practice is intended to make hospitality to strangers a more intentional part of our lives and to cultivate the "one another" and "outward" cardinal directions.

- To begin, come before God and consider your experiences of others' hospitality. Make a list of times you felt welcomed, received, and set at ease by others. These may be from long ago or more recent, among family and close friends, or among casual acquaintances or strangers. Reflect and journal on two or three of these times. What made you feel welcome and at ease? What about your hosts, the setting, the food and drink, or anything else about these times strikes you as being essential to warm hospitality? Why do these experiences stand out for you?

- Now consider memorable meals you've eaten. These may be meals you or others served or meals eaten out. Call to mind meals where you most experienced God's grace. What about the setting, the people present, the overall atmosphere, or the specific food and drink most moved you? Journal about two or three of these experiences.

- Next, consider people in your life who you have never extended hospitality to. They may be neighbors, colleagues at work, distant relatives, or people you know in some other way. Ask God to help you choose one or more of these people to invite into your home in the coming weeks—aim for someone beyond your normal circles. The invitation can be for anything: coffee and dessert, a backyard fire, a meal, a movie, a neighborhood walk, etc. Include in these acts of hospitality some of the elements noted above—those things that helped you feel most welcome and at ease. If your situation does not allow you to host anyone in your own space, visit someone in theirs or extend hospitality to them through a simple gift or by inviting them out for a meal, drinks, or a walk.

- After extending hospitality to someone new, reflect on the experience and journal your observations. In what ways did you or did you not encounter God? What went according to plan and what did not? What is your sense of how your guest experienced your time together?

PRACTICE 12
Imaginative Reading of Scripture

Imaginative reading of Scripture, also called imaginative prayer, uses one's five senses and imagination to build upon reflective approaches to Bible reading such as *lectio divina*. The Bible—particularly narrative passages—often describes events that actually took place, and even when passages are more metaphorical, poetic, or apocalyptic, there is a great deal of imagery that allows us to imaginatively engage our senses.

Incorporating our whole being into Scripture reading, including our imagination and our senses, is one way to fulfill the Great Commandment: to love God with all our heart, all our soul, all our mind, and all our strength (cf. Mark 12:30–31 etc.). And it opens the Scriptures to us in new ways. Imaginatively reading Scripture can often lead us to a more intimate encounter with God—Father, Son, and Holy Spirit. And even with passages we've read many times before, an imaginative reading may reveal details we have never noticed before, as though we are encountering them for the first time.

Imaginative reading of Scripture takes no more than 30 minutes and includes the following steps:

1. Choose a passage of Scripture—the Gospels, the Book of Acts, Genesis, Exodus, and other Old Testament historical and narrative books are a good place to start. (3 minutes)

2. Ask the Holy Spirit for guidance as you read and imaginatively reflect on the passage. (1 minute)

3. Read the passage slowly out loud two or three times, letting the narrative gently impact you. (10 minutes)

4. Choose one character in the story and imagine yourself as that person. (1 minute)

5. Engage all five of your senses as you imagine yourself in the scene as that person. What do you see, hear, smell, taste, and touch? What are your thoughts and feelings? (5 minutes)

6. Respond to God about what you have noticed. Speak out a simple prayer of response or thanksgiving. (1 minute)

7. Journal in words or pictures some of what you imagined, or a response to God. Consider expressing your journal entry in the words of the person you chose to identify with. (5 minutes)

8. Finally, rest before God and savor the overall passage and the impact of imaginatively reading it. Thank God for what he revealed to you. Choose the one thing that most moved you and close with a prayer asking God to shape you in keeping with that one thing. (3 minutes) ✠

PRACTICE 13
Contemplative Prayer

Contemplative Prayer Defined

Contemplative prayer is simply a wordless turning to God, a gazing upon and listening to God, and a quiet waiting before God as God gazes upon us. In addition to the many ways of praying using words (historically referred to as *cataphatic* prayer), contemplative prayer (historically referred to as *apophatic* prayer) does not normally rely on words, thoughts, and images, but it does help us expand the ways we can live into the Apostle Paul's admonition to "pray without ceasing" (1 Thess. 5:17 NASB).

Contemplative prayer aims to help us:

- Still our inward and outward stream of thoughts, words, and deeds.
- Cultivate our ability to turn inwardly to the Triune God moment by moment at all times, whether we are speaking or not.
- Maintain interior and exterior silence as we gaze upon, adore, and open ourselves to God's presence.
- Grow in our ability to simply be present before God and to savor his beauty and love without striving.

The Biblical Basis for Contemplative Prayer

David and the other psalmists savored times of rest and silence in the presence of God. The practice of contemplative prayer hearkens back to words like these in the Psalms:

> One thing I have asked from the Lord, that I shall seek:
> That I may dwell in the house of the Lord all the days of my life,
> To behold the beauty of the Lord
> And to meditate in His temple. (Ps. 27:4 NASB)

> "Cease striving and know that I am God; I will be exalted among the nations, I will be exalted in the earth." (Ps. 46:10 NASB)

> Surely I have composed and quieted my soul;
> Like a weaned child rests against his mother,
> My soul is like a weaned child within me.
> (Ps. 131:2 NASB)

Likewise, elsewhere in Scripture we are turned toward contemplative prayer:

- Ecclesiastes affirms "a time to be silent and a time to speak" (Ecc. 3:7b NASB). While our faith clearly involves labor of thought, word, and deed, the practice of silently sitting before God teaches us that in quietness and stillness we maintain a deep connection with God.

- Like Jesus' friend Mary, we choose "what is better" when we simply sit at his feet and listen (John 10:42 NIV).

- And Isaiah affirms:

  For thus the Lord God, the Holy One of Israel, has said, "In repentance and rest you will be saved, In quietness and trust is your strength." (Is. 30:15a NASB)

Rooted in Scripture, contemplative prayer has been part of Christian faith and practice since the early church and the beginnings of monasticism. It holds a longstanding place in Catholic, Orthodox, and a wide range of Protestant traditions.

The Practice of Contemplative Prayer

Duration:
Start with five minutes and eventually work up to at least 20 minutes.

Setting:
Find a quiet place where you can sit alone and uninterrupted.

Considerations:

1. Choose a simple word or phrase to use as an anchor prayer for when you find your mind drifting and your thoughts stirring. Often a phrase like "Lord, have mercy," "Come, Lord Jesus," or another short breath prayer will serve well.

   Alternatively, choose one of the many names for God found in the Scriptures or perhaps a brief phrase taken from the Lord's Prayer. Don't overthink your selection, and once you have chosen, stick with what you have decided.

   While a short verbal anchor prayer of this sort will make this way of praying easier in the beginning, you may eventually be able to forgo it and simply aim for complete inward and outward silence as you pray.

2. If you pray in tongues, consider quietly doing so as you practice contemplative prayer. While praying in tongues is not given to all believers as a gift and is not essential to a rich life of prayer, for those able to pray in this way it is a helpful way to engage with God contemplatively and to be "strengthened personally" (1 Cor. 14:4a NLT).

3. You will find it difficult at first to still your inner voice. Don't lose heart, and don't condemn yourself when your mind drifts. It will get easier, and you will likely notice over time this practice positively impacting your ability to inwardly turn toward God in the ordinary moments of your life.

4. Finally, do not expect the time of contemplative prayer itself to be a mountaintop experience. Rather, commit to persevering in the practice. Over time, and with God's help, you will see it bear fruit more broadly and give rise to a more unbroken, settled, moment-by-moment openness to God in your life overall.

Method:

1. Sit down and still your body

2. Set a timer for 5–20 minutes.

3. Choose a word, phrase, or name of God as an anchor prayer.

4. Close your eyes and turn your attention toward God.

5. When you're distracted or your thoughts drift, quietly repeat your anchor prayer, and ever-so-gently turn your quiet attention toward God. ✠

PRACTICE 14
Examen of Words

Jesus says: "The mouth speaks out of that which fills the heart" (Matt. 12:34 NASB), and "by your words you will be justified and by your words you will be condemned" (Matt. 12:37 NASB). "Death and life are in the power of the tongue" (Prov. 18:21a NASB), the Proverbs tell us, and James laments that both sweet and bitter water—both blessing and cursing—can flow from the same spring, our mouth (James 3:9-12).

The words we choose to speak or not to speak reflect the extent to which we have embraced and internalized what James calls "the wisdom from above" (James 3:17 NASB). We must give our words due attention and yield to God's recurring admonition to guard our tongues and to pay close attention to what we allow to flow from our lips (Prov. 13:3, 21:23, Eph. 4:29, etc.). It is fitting to make this prayer our own:

> "Set a guard, O Lord, over my mouth;
> Keep watch over the door of my lips.
> (Ps. 141:3 NASB)

An "Examen of Words" is one way to embody this prayer. This practice helps us become intentionally more aware of what we say or don't say in a given day, with the aim of allowing God to increasingly shape our ways with words.

Begin your time with the prayer above from Psalm 141:3. Next, pray along these lines: "God, as I review my day before you, help me notice my words, both spoken and written. When were my words, in both tone and substance, pleasing to you and a grace to others? When were they not? Show me, Lord, if there is anything I should have said, but did not, or if there is anything I said that would have been better said in a different way, or not at all."

Then simply review your day as though practicing the traditional prayer of examen but with a focus on the words you said and didn't say to others, and the ways that you said them, in either speech or writing. Briefly journal what you notice about your words that day and the way they impacted others.

As you engage in this practice, note patterns in your words over time and how those patterns intersect with God's heart and mind as revealed by his word and his Spirit. Seek God for ways to bring your words into alignment with his heart and mind and to increasingly bring grace to those who hear (Eph. 4:29).

PRACTICE

15

Core Books

One way to learn a lot about yourself and the way God has made you is to notice the books of Scripture that you are most drawn to and that have most impacted you over the course of your life with Jesus. Take some time to pray and consider your personal "core books" from the Bible—those books of Scripture that have made a deep and recurring impression on you as you've walked with Jesus—the books that you find yourself turning to again and again to stir your soul, give you direction, and restore and realign your life with God. Make a list of these books in your journal, aiming for five to twelve in total.

Next, take a few minutes to reflect and jot down a few thoughts on why you have chosen these particular books.

- What about God and his kingdom do these books reveal to you?

- What do your choices reveal about you, your personality, your gifting, and the calling God has placed on your life?

- What do they show about the way Scripture inspires, challenges, and encourages you?

- What do they reveal to you about your areas of weakness and sin?

Finally, choose one of your core books to read through this month at least once, and make your core books part of your regular Scripture reading this year.

MY CORE BOOKS

PRACTICE 16
Core Calling

For this journaling exercise, recall the books you chose in the earlier Core Books exercise. Reflect again on why you chose those books and the texts you chose from within those books. What does this reveal to you about who you are and the things God has likely called you to?

Shifting from books of the Bible to people of the Bible, choose one to three of the figures below and focus your Bible reading, reflection, and study on that person this month. Feel free to choose a biblical character not included here; this list is simply a guide.

Old Testament

- Abraham, father of many nations (Gen. 12–25, etc.)
- Sarah, Abraham's wife (Gen. 17–23, etc.)
- Hagar, Sarah's handmaid and mother of Ishmael (Gen. 16, 21, etc.)
- Isaac, promised son of Abraham (Gen. 17–25, etc.)
- Rebekah, wife of Isaac (Gen. 24–28)
- Jacob, son of Isaac and father of the 12 tribes of Israel (Gen. 25, 27–37, 42, 45–50, etc.)
- Rachel, first wife of Jacob (Gen. 29–31)
- Leah, second wife of Jacob (Gen. 29:16–33)
- Esau, son of Isaac and brother of Jacob (Gen. 25–28, 32–33, 35–36, etc.)
- Joseph, son of Jacob (Gen. 37–50, etc.)
- Moses, receiver of the Law and leader of Israel (Ex., Lev., Num., Deut., etc.)
- Bezalel and Oholiab, chief artists and builders of the tabernacle (Ex. 31–38)
- Deborah, warrior and judge (Judg. 4–5)
- Daniel, wise youth, exile to Babylon, prophet (Book of Daniel)
- Ruth, daughter-in-law of Naomi; wife of Boaz (Book of Ruth)
- Hannah, mother of Samuel (1 Sam. 1–2)
- Esther, Queen of Persia and deliverer of Israel (Book of Esther)
- David, shepherd, poet, warrior, king, and man after God's own heart (1 Sam. 16–1, Kings 2, Book of Psalms, etc.)
- Samuel, prophet and kingmaker in Israel (1 Sam., etc.)
- Solomon, king of Israel, son of David and Bathsheba (1 Kings 1–11, Prov., Ecc., etc.)
- Abigail, widow of Nabal and wife of David (1 Sam. 25, 30, etc.)

- Elijah, mighty prophet of Israel (1 Kings 17–19, 21; 2 Kings 1–2)
- Elisha, successor to Elijah the prophet (1 Kings 19:19–2 Kings 13:21)
- Jeremiah, the weeping prophet (Book of Jeremiah)
- Isaiah, the greatest writing prophet of Israel (2 Kings 19, 20, Book of Isaiah, etc.)

New Testament

- Joseph, husband of Mary and stepfather of Jesus (Matt. 1–2, etc.)
- Simeon, righteous man, who blessed Jesus in the temple after his birth (Luke 2:21–36)
- Anna, prophetess in the temple after the Lord's birth (Luke 2:21–36)
- Mary, mother of Jesus (Luke 1–2, Matt. 1–2, etc.)
- Mary Magdalene, follower of Jesus and witness to the resurrection (Matt. 27–28; Mark 15–16; Luke 8, 24; John 19–20; etc.)
- Mary, sister of Lazarus, sister of Martha, friend of Jesus (Luke 10, John 11, etc.)
- Martha, sister of Lazarus, sister of Mary, friend of Jesus (Luke 10, John 11, etc.)
- John the Baptist, forerunner of Jesus and prophet in the way of Elijah (Matt. 3, 11, 14; Luke 3, 7, etc.)
- John, the beloved Apostle, brother of James (throughout all four Gospels; 1, 2, and 3 John; Book of Rev., etc.)
- Timothy, beloved colleague and co-laborer of the Apostle Paul (throughout Book of Acts; 1 and 2 Timothy; multiple references in other Pauline Epistles, etc.)
- Priscilla, colleague and co-laborer with the Apostle Paul (Acts 18)
- Peter, impetuous apostle (throughout all four Gospels, 1 and 2 Peter, etc.)
- Matthew, tax gatherer, disciple of Jesus, Gospel writer (Book of Matthew, etc.)
- Barnabas, encourager of the saints and co-worker with the Apostle Paul (Acts 11:22–15:35)
- Luke, beloved physician, companion of Paul, writer of Luke and Acts (Acts 16:10–17, 20:5–15, 21:1–18, 27:1–37, 28:1–16; Luke 1; Col. 4:14; etc.)
- Simeon (Niger), Lucius, and Manaen, diverse prophets in the Antioch church (Acts 11:19-30, 13:1–3 ff.)
- James, brother of the Apostle John (throughout all four Gospels, etc.)
- James, half-brother of Jesus, leader of the Jerusalem church, author of Epistle of James (Epistle of James, Acts 15, etc.)
- Paul, Apostle to the Gentiles (Book of Acts, Pauline Epistles, etc.)
- Apollos, eloquent co-worker with the Apostle Paul (Acts 18:18–19:1, etc.)
- Tabitha (Dorcas) beloved sister in the church in Joppa (Acts 9:36–42) ✥

PRACTICE 17
Giving Gifts

The 1924 Olympic gold medalist Eric Liddell was both deeply devoted to God and a gifted athlete. In the 1981 film, *Chariots of Fire*, in defending his decision to delay returning to China for missionary service over the objections of his sister in order to compete in the Olympics, Eric remarked, "He made me His, but He also made me fast. When I run, I feel His pleasure."

Throughout the Scriptures, as well, different ones of God's people are recognized and celebrated as possessing creative gifts that benefit both the people of God and the world. Bezalel is set apart along with others in Exodus 31–36, and he is filled "with the Spirit of God, with wisdom, with understanding, with knowledge and with all kinds of skills—to make artistic designs for work in gold, silver and bronze, to cut and set stones, to work in wood, and to engage in all kinds of crafts" (Ex. 31:3–5 NIV). In Acts 9, Tabitha (Dorcas in Greek) was celebrated and remembered both for helping the poor and for the robes and other clothing she had made before she died. Asaph and his descendants were musicians and songwriters in service of God. David himself was a poet. And among the prophets and people of God we find myriad skills and gifts—men and women skilled in farming and animal husbandry, vine dressing and various trades—even the Lord himself was a carpenter. God has given each of us, who have all been created in the image of the Creator, gifts and graces he intends us to use as co-creators to bless and benefit ourselves, our communities, and the world.

In light of this, with an openness to the particular creative gifts God has given each of us, we will all prepare gifts to share with our 12-for-12 group.

To prepare:

- Consider how you would fill in the blank: "When I _____, I feel his pleasure." What activities put you most in touch with who God made you to be? What sorts of things do you make and do that give you a sense of God's pleasure and delight? Even if you do not consider yourself particularly creative, seek God to notice the ways he has made you a co-creator with him and choose a modest creative project to work on this month.

- Then, create a gift for God that you can in some way share with the group and perhaps give to someone else as a gift. It can be anything: something handmade or written, food, visual art, something you have grown, performance art, crafts, photography, dance, music, a building project, etc.—finish a writing project, make a dish you've been meaning to cook, dust off your paintbrushes or shop tools, speak the words you've been storing up, write the song you've been composing in your head, etc. Whatever you choose, it should flow out of something important to you and essential about who you are. Each member will have 10–15 minutes to share at your next meeting.

PRACTICE 18
Postures of Prayer

Throughout the Scriptures, people respond to and engage with God in profoundly physical ways. Our inner posture informs our outward response to God, and our outward posture similarly shapes our inward orientation to him. Since we are both body and spirit, it is an important part of spiritual formation to develop and integrate both our inner life with God and our outward physical expressions of it. This practice brings these two essential parts of ourselves together in private worship and prayer.

Church traditions approach physical expression during corporate worship in very different ways. Many traditions invite bowing of heads, folding of hands, and kneeling. In other traditions, people lift a single hand during corporate worship, and in many Pentecostal and Charismatic settings, it is normal to clap, open, or lift both hands, and even dance during group worship. In some Orthodox liturgies, the congregation prostrates before God by kneeling and bowing one's head to touch the floor.

No matter what norms our own church or cultural tradition embraces in corporate worship, there is great value in using our physical bodies in private worship. Here are a few examples from Scripture:

- When Ezra reads the Law upon the walls' restoration and the exiles' return to Jerusalem, the people lift their hands, bow low, and worship with their faces to the ground (Neh. 8:6).

- When God appears to Abram in Genesis 17, Abram falls on his face, and God talks with him. (Gen. 17:3)

- At the Lord's Transfiguration in Mathew 17, Peter, James, and John fall face down to the ground before the Lord. (Matt. 17:6)

- The Psalms and other scriptures regularly model and encourage us to lift our hands, bow down, kneel, etc. in prayer and worship (Ps. 63: 4, 95:6, 121:1, 123:1, 134:2; Lam. 2:19, 3:41; 1 Tim. 2:8, etc.).

- At the temple's dedication, Solomon alternately stands and kneels before God, lifting his hands to heaven as he prays (1 Kings 8:22, 54).

- In defiance of the king's edict, Daniel continues to kneel and pray three times a day, his windows open toward Jerusalem (Dan. 6:10).

- In Luke 18, the tax collector beats his breast, unwilling to lift his eyes to heaven as he prays (Luke 18:13).

- During the High Priestly Prayer in John 17, Jesus lifts his eyes to heaven, and in multiple places throughout Scripture, God encourages people to lift their eyes to notice what he is doing (Deut. 3:27, Is. 40:26, John 4:35, etc.).

Throughout the ages God's people spontaneously and liturgically engage their bodies in worship and prayer, and God encourages them to do so. And beyond bodily expressions of worship, people sing, shout, weep, wail, fast, wear sackcloth and ashes; and use incense, art, ornamentation, and other outward expressions in their worship. This practice focuses on helping you become more comfortable using your physical posture in your worship of God.

Slowly move through the different movements of prayer outlined below. Before transitioning from one movement to the next, pause for 15–30 seconds to notice thoughts, feelings, physical sensations, and words that arise, and to offer a simple prayer arising from both your interior and exterior posture before God. Breath prayers tend to work well. Adjust your movements as needed to accommodate physical limitations, or imaginatively hold yourself before God in the suggested posture. Alternatively, sit in a straight-back chair to move through the various postures of prayer from a sitting position. Whatever you choose, remember to pause between each movement in order to notice and pray.

1. Stand in a relaxed posture before God, hands at your sides, eyes open, and looking straight ahead.

2. Open your hands, palms raised.

3. Cross your hands over your chest, lower your head slightly, and close your eyes. Then bring your hands back down to your sides, resuming a relaxed standing posture, looking ahead with eyes open.

4. Lift your arms up, palms up and outward, head facing upwards, eyes open.

5. Bring your hands back to your sides and then kneel, toes to the ground, sitting on the back of your feet, hands down on your thighs, facing forward with eyes open.

6. Cross your hands over your chest again, lower your head to your chest, and close your eyes.

7. Return to a simple kneeling posture, hands down on your thighs, facing forward with eyes open. Now put your hands down on the floor in front of you, leaning over as far as you are able, closing your eyes and touching your forehead to the floor between your hands. Hold for a few seconds or move two or three times between the posture of kneeling and prostrating.

8. Sit before God with legs crossed, hands folded in your lap, looking ahead with eyes open. Lean back, supporting yourself with your hands, and stretching your legs out in front of you, head up and eyes open.

9. Finally, stand up, cross your hands over your chest, lower your head to your chest with eyes open, and offer a final prayer of consecration to God, asking him to fill you with his Holy Spirit.

After working through the movements, reflect on your experience. How did your thoughts, feelings, and prayers change as your physical posture changed? When did you most sense God's presence, greatness, beauty, authority, or love? When did you feel most or least comfortable before God? Journal your reflections and observations.

Feel free to rearrange, adapt, and add to the movements to become even more comfortable employing your physical body in private worship and prayer and in order to love God in increasing measure with all your heart, soul, mind, and strength. ✠

PRACTICE 19
Selective Abstaining

Fasting places temporary limits on food and drink consumption in order to give ourselves more fully to God and pursue his plans and purposes in our lives. Throughout the Old Testament (e.g., Jud. 20:26, 1 Sam. 7:6, 2 Sam. 1:12, 2 Sam. 12:16 and 21-23, Ezra 8:21, Neh. 1:4, Est. 4:16, Ps. 35:13, Dan. 9:3, Joel 2:12, Jon. 3:5, Zec. 8:19, etc.), people seek God through fasting—sometimes sincerely, sometimes for the wrong reasons. The prophet Isaiah offers an important corrective to the practice: fasting isn't merely a task on a religious to-do list; its aim is to transform us both as individuals and as a society (Is. 58:1–9).

In the New Testament, Jesus' public ministry is preceded by a 40-day fast (Matt. 4:1–11). In his Sermon on the Mount, assuming people fast, Jesus provides guidelines (Matt. 6:16–18). In Acts (13:2-3, 14:23), the early church fasts as they seek God for important decisions. Across time and tradition, God's people fast, especially during the 40 days of Lent. With origins in both Scripture and tradition, fasting plays an important role in faith and our pursuit of God.

While food and drink are the traditional focus of fasting, laying aside other routine activities also helps "unclutter" our external and internal landscape to open ourselves more fully to God. Solitude and silence are ways to fast from social activity and the noise of everyday life. A "device fast" or "media fast" is similarly helpful. And as many Christians do during Lent, a fast from certain foods or activities is beneficial. Whether it is abstaining from meat or sweets, social media or online games, watching sports or reading the news, these newfound, often uncomfortable gaps turn us godward to a place of greater attentiveness and permeability and can open us once again to God's gaze.

To engage this practice:

1. Ask God to help you identify the things that would best impact your life with him if you were to lay them aside for a time. Don't overthink it; trust God to lead you.

2. Choose one "time and attention magnet" in your life—an activity that if removed creates breathing room in both your schedule and your thoughts—and one "longing and desire magnet"—something you regularly consume or do that when absent leaves you desiring it. Choose something you will feel the loss of, not something you won't miss.

3. Decide upon the frequency and duration for abstaining from the things you have chosen. For broader things like a complete food or tech fast a few hours or days may have meaningful impact. For more specific things like online shopping, social media, and select food and drink, a week, a month, or even 40 days may be a more fitting time frame. You may decide to make your fast periodic—every Wednesday, for example, or the first Sunday of every month.

4. After choosing the two things you will abstain from and the time intervals for each, it's time to practice abstaining. As you do so, consider and journal about the following:

- Notice your emotions. Are you in a place of consolation or a place of desolation? In the face of negative emotion (anxiety, boredom, etc.) what turns you toward God? What turns you away from him? What are these encounters with God like? Are there any unexpected joys or breakthroughs? How has God surprised you?

- In what ways do you resist abstaining or find it too challenging? Be gentle with yourself as you recount failures. Ask God to shed light on the reasons for them and on what they reveal about your life with him.

- What impact does abstaining make on your life with God and others? Is there anything you'd like to abstain from more regularly or for a longer period of time?

- Regularly express emotions, struggles, and joys to God as you continue to practice abstaining. Over time you will develop a better sense of what best opens you to God's presence and his work in and through you, and most helps you shape and master your own desires.

PRACTICE 20
Building for Life

Introduction

This exercise will help you plan for seasons ahead. It is meant to help clarify your gifts, graces, calling, and future aims. Before working on details of this exercise, get familiar with the framework by reading it through to the end. Then ask for God's guidance as you slowly work through it. May God use this process to open new ways of fruitfulness and joy in your life and work!

The Planning Framework

In keeping with the metaphor of a building, from the Lord's parable of "The House Built on the Rock" in Matthew 7, this planning framework assumes we build our lives on the Lord. But even when a building is set on solid ground, it consists of several essential parts: *footings, foundation, framing, and finishing.*

Footings

Footings (sometimes called footers or piers) are pillar-like structures, often of concrete and steel, sunk deep into the ground to support and to distribute the load of the structure above. In the construction of wooden decks, concrete footings are often poured to support the foundational framing of the deck. In the case of skyscrapers, footings may extend into the bedrock several stories beneath the ground in order to support and stabilize the immense building above. Footings are hidden and virtually never change—once poured, they remain for the life of the building and are modified only in highly unusual circumstances. By analogy, the footings of life are the core commitments we make to God, as well as the core calling we sense from God on our life.

Life's footings can take the form of a *mission statement*—a simple declaration of the core commitments we make to God and others. It keeps us stable and solid, connected to God, and walking in wisdom and grace. It also summarizes our core sense of calling. It is derived from an accurate understanding of who God made us to be and of what he has made us to do, and it serves as a steadfast point of reference as we move through the changes and complexities of life.

A life is only as good as its footings. If we do not designate God as our bedrock, or if our mission statement is based upon a poor understanding of who God has made us to be, then whatever we build upon it is sure to be weak. Improperly poured footings risk damage to a structure or cause its collapse.

Foundation

The *foundation* is as crucial to stability as a footing. A poorly laid foundation cannot bear the weight of the building it supports. Our life's foundation comprises core commitments we adhere to regardless of changes in employment, relationships, location, etc. Our life's foundation attends to physical, mental, emotional, spiritual, and relational health. It ought to be holistically nourishing, including connection to God, relationships with family and intimate friends, rest and renewal, etc. Like life's footing, the foundation remains relatively constant all of our lives. Its attributes rarely, if ever, change.

A foundation provides underlying soundness and stability to our outward life—one marked by love, service, and calling. A neglected foundation—too little connection with God, spouse, family, and friends; too little sleep; too little time off, and so on—is a recipe for burnout. A strong and well-tended foundation prevents burnout. We do not maintain a foundation for its own sake. Nor do we maintain it in place of work and service. A foundation exists in support of work and service. But the order is crucial—foundation first, then the building above it.

Framing

Framing is a building's skeleton. It stands above ground to support the finishing—the finished surfaces, including the walls, ceilings, and roof. Depending on era, region, and size of the building, framing material is usually wood, brick, concrete, or steel. While a building's frame is modified more frequently than either its footings or its foundation, such an undertaking occurs only after significant deliberation and only at significant cost.

Similarly, life's framing consists of roles and responsibilities that remain unchanged for months or years. This includes jobs, family responsibilities, volunteer work, and avocational callings. These responsibilities are typically substantial and are taken up or laid aside only after significant deliberation and at significant cost in time, money, and effort.

There is a limit to how many framing items one can realistically maintain in their life. A person with too many significant roles and responsibilities will either neglect substantial dimensions of them or neglect maintenance of their foundation. No one can sustain either scenario without risking burnout; one or more responsibilities must be dropped.

Finishing

Finishing consists of a building's interior and exterior surfaces, fixtures, and decorations. These details are critical to the usefulness and value of the building. Jesus' parable of the man who fails to complete construction of a tower illustrates the futility of unfinished buildings. The bare skeleton of a building whose walls, roof, flooring, and fixtures have never been attached is a depressing sight—so much potential lost.

The finishing is what we see, walk on, and handle every day. It gets the most wear and tear and requires the most frequent modification and maintenance. Our life's finishing consists of the activities we do every day, or multiple times per day. These daily and weekly tasks are adjusted frequently, often on the fly. We alter, add to, or eliminate them with far less deliberation than we do life's footings, foundation, and framing. They are dictated by specific commitments at specific times for specific people or objectives. Finishing might be an extra daily hour set aside for prayer and discernment in the days leading up to an important decision, helping your high schooler study for a test, or cooking a meal for a convalescent neighbor. Life's well-established footings, foundation, and framing, and the values expressed in them, inform its finishing.

A Word About Balance

One may assume a person who invests all effort in foundational activities—time with the Lord, time with family, rest, renewal, etc.—has the strongest life. But this is not so. Life's footing and foundation exist to provide a solid basis for fruitful action. A fool lays a foundation only to spend the next several years scrubbing, painting, and admiring it, but never building a house upon it. Likewise, for most of us, our lives are incomplete if we never do anything beyond our family and devotional life.

Conversely, a person who spends a disproportionate amount of time on framing—job, ministry, volunteer work, etc.—is like one who pours a foundation far too light and shallow. Unable to support the building he has placed upon it, it is only a matter of time before disaster strikes.

Proportionality is key. The Lord wants the time we spend on foundation work to adequately support life's framing and finishing. Keeping in mind sleep and time with family are foundational activities, a 1:2 ratio of framing and finishing activities to foundation activities is generally beneficial and sustainable. With 168 hours available to us each week, this amounts to roughly 56 hours for framing and finishing and 112 hours for foundational activities. For those who require less sleep, have fewer family responsibilities, etc., the ratio may approach 2:3, but 1:2 should be the initial aim. When the ratio exceeds these limits, our families, spiritual lives, and physical and emotional health often suffer, which ultimately impacts our ability to complete the framing activities we have consistently overemphasized.

There will be seasons where framing requires more of our time. Project deadlines, conferences, financial demands, and emergencies may shift the ratio. But if for months you find yourself saying, "It's a busy season," or "Next week I'll spend time with my spouse and kids and with God," then there is likely a problem of disproportionality. Left uncorrected, disproportionalities bear bitter fruit.

Seasons of Caregiving

Intensely service-oriented household responsibilities such as raising young children, caring for an elderly parent or special-needs child, and helping a family member recover from illness or injury should be considered framing, not foundational activity. These activities require substantial physical, spiritual, and emotional energy to undertake, and they are often more demanding than careers and endeavors conducted outside the home. Unfortunately, however, they are rarely recognized as such.

In this planning model, those whose primary work responsibilities are at home with their family should count these activities as *framing*, not *foundational*. Therefore, it is crucial that those in this situation prioritize foundational activities that are physically, spiritually and emotionally renewing so as to prevent burnout. Spouses must be sensitive to this reality in each other's lives and be sure to guard one another's foundations. If you are close with someone—especially a single parent—in a season of caregiving, look for ways to share the load. It is incumbent on the church, the community of faith, to provide practical support to single parents so they can flourish in both the foundational and framing dimensions of their lives.

The Planning Process

If possible, set aside uninterrupted time to complete this assignment.

Pouring the Footings

Identify the footings in your life by prayerfully working through the following questions.

1. What activities do you most enjoy in your personal life?

2. What activities do you most enjoy in your professional life?

3. In what activities does God use you most powerfully and effectively?

4. What are your spiritual gifts?

5. What other skills, talents, and abilities do you have?

6. Over the past several years, what has motivated you, interested you, and stirred up your passion? When do you most consistently experience God's pleasure?

7. What are the best contributions you make to your family and community?

8. How would you like to spend most of your time?

9. What, if any, calling do you sense from God?

10. Who are your heroes—those who inspire you to live fully and according to your calling? Which biblical figures did you chose in the Core Calling exercise? Why do they inspire you?

In light of your answers above, draft and finalize a personal lifelong mission statement comprising your *footing*. Make it short enough (less than 50 words) to memorize and repeat but long enough to cover the major emphases in your answers above.

By way of example, the author's longstanding mission statement is:

My life's mission is to love God, to love my neighbor, to pursue truth in my innermost being at all times, and to use my life, and especially my words, to lead others to do the same.

Once your mission statement feels complete, write it on the following page.

MY LIFE'S MISSION

Laying the Foundation

Now consider your areas of regular focus and renewal that rarely, if ever, change and that serve to support your life's more malleable roles and responsibilities, such as jobs, volunteer work, ministry responsibilities, etc. Foundation items most believers have in common include relationship with God (including spiritual disciplines), involvement in the life of the church, relationship with family and close friends, vocation, and rest and recreation (including Sabbath and care for yourself). While foundational activities involve all four of the cardinal directions, the outward direction will take precedence in the next section, the framing.

One or more other activities unique to the individual also often comprise one's foundation, serving as a constant source of encouragement and renewal. For the author, such reading and writing form a separate part of the foundation because they play a central role in renewing mind and spirit. For you, playing music or making art may fill this role, as may a physical activity such as running or racquetball. Be sure to list these in your foundation.

My foundation consists of:

1. _____

2. _____

3. _____

4. _____

5. _____

6. _____

Erecting the Framing

Consider roles and responsibilities that are not part of your foundation but ones you embrace as major areas of activity for months or years. While framing sometimes includes things on your foundation list, these tend to be more specific activities that fall into the fourth cardinal direction—the outward. These include our job or profession, vocational and avocational callings, volunteer or service roles, and domestic labor.

List your framing activities below. Add as many as you need to.

1. _____

2. _____

3. _____

4. _____

5. _____

6. _____

Attaching the Finishing

This most detail-oriented part of the entire planning process requires perseverance. Apart from finishing, your life's footing, foundation, and framing are only theoretical. Finishing consists of specific action items that take real time in your weekly routines.

Completing the finishing also takes into account foundation and framing items and sets specific, but not inordinately fastidious, goals for each one. Every aspect of finishing should have either a deadline or a frequency of occurrence, with a grace-filled recognition that we will only partly complete what we purpose to do. Examples of finishing might look like the following:

1. With respect to foundational items: Relationship with family and close friends

   - Weekly family game/movie night
   - At least one weekly focused time (reading, activity, etc.) with each child
   - Weekly date night
   - Weekly visit with at least one close friend
   - At least two meaningful conversations with friends or family per week
   - Annual extended visit with intimate friends and family
   - Quarterly long weekend away with family

2. With respect to framing items: Reading and writing

   - Complete a spiritual formation book or curriculum by a certain date
   - Outline a wisdom book from the Bible by a certain date
   - Write two poems a month
   - Read a book about a multiethnic church by a certain date
   - Read four books of poetry or philosophy this year

Complete something like the above examples for each of your foundation and framing items. This may require multiple sessions, with one or two foundation or framing items completed at each sitting. The end result should be a list of clearly defined targets for each of your foundation and framing items.

Sorting the Finishing

You now have a list of finishing items for every foundation and framing item. With completion times ranging from specific deadlines to daily items, weekly items, monthly items, annual items, etc., it will be difficult to translate the finishing into reality if you do not further sort them by completion time.

Sort your finishing items according to categories such as:

- Daily goals
- Weekly goals
- Monthly goals
- Quarterly goals
- Annual goals

Map these lists into your schedule, however you organize that. As you work toward specificity, resist the temptation to anxiously grip too tightly to your agenda—"We can make our plans, but the Lord determines our steps" (Prov. 16:9 NLT). Depending on your personality and disposition, God will give you grace by leading you into greater or lesser specificity. As you work through this exercise, may he meet you and lead you into deeper ways of grace and flourishing for many years to come! ✣

APPENDIX B

*Encounters with the Love of God:
A Visio Divina Exercise*

TABLE OF CONTENTS

1.
The Creation

B8

ARTWORK
Creation of the World XIII
by Mikalojus Konstantinas Ciurlionis

2.
Abraham and Isaac

B10

ARTWORK
Sacrifice of Isaac
by Caravaggio

3.
The Crossing of the Red Sea

B12

ARTWORK
Exodus
by Marc Chagall

4.
Elijah in the Wilderness

B14

ARTWORK
Elijah Fed
by Ferdinand Bol

5.
Ruth and Naomi

B16

ARTWORK
Naomi Entreating Ruth and Orpah
by William Blake

6.
The Annunciation

B18

ARTWORK
The Annunciation
by Henry Ossawa Tanner

7.
The Good Samaritan

B20

ARTWORK
The Good Samaritan
by Vincent van Gogh

8.
The Prodigal Son

B22

ARTWORK
Return of the Prodigal Son
by Rembrandt van Rijn

9.
Jesus and the Woman at the Well

B24

ARTWORK
Jesus and the Woman at the Well
Artist Unknown

10.
Jesus and the Woman Caught in Adultery

B26

ARTWORK
Jesus and the Woman Caught in Adultery
by Lucas Cranach the Elder

11.
Jesus on the Cross

B28

ARTWORK
The Crucifixion
by Matthias Grünewald

12.
The Restoration of Peter

B30

ARTWORK
The Restoration of Peter
Icon, Artist Unknown

Encounters with the Love of God: A *Visio Divina* Exercise

Using a piece of art to help us pray is often referred to by the Latin term *visio divina* (literally, "divine seeing"). This practice simply involves looking at and reflecting on a work of art, sometimes along with a related text of Scripture, and seeking God to guide our hearts and our prayers as we do so.

Visio divina helps engage both our imaginations and our sense of sight as we seek to draw near to God. Historically, Christian art, architecture, iconography, and even the long tradition of stained glass in churches and cathedrals, has helped people engage both their eyes and their imaginations as they seek God using the "eye of their heart." In times and cultures where many people are either illiterate or non-literate, this is a particularly helpful practice.

To practice *visio divina,* take some increments of time over the course of this month to sit with each image below. Find a quiet, relaxing place and ask God to open your heart and mind to him, and to guide your time. Then simply look at the image before you and seek to encounter God as you do so. Slowly read out loud the brief text that accompanies each image. Without rushing, let the text and the picture impact you, and pay attention to what you sense God saying and stirring in you.

This *visio divina* exercise involves a selection of twelve events or narratives in the Scriptures drawn from both the Old and the New Testaments that are organized roughly in the order of their appearance. The unifying theme of these events is "the love of God," and the aim of this exercise is to help you reflect on the ways the unchanging love of God has been expressed to his broken and wandering people through the ages.

These images include events that are winsome and tender, striking and sorrowful, and even violent. It may not be immediately clear how God's love is demonstrated through a particular image. Even in those instances where you find yourself experiencing resistance to the selected image or text, press in to see if God reveals something that eluded you at first glance.

AS YOU ENGAGE EACH IMAGE AND ITS ACCOMPANYING TEXT, USE THESE PROMPTS TO GUIDE YOU IN YOUR TIME:

1.

What most stands out to you in this picture? Why?

2.

What feelings and thoughts does this picture stir in you?

3.

What is the most striking physical, spiritual, or emotional need represented in this picture? Does this connect with your own sin, weakness, or need in any specific ways? How?

4.

What facet of God's love is most deeply expressed to you through this picture? How does that make you feel?

5.

Write a short prayer to God that expresses your reactions to and reflections on this image and text.

1.
The Creation

✣

Genesis 1:1–5 NASB

In the beginning God created the heavens and the earth.

The earth was formless and void, and darkness was over the surface of the deep, and the Spirit of God was moving over the surface of the waters.

Then God said, "Let there be light"; and there was light.

God saw that the light was good; and God separated the light from the darkness.

God called the light day, and the darkness He called night. And there was evening and there was morning, one day.

Creation of the World XIII, by Mikalojus Konstantinas Ciurlionis

Creation of the World XIII, 1906-Mikalojus Konstantinas Ciurlionis-WikiArt.org

2.
Abraham and Isaac

✣

Genesis 22:10–14 NIV

Then he reached out his hand and took the knife to slay his son. But the angel of the Lord called out to him from heaven, "Abraham! Abraham!"

"Here I am," he replied.

"Do not lay a hand on the boy," he said. "Do not do anything to him. Now I know that you fear God, because you have not withheld from me your son, your only son."

Abraham looked up and there in a thicket he saw a ram caught by its horns. He went over and took the ram and sacrificed it as a burnt offering instead of his son. So Abraham called that place The Lord Will Provide. And to this day it is said, "On the mountain of the Lord it will be provided."

Sacrifice of Isaac, by Caravaggio

3.
The Crossing of the Red Sea

✥

Exodus 14:29–31 NIV

But the Israelites went through the sea on dry ground, with a wall of water on their right and on their left.

That day the LORD saved Israel from the hands of the Egyptians, and Israel saw the Egyptians lying dead on the shore.

And when the Israelites saw the mighty hand of the LORD displayed against the Egyptians, the people feared the LORD and put their trust in him and in Moses his servant.

Exodus, by Marc Chagall

Exodus, 1952-1966-MarcChagall-WikiArt.org

4.
Elijah in the Wilderness

✣

1 Kings 19:3–7 NIV

Elijah was afraid and ran for his life. When he came to Beersheba in Judah, he left his servant there, while he himself went a day's journey into the wilderness. He came to a broom bush, sat down under it and prayed that he might die. "I have had enough, Lord," he said. "Take my life; I am no better than my ancestors." Then he lay down under the bush and fell asleep.

All at once an angel touched him and said, "Get up and eat." He looked around, and there by his head was some bread baked over hot coals, and a jar of water. He ate and drank and then lay down again.

The angel of the Lord came back a second time and touched him and said, "Get up and eat, for the journey is too much for you."

Elijah Fed, by Ferdinand Bol
http://ivehadanepiphany.blogspot.com/2018/07/bread-for-journey.html

5.
Ruth and Naomi

✣

Ruth 1:16–17 NIV

But Ruth replied, "Don't urge me to leave you or to turn back from you. Where you go I will go, and where you stay I will stay. Your people will be my people and your God my God. Where you die I will die, and there I will be buried. May the Lord deal with me, be it ever so severely, if even death separates you and me."

Naomi Entreating Ruth and Orpah, by William Blake

https://commons.wikimedia.org/wiki/File:1795-William-Blake-Naomi-entreating-Ruth-Orpah.jpg

6.
The Annunciation

✣

Luke 1:26–31, 34–35, 38 NIV

In the sixth month of Elizabeth's pregnancy, God sent the angel Gabriel to Nazareth, a town in Galilee, to a virgin pledged to be married to a man named Joseph, a descendant of David. The virgin's name was Mary.

The angel went to her and said, "Greetings, you who are highly favored! The Lord is with you." Mary was greatly troubled at his words and wondered what kind of greeting this might be. But the angel said to her, "Do not be afraid, Mary; you have found favor with God. You will conceive and give birth to a son, and you are to call him Jesus.

"How will this be," Mary asked the angel, "since I am a virgin?" The angel answered, "The Holy Spirit will come on you, and the power of the Most High will overshadow you. So the holy one to be born will be called the Son of God.

"I am the Lord's servant," Mary answered. "May your word to me be fulfilled." Then the angel left her.

The Annunciation, by Henry Ossawa Tanner

The Annunciation, 1898-Henry Ossawa Tanner-WikiArt.org

7.
The Good Samaritan

✣

Luke 10:30–37 NIV

Jesus said: "A man was going down from Jerusalem to Jericho, when he was attacked by robbers. They stripped him of his clothes, beat him and went away, leaving him half dead. A priest happened to be going down the same road, and when he saw the man, he passed by on the other side. So too, a Levite, when he came to the place and saw him, passed by on the other side. But a Samaritan, as he traveled, came where the man was; and when he saw him, he took pity on him. He went to him and bandaged his wounds, pouring on oil and wine. Then he put the man on his own donkey, brought him to an inn and took care of him. The next day he took out two denarii and gave them to the innkeeper. 'Look after him,' he said, 'and when I return, I will reimburse you for any extra expense you may have.'

"Which of these three do you think was a neighbor to the man who fell into the hands of robbers?"

The expert in the law replied, "The one who had mercy on him." Jesus told him, "Go and do likewise."

The Good Samaritan, by Vincent van Gogh

https://www.immanuelpc.org/sermon/luke-the-good-samaritan/

8.
The Prodigal Son

✣

Luke 15:20–24 NIV

"So he got up and went to his father.

But while he was still a long way off, his father saw him and was filled with compassion for him; he ran to his son, threw his arms around him and kissed him.

"The son said to him, 'Father, I have sinned against heaven and against you. I am no longer worthy to be called your son.'

"But the father said to his servants, 'Quick! Bring the best robe and put it on him. Put a ring on his finger and sandals on his feet. Bring the fattened calf and kill it. Let's have a feast and celebrate. For this son of mine was dead and is alive again; he was lost and is found.' So they began to celebrate."

Return of the Prodigal Son, by Rembrandt van Rijn

https://en.wikipedia.org/wiki/The_Return_of_the_Prodigal_Son_(Rembrandt)

9.
Jesus and the Woman at the Well

✣

John 4:7–18 NIV

When a Samaritan woman came to draw water, Jesus said to her, "Will you give me a drink?" (His disciples had gone into the town to buy food.)

The Samaritan woman said to him, "You are a Jew and I am a Samaritan woman. How can you ask me for a drink?" (For Jews do not associate with Samaritans.)

Jesus answered her, "If you knew the gift of God and who it is that asks you for a drink, you would have asked him and he would have given you living water."

"Sir," the woman said, "you have nothing to draw with and the well is deep. Where can you get this living water? Are you greater than our father Jacob, who gave us the well and drank from it himself, as did also his sons and his livestock?"

Jesus answered, "Everyone who drinks this water will be thirsty again, but whoever drinks the water I give them will never thirst. Indeed, the water I give them will become in them a spring of water welling up to eternal life."

The woman said to him, "Sir, give me this water so that I won't get thirsty and have to keep coming here to draw water."

He told her, "Go, call your husband and come back."

"I have no husband," she replied.

Jesus said to her, "You are right when you say you have no husband. The fact is, you have had five husbands, and the man you now have is not your husband. What you have just said is quite true."

Jesus and the Woman at the Well, artist unknown
http://bojackson54.com/tag/woman-at-the-well/

10.
Jesus and the Woman Caught in Adultery

✣

John 8:6b–11 NIV

The teachers of the law and the Pharisees brought in a woman caught in adultery. They made her stand before the group and said to Jesus, "Teacher, this woman was caught in the act of adultery. In the Law Moses commanded us to stone such women. Now what do you say?"

But Jesus bent down and started to write on the ground with his finger. When they kept on questioning him, he straightened up and said to them, "Let any one of you who is without sin be the first to throw a stone at her." Again he stooped down and wrote on the ground.

At this, those who heard began to go away one at a time, the older ones first, until only Jesus was left, with the woman still standing there. Jesus straightened up and asked her, "Woman, where are they? Has no one condemned you?"

"No one, sir," she said.

"Then neither do I condemn you," Jesus declared. "Go now and leave your life of sin."

Jesus and the Woman Caught in Adultery, by Lucas Cranach the Elder

https://wsimag.com/museumkunstpalac/artworks/95138w

11.
Jesus on the Cross

✠

Luke 23:34, Mark 15:33–34 NIV

Jesus said, "Father, forgive them, for they do not know what they are doing." And they divided up his clothes by casting lots.

At noon, darkness came over the whole land until three in the afternoon. And at three in the afternoon Jesus cried out in a loud voice, "Eloi, Eloi, lema sabachthani?" (which means "My God, my God, why have you forsaken me?")

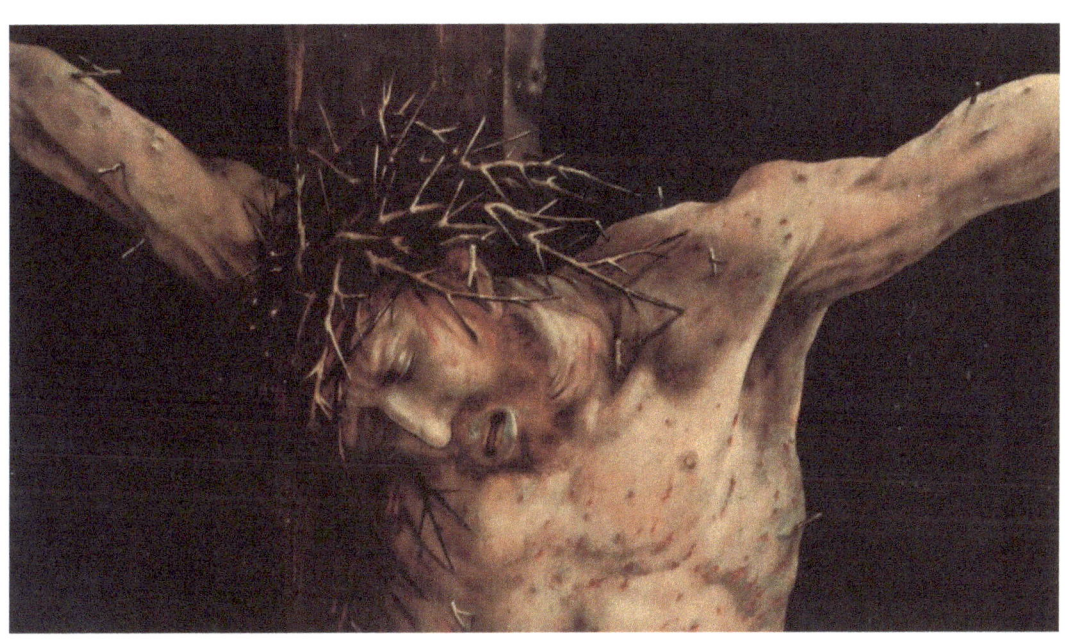

The Crucifixion (detail from the Isenheim Altarpiece), by Matthias Grünewald

The Crucifixion (detail from the Isenheim Altarpiece), c.1512–c.1515-Matthias Grünewald-WikiArt.org

12.
The Restoration of Peter

✣

John 21:9–15 NLT

When they got there, they found breakfast waiting for them—fish cooking over a charcoal fire, and some bread. "Bring some of the fish you've just caught," Jesus said. So Simon Peter went aboard and dragged the net to the shore. There were 153 large fish, and yet the net hadn't torn.

"Now come and have some breakfast!" Jesus said. None of the disciples dared to ask him, "Who are you?" They knew it was the Lord. Then Jesus served them the bread and the fish. This was the third time Jesus had appeared to his disciples since he had been raised from the dead.

After breakfast Jesus asked Simon Peter, "Simon son of John, do you love me more than these?" "Yes, Lord," Peter replied, "you know I love you." "Then feed my lambs," Jesus told him.

Jesus repeated the question: "Simon son of John, do you love me?" "Yes, Lord," Peter said, "you know I love you." "Then take care of my sheep," Jesus said.

A third time he asked him, "Simon son of John, do you love me?" Peter was hurt that Jesus asked the question a third time. He said, "Lord, you know everything. You know that I love you." Jesus said, "Then feed my sheep."

The Restoration of Peter

Icon, Artist Unknown https://theencouragingthomist.blogspot.com/2019/05/sunday-homily-may-5th-2019-dont-judge.html

APPENDIX C

Resources

TABLE OF CONTENTS

RESOURCE

1

Books

A Month-by-Month Reference

C6

RESOURCE

2

The Word Implanted

A Month-by-Month Reference

C12

RESOURCE

3

Films

A Month-by-Month Reference

C14

RESOURCE

4

12-for-12 Leader's Guide

How to Form and Lead a Group

C18

RESOURCE

5

Bibliography

C30

RESOURCE

1

Books

A Month-by-Month Reference

Instruct the wise and they will be wiser still;
teach the righteous and they will add to their learning.
The fear of the Lord is the beginning of wisdom,
and knowledge of the Holy One is understanding.
For through wisdom your days will be many,
and years will be added to your life.
(Prov. 9:9–11 NIV)

Chapter 1

Sacred Companions: The Gift of Spiritual Friendship and Direction
by David G. Benner (2002)

In *Sacred Companions,* Benner provides a winsome introduction to the value and characteristics of true Christian community and spiritual friendship, as well as a helpful introductory guide to approaches to spiritual direction in community, all framed in the context of what he calls "the transformational journey."

Chapter 2

Life Together
by Dietrich Bonhoeffer (1954)

A modern classic written by a martyred German theologian in the years before WWII during the dark days of Nazi rule under Adolf Hitler, *Life Together* explores the rhythms of a life lived in close proximity and relationship to other Christian believers. This book is essential reading for anyone reflecting on the essence of Christian community in our own day and time.

Chapter 3

The Practice of the Presence of God
by Brother Lawrence (1982)

This humble collection of the letters, conversations, and reflections of Brother Lawrence of the Resurrection, a 17th century French Carmelite monk, continue to bear witness to a simple life given over to the pursuit of the presence of God in the most ordinary of everyday circumstances. Brother Lawrence's earthy approach to "practicing the presence" has much to teach us about pursuing union with God through the moment-by- moment experience of his abiding presence. This book is widely available online and in libraries for free, as well as in multiple digital and print editions at low cost.

The Sacrament of the Present Moment
by Jean-Pierre de Caussade (1989)

De Caussade's work focuses on what he considers the central duty of the Christian—"to keep one's gaze fixed on the master one has chosen and to be constantly listening so as to understand and hear and immediately obey his will." Originally written in the 18th century, though not appearing for the first time until 1861 under the title *Self-Abandonment to Divine Providence*, *The Sacrament of the Present Moment* still stands as a wonderful resource for anyone who wants to learn to redeem the sacredness of ordinary moments in an ordinary life.

Beginning to Pray
by Anthony Bloom (1970)

Written by an atheist convert to the Christian faith who went on to become a Russian Orthodox priest and bishop, this little volume has come to be viewed as a modern classic on prayer. Original in tone, and with short chapters entitled "The Absence of God," Knocking at the Door," "Going Inward," "Managing Time," and "Addressing God," as well as a wonderful autobiographical introduction, Beginning to Pray leads us in refreshingly simple and practical ways to embrace an increasingly godward life, and is very much worth its barely over a hundred pages.

Chapter 4

The Knowledge of the Holy: The Attributes of God,
Their Meaning in the Christian Life
by A.W. Tozer (1961)

The Knowledge of the Holy stands as a classic modern treatment of the attributes of God by acclaimed Chicago pastor, author, and mystic A.W. Tozer. With helpful opening prayers in many chapters, Tozer leads us in both theological reflection and direct encounter with God in light of his character and attributes and begins his book with the arresting line, "What comes into our minds when we think about God is the most important thing about us."

Chapter 5

The Gift of Being Yourself: The Sacred Call to Self-Discovery
by David G. Benner (2015)

Benner asserts in *The Gift of Being Yourself* that there can be no deep knowledge of God without deep knowledge of oneself and spends the bulk of this book helping us notice and understand the working of both grace and sin in our lives in light of the abiding love of God. This book is particularly helpful in identifying sin, not merely as patterns of external behavior, but as ways rooted more deeply within us, and it provides practical instruction to help us overcome sin and embrace our identity as defined by God.

Chapter 6

Searching For and Maintaining Peace: A Small Treatise on Peace of Heart
by Jacques Philippe (2002)

This little book, written by a French Catholic priest and retreat leader, is a simple yet profound treatise on peace of heart and offers gentle, practical ways to encounter and receive from God amid the most ordinary life situations. Divided into three helpful sections, *Searching for and Maintaining Peace* first addresses the central importance of maintaining a peaceful heart in our life with God; identifies common reasons for us to lose our peace as well as practical ways to maintain it; and then provides a selection of texts by various authors through the ages who speak to these same themes.

Interior Freedom
by Jacques Philippe (2007)

Jacques Philippe's stated purpose in this little book is that "every Christian needs to discover that even in the most unfavorable outward circumstances we possess within ourselves a space of freedom that nobody can take away, because God is its source and guarantee. Without this discovery we will always be restricted in some way..." (p. 9). The rest of the book explores the nature of this "interior freedom" that is available to us all as a gift from God and how in practical terms we can more fully lay hold of it.

Chapter 7 and 8

Watership Down
by Richard Adams (1972)

Based on the author's experience in the British army, this celebrated novel follows the epic adventures of a band of rabbits in the English countryside and has much profound wisdom to offer regarding leadership and community in the context of mission. Though perhaps an unlikely selection for a spiritual formation group, *Watership Down* makes its way into the work of theologians like Stanley Hauerwas and is included in seminary curriculums.

Chapter 9

The Way of Discernment: Spiritual Practices for Decision Making
by Elizabeth Liebert (2008)

A deep and yet very readable book, *The Way of Discernment* presents a whole-life framework for becoming a discerning person and also provides a number of practical exercises to assist with larger life decisions. Liebert's presentation is thoughtful and theologically rich and lays out both a case and a gentle process for how to grow and become a mature disciple of Jesus who learns to make wise decisions in both the smallest and largest matters of life.

Markings
by Dag Hammarskjöld (1964)

This modern classic contains the posthumously published journals of the celebrated Swedish economist, diplomat, and Secretary General of the United Nations between 1953 and his death in a plane crash in 1961. Hammarskjöld, a public man of deep private faith, offers years of personal reflections, poetry, and spiritual wrestling. His writing is of great value to anyone desiring to incorporate Christian faith into a more public calling.

Every Good Endeavor: Connecting Your Work to God's Work
by Timothy Keller (2012)

Titled after the words of jazz great John Coltrane, this approachable book by bestselling author and former pastor of New York's Redeemer Presbyterian Church provides a biblical theology of work and calling and offers much practical wisdom in the pursuit of God in the context of career. In three helpful sections, Keller addresses God's plan for work, problems we face regarding work, and how the gospel redeems our work for God's good purposes in the world. It ends with an epilogue on approaches to integrating faith and work.

Chapter 10

The Church of Mercy: A Vision for the Church
by Pope Francis (2013)

In this collection of essays, homilies, and other excerpts taken from the first year of his papacy, Pope Francis weaves all four of the cardinal directions into a winsome and practical vision for the church in the world. As both the first Jesuit pope and the first pope from South America, Francis seeks a church whose people have personal union with Christ, live in the unity of love with God's people, and who humbly and courageously engage with the world in Christ's mission.

Cry the Beloved Country
by Alan Paton (1948)

Written by a white South African author during the horrors of apartheid, this modern classic tells the fictional story of two fathers whose lives intersect when the son of one, a Black pastor, murders the son of the other, a white landowner and farmer. The story of grace and reconciliation unfolds in the face of great pain, systemic racism, poverty, and loss, and it leads us to a place of rooted and transformational hope in the way of Jesus.

How the Irish Saved Civilization: The Untold Story of Ireland's Heroic Role from the Fall of Rome to the Rise of Medieval Europe
by Thomas Cahill (1995)

This book tells the remarkable story of St. Patrick's 5th century call to return to his Irish enslavers and how the ensuing Irish missional and monastic movement emerged in the following centuries, winning many to faith, promoting education and justice among the poor and marginalized of Europe, and preserving Classical Greek and Latin texts along the way. This book stands as a popular approach to the history of mission, and testifies to the power of Christian mission to holistically impact the world for good.

Death Comes for the Archbishop
by Willa Cather (1927)

Among Cather's most celebrated novels, *Death Comes for the Archbishop* tells the story of a devoted Catholic missionary priest in the 19th century American Southwest. Without sentimentality or idealism, this simple story illuminates qualities of perseverance, resourcefulness, and grace in a cross-cultural missional context.

The Art of Neighboring: Building Genuine Relationships Right Outside Your Door
by Jay Pathak and Dave Runyon (2012)

In *The Art of Neighboring*, Pathak, a local pastor and National Director of Vineyard USA, provides a winsome and practical approach to connecting in the way of Jesus with the people in our own neighborhoods. Living missionally, according to Pathak, best begins when we pay attention and make ourselves available to the people we see every day in our own neighborhoods.

Chapter 11

"Neighbor Rosicky"
by Willa Cather (1930)

First published in *Woman's Home Companion* in 1930, this gentle short story tells the story of Czech immigrant Anton Rosicky and his family on their humble farm in Nebraska. Told from the perspective of the local country doctor and containing flashbacks of Anton Rosicky's days in London as a poor immigrant, "Neighbor Rosicky" considers the life of a man and a family given to relationship and simple domestic graces rather than ambitious pursuit of profit.

The Sabbath: Its Meaning for Modern Man
by Abraham Joshua Heschel (2005)

This modern classic by a celebrated Jewish scholar, mystic, activist, and theologian uses metaphor, imagery, narrative, and verse to frame Sabbath as a "palace in time" where we reconnect with eternity and with God himself. No serious 21st-century consideration of Sabbath is complete without Heschel's deeply mystical yet profoundly practical work.

Sabbath Keeping: Finding Freedom in the Rhythms of Rest
by Lynne M. Baab (2005)

By addressing Sabbath resistance and sharing testimonies from her congregation, this book by Presbyterian minister Lynne Baab stands as a practical guide to embracing Sabbath and provides simple tools to help discern the ways of Sabbath in the context of ordinary life.

RESOURCE 2
The Word Implanted
A Month-by-Month Reference

Let the word of Christ richly dwell within you ... (Col. 3:16a NASB)

Chapter 1

- Ephesians 4:21–5:2
- Philippians 2:12–16
- 2 Peter 1:1–8
- Psalm 16
- 2 Corinthians 4:6–11
- Mark 12:28b–31

Chapter 2

- Psalm 133
- Romans 12:1–8
- John 13:34–35
- Acts 2:42–47
- I Timothy 1:5

Chapter 3

- Psalm 24
- Psalm 27
- Psalm 46
- Psalm 104

Chapter 4

- Psalm 103
- Isaiah 40
- Romans 1:18–20
- Colossians 1:15–20
- Hebrews 1:1–4
- 1 John 4:7–16

Chapter 5

- Psalm 103:8–18
- Lamentations 3:21–26
- John 17:20–26
- 1 Peter 4:10–11
- 1 John 4:16–19

Chapter 6

- Psalm 51
- Psalm 139
- Isaiah 6:1–8
- Luke 18:9–14
- Hebrews 12:1–6

Chapter 7

- Genesis 18:1–15
- 1 Kings 17:1–16
- John 21:1–17
- Ephesians 2:11–22
- James 5:16–18
- 1 Peter 4:7–9

Chapter 8

- Job 28
- Psalms 90
- Proverbs 2:1–15
- Matthew 12:33–37
- James 1:2–8; 3:13–18

Chapter 9

- Proverbs 6:6–11, 10:4-5, 16:3, 31:1–31
- Luke 2:39–52
- Luke 6:12–16
- 1 Corinthians 12 and 13
- 1 Thessalonians 4:9–12

Chapter 10

- Genesis 12:1–3
- Psalm 67
- Isaiah 58:6–12
- Matthew 28:18–20
- Revelation 5:9–10, 7:9–12

Chapter 11

- Exodus 20:8–11
- Psalm 127
- Ecclesiastes 3
- Isaiah 58
- Matthew 7:24–27
- Ephesians 5:15–16

RESOURCE

3

Films

A Month-by-Month Reference

I devoted myself to study and to explore by wisdom all that is done under heaven. (Ecc. 1:13a NIV)

Chapter 2

Of Gods and Men (2010)

Based on a true story, this winner of the Grand Prize at the Cannes Film Festival tells the story of a community of French Cistercian monks during a time of significant social and religious unrest in Algeria in the 1990's. Following the lives of the monastic community as a whole, its individual members, and the Algerian Muslim community of which they are a part, this film has much to teach about discerning the will of God, no matter the cost, in missional community with others.

Chapter 3

Tender Mercies (1983)

Robert Duvall won Best Actor honors for his performance in this film, which focuses on the failure and redemption of a country singer in small town Texas and whose title hearkens from the language of the King James translation of the Psalms. While avoiding simplistic answers, this quiet film sheds light on the tender mercies of God in the life of Mac Sledge, a down-on-his-luck country singer, his new wife, Rosa Lee, and her son, Sonny, who together work out their own senses of loss, failure, and God's love in earthy ways. Much of the background music in this film is performed by Duvall himself.

Chapter 4

Signs (2002)

This M. Night Shyamalan science fiction film tells the story of Graham Hess, a preacher who has lost his faith after his wife dies in a terrible auto accident. Father Hess, his son, his daughter, and his brother Merrill, who live together in a farmhouse in eastern Pennsylvania, encounter a group of aliens whose presence first becomes known through mysterious crop circles in the surrounding cornfields. The action centers on how the family protects themselves from the aliens and on how these events shape Father Hess's understanding of God.

Chapter 5

Chariots of Fire (1981)

This Academy-Award-winning film tells the true story of the celebrated British running team in the 1924 Paris Olympics. It focuses on the lives of two members of that team—Eric Liddell, born in China into a devout missionary family, and Harold Abrahams, a brilliant secular Jewish man with a background in business and finance. The film has much to say about submission to God and good stewardship of our graces and gifts.

The Last Emperor (1987)

Winner of nine Academy Awards, this epic biographical film focuses on the life of Puyi, the last emperor of China, who was removed from his reign during profound changes in China in the first half of the 20th century. Employing brilliant cinematography and expansive historical sweep, this film tells the story of how a man wrestles with his own identity in the face of massive upheaval and external change and how he comes to understand himself in the end. Check the IMDb listing before watching.

Chapter 6

The Painted Veil (2006)

This film starring Naomi Watts and Edward Norton tells the story of the fracture and ultimate healing of the marriage of Dr. Walter Fane and his wife, Kitty. Based on a novel by W. Somerset Maugham and set in China in the 1920's, it addresses themes of sin and forgiveness, suffering and transformation, life, death, and love, and serves as an excellent story of how we come to know ourselves and others, and how we learn to give and receive love, even as we come face to face with our deepest failures and sins. Check the IMDb listing before watching.

The Remains of the Day (1993)

This excellently acted and directed Merchant Ivory film stars Anthony Hopkins and Emma Thompson and centers on the life of James Stevens, a faithful butler to a wealthy, though naïve and tragically misguided English Lord. The story is a tale of regret, of the daunting quest of coming to grips with the truth about oneself and one's sins and failures, and about what it might look like to deal—or not deal—truthfully with what one discovers.

Chapter 7

A Raisin in the Sun (1961)

This celebrated and brilliantly acted Sidney Poitier film tells the story of an extended Black family in Chicago caught in the throes of grief and conflict. As they seek to resolve their differences, the family experiences failure, forgiveness, racial bias, and personal transformation, while its main character, Walter, comes to a deeper and more settled understanding of himself.

Seabiscuit (2003)

Based on true events, this film tells the Great Depression-era story of a group of unlikely people united by long-shot aspirations for an undersized and injured racehorse named Seabiscuit. It is a tale of how hurt and broken people can help each other grow, change, and step back into the identity and purpose each person was originally designed for.

Chapter 8

12 Angry Men (1957)

This film focuses on the jury deliberations in a murder trial in Chicago and takes place almost entirely in the locked room where they are deciding the fate of the accused man, an 18-year-old immigrant man accused of murdering his father. Through their sometimes-heated conversations, the twelve jurors come to better understand themselves and their own biases and ultimately arrive at a verdict that is both different and wiser,than they had first expected. This film bears witness to the power of attentive conversation to shape us, as well as to how courage, conscience, bias, and our commitment, or lack of commitment to paying attention impacts our ability to discern the truth.

Inside Out (2015)

This animated film focuses on the emotions—joy, fear, anger, disgust, and sadness—in the life of a young girl experiencing a major family move, and sheds helpful light on how the ways we identify and navigate these emotions in our own lives contributes to our ability to make good choices, and to live wisely and well.

Chapter 9

A Man for All Seasons (1966)

Winner of six Academy Awards, including Best Picture, Best Actor, and Best Director, this film tells the story of Sir Thomas More, celebrated English author, statesman, philosopher, and ultimately Lord Chancellor of England under Henry VIII. More's unyielding integrity in undertaking his public post cost him his life in 1535 when he was beheaded by the king for refusing to support him in his self-proclaimed supremacy over the English church and the right to annul his marriage with Catherine of Aragorn, the first of Henry's eight wives. This film stands as an excellent study in maintaining personal integrity in the context of a public calling and political career.

Concussion (2015)

Based on actual events, this film starring Will Smith tells the story of Nigerian American forensic pathologist Dr. Bennett Omalu, who first discovered and published findings linking repeated head trauma among NFL players with chronic traumatic encephalopathy, a destructive and sometimes fatal neurodegenerative disease. Against the opposition of NFL leadership, Omalu persists in researching and publishing his findings, and his story is a helpful glimpse into a career yielded to God and committed to integrity and truth.

Something the Lord Made (2004)

Also based on actual events, this film starring Mos Def and Alan Rickman tells the story of skilled African American carpenter Vivien Thomas, who becomes the unlikely partner to the celebrated Dr. Alfred Blalock in the development of bypass surgery in the care of so-called "blue babies." Without medical training, but with remarkable gifting and intuitions in the work of surgery, Thomas rose from the position of janitor to lab technician to Instructor of Surgery at the Johns Hopkins School of Medicine; he worked for 34 years with Blalock, who initially received disproportionate credit for their achievements. This film stands as a helpful example of a humble man of faith who employs his God-given abilities on an unexpected path for the public good.

Arrival (2016)

Nominated for Best Picture, this science fiction film tells the story of linguistics professor Louise Banks, played by Amy Adams, as she leads a team seeking to understand the written language of extraterrestrial visitors in the quest to communicate with them and avoid potential war. Focused on a committed professional faithfully practicing her craft in a high-stakes context, this film provides much to reflect on regarding the use of vocation to bring good into the world.

Chapter 10

The Mission (1986)

Nominated for seven Academy Awards and winner of Best Cinematography, this 1986 film starring Robert DeNiro and Jeremy Irons focuses on the establishment of a Jesuit mission in the heart of the Amazon in the late 18th century and its protection of the indigenous population from pro-slavery Portuguese colonial powers. This film raises important questions about the complex relationship between Christian mission, evangelism, justice, culture, power, and money.

Cry the Beloved Country (1995)

Based on Alan Paton's novel of the same name, *Cry the Beloved Country* tells a moving story of death, loss, justice, mercy, and redemption in the face of horrific racial injustice under South African apartheid. Of particular note is how Reverend Theophilus Msimangu's words and actions model missional living in the way of Jesus and bring about an unlikely reconciliation.

Just Mercy (2019)

This 2019 film tells the true story of Bryan Stevenson, Harvard-educated attorney and founder of the Equal Justice Initiative, who rather than pursuing lucrative opportunities, moves to Alabama to defend wrongly convicted prisoners. This film focuses on the defense and ultimate exoneration of Alabama death row prisoner, Walter McMillian. Stevenson's celebrated social justice work is deeply influenced by his Christian faith and early formation in the African Methodist Episcopal Church.

RESOURCE

4
12-for-12 Leader's Guide
How to Form and Lead a Group

...not giving up meeting together... but encouraging one another—and all the more as you see the Day approaching... (Heb. 10:25 NIV)

Leading a 12-for-12 group is a rewarding opportunity to walk with a group of committed sisters and brothers for a year of focused spiritual formation in community. It is a singular privilege to share in the sacred times of transparency, authenticity, and openness to God, and to see God at work in, among, and through a 12-for-12 group over the course of a year. As you grow in experience, you will develop intuitions and become increasingly comfortable with the rhythms of a normal group. This guide consists of five sections:

1. General guidelines for forming groups.

2. General guidelines for leading groups.

3. Monthly meeting agendas for easier planning.

4. Tools and resources to use during your group meetings.

5. Suggested psalms, prayers, check-in prompts, etc.

SECTION 1: How to Form a Group

Participate first

Be part of a 12-for-12 group before leading one. When this is not possible, practice and familiarize yourself with the content prior to starting a group and stay at least a month or two ahead on homework assignments.

Have a co-leader

Even if one person takes the lead during most meetings, two people share the load of planning, preparing, and hosting, and provide support and accountability to one another. Commit to a co-leader at least a few months before the group begins. Generally, co-ed groups are best led by both a man and a woman.

Take time to form a group

Usually, it takes about three to four months to build a group. A 12-for-12 group is a big commitment; potential group members need time to process and consider whether they can join. Personal invitations often work best. A range of different types of groups can work well—co-ed groups, men's groups, women's groups, singles groups, multigenerational groups, lay leader groups, young adult groups, etc.—and it is important to consider in advance the kind of group you sense God leading you towards before you begin building it. When forming groups, try not to include isolated individuals from any one ethnic group, age group, gender, etc., but work to have at least two or three representatives of any given demographic in the group as well. A simple group application is helpful and provides an opportunity for you to learn a bit about your group members in advance, to invite reflection on their part as they consider joining the group, and to filter out people who find themselves resistant to or unable to complete even the reflective work of the initial application.

Determine your meeting location

Generally, a group leader or group member serves as host by opening their home for monthly gatherings. Whatever the location, it should be comfortable, quiet, and if possible, have room for members to occasionally break up into small groups or individually for reflection, etc.

Share the schedule

Share the year's meeting schedule with all prospective members. Meetings should happen at roughly the same time each month (e.g. the first the first Friday evening of each month, etc.). If someone knows they will miss more than 2–3 meetings, or if they will miss more than one of the first three meetings, it is probably best for them to join a group at a later date or one with a different schedule.

Helpful application questions include

- Is there anything in the 12-for-12 group description you are particularly drawn to? Please explain.

- Describe any ways you have recently sensed God inviting you to deepen your relationship with him, as well as how you find yourself responsive or resistant to that invitation.

- How long have you been in a personal relationship with God? How do you presently spend time with God? Briefly describe your current season of life overall and your current season of relationship with God.

- In worship and life, what do you find yourself most passionate about? When do you feel most drawn to worship God? What kinds of things draw you close to him?

- What are your particular desires for spiritual growth in the year ahead?

- List any books on spiritual formation that have impacted you.

- Describe any previous experiences you have had with spiritual formation practices and groups.

- Are you able to commit the time necessary for the meetings and homework in the year ahead? Please list any scheduling or other conflicts you are aware of.

- Are you able to pitch in for meals and to a fund for childcare for other members of the group? Would you benefit from a fund like that for your own childcare needs?

SECTION 2: How to Lead a Group

Set the tone
You steward the atmosphere and direction of this group the entire year. Take the role seriously. Model transparency and vulnerability.

Before Meeting 1
- Confirm all group members.
- Ensure members obtain this handbook at least 3–4 weeks prior to the first meeting.
- Assign the reading for the Introduction and Chapter 1 of this handbook.
- Assign the Introduction homework.

Pray
Regularly and reflectively pray for group members.

Homework
If you have not recently completed a chapter's assignments, do the homework with your group.

Research
Research liturgical sources for materials to introduce to your group. *The Book of Common Prayer* (available at bcponline.org) is particularly rich in resources, as are prayer books, hymnals, and liturgical guides from a variety of church traditions.

Keep time
Keep time during meetings, especially during individual sharing times, as some members speak less than the allotted time while others share more. A phone timer is helpful; it gently reminds people that their time is up. (Be sure to select a gentle alarm tone.)

Discourage crosstalk
Authentic sharing is a gift, as is attentive listening. Advice, comments, and interjections interfere with the sacred exchange.

Share a meal
Begin each meeting with a potluck meal or order food in. You or someone from your group can coordinate sign ups. Often, the host serves an entrée. Find out in advance about any members' food restrictions, cultural practices, etc. that might impact how you organize your meals. Pass the hat for meal costs if you order food in.

Childcare
To share the load of members' childcare costs, collect a suggested donation of $5–10 per month per member.

SECTION 3: Suggested Monthly Meeting Agendas

General Format
Each monthly meeting takes about 3–3.5 hours. During these meetings, you will:

- Share a meal
- Settle before God
- Share authentically and transparently
- Listen attentively to others as they share
- Review experiences with the homework
- Engage in a new practice
- Review next month's homework
- Pass the hat for the childcare and/or meal fund

While this is the typical agenda, feel free to adjust items and timelines as needed.

Month-by-month Agendas
The following agendas will help you plan your meetings. Feel free to adjust them as needed.

Meeting 1

- Gather; open with a psalm or song, etc., pray, and share a meal together. (45 minutes)

- Opening prayer (5 minutes)

- Practice "Five Minutes of Stillness," Practice 1 in Appendix A. (5 minutes)

- Check in using the "Three Words" prompts from section 4 of this chapter. (20 minutes)

- Review the cardinal directions and guidelines and ethos of 12-for-12 groups from the Introduction. (10 minutes)

- Five minutes of personal sharing from homework prompt in Introduction (60 minutes)

- Read Chapter 1 poem aloud. (5 minutes)

- Introduce Chapter 1 theme and homework. (10 minutes)

- Leaders share their spiritual autobiographies. (20 minutes)

- Close with a brief psalm, song, benediction, or prayer. See section 5 of this chapter for suggestions and options. (5 minutes)

- Remind group members to pray for one another this month and pass the hat for the childcare and/or meal fund.

Meeting 2

- Gather; open with a psalm or song, etc., pray, and share a meal together. (45 minutes)

- Opening prayer (5 minutes)

- Practice the "Prayer of Examen," Practice 3 in Appendix A. (10 minutes)

- Check in using the "Three Words" prompts from section 4 of this chapter. (15 minutes)

- Read Chapter 2 poem aloud. (5 minutes)

- Discuss Chapter 1 homework. (30 minutes)
  - What one thing stands out as particularly significant this month? Why?
  - What was the biggest obstacle or area of resistance as you approached the homework?
  - Review and briefly discuss each section of the homework.

- Share 4–5 spiritual autobiographies. After each autobiography, pause for a few moments in silence to savor what was shared and to thank God for the person's story. (55 minutes)

- Introduce Chapter 2 theme and homework. (10 minutes)

- Close with a brief psalm, song, benediction, or prayer. (5 minutes)

- Remind group members to pray for one another this month and pass the hat for the childcare and/or meal fund.

Meeting 3

- Gather; open with a psalm or song, etc., pray, and share a meal together. (45 minutes)

- Opening prayer (5 minutes)

- "Five Minutes of Stillness" and 3-word check-in prompt. (5 minutes)

- Read Chapter 3 poem aloud. (5 minutes)

- Review the cardinal directions and group progress thus far. (5 minutes)

- Discuss Chapter 2 homework. See review questions from Meeting 2. (30 minutes)

- Share 4-5 spiritual autobiographies, pausing after each one, as already noted. (55 minutes)

- Introduce and take turns reading "Breath Prayers," Practice 4 in Appendix A, aloud slowly as a group. (10 minutes)

- Introduce Chapter 3 theme and homework. (10 minutes)

- Close with a brief psalm, song, benediction, or prayer. (5 minutes)

- Remind group members to pray for one another this month and pass the hat for the childcare and/or meal fund.

Meeting 4

- Gather; open with a psalm or song, etc., pray, and share a meal together. (45 minutes)

- Opening prayer (5 minutes)

- Practice *Lectio Divina*, Practice 6, as a group with one of this month's Word Implanted texts, inviting group members simply to speak out the words and phrases that impact them—but not to elaborate further on them. (20 minutes)

- Share any remaining spiritual autobiographies, pausing after each one, as already noted. (30 minutes)

- Discuss Chapter 3 homework. See review questions from Meeting 2. (30 minutes)

- Share "Prayer of Examen" journal entries. (20 minutes)

- Take turns slowly reading aloud the prayers in "Who Is God? Who Are We?," Practice 5 in Appendix A. (15 minutes)

- Introduce Chapter 4 theme and homework. (10 minutes)

- Close with a brief psalm, song, benediction, or prayer. (5 minutes)

- Remind group members to pray for one another this month and pass the hat for the childcare and/or meal fund.

Meeting 5

- Gather; open with a psalm or song, etc., pray, and share a meal together. (45 minutes)

- Opening prayer (5 minutes)

- Check in using the "Three Encounters, Two Regrets, One Focus (3, 2, 1)" prompts in section 4 of this chapter. (50 minutes)

- Read Chapter 5 poem aloud. (5 minutes)

- Discuss Chapter 4 homework. See review questions from Meeting 2. (30 minutes)

- Individually engage with one *visio divina* image and text of each person's choosing from the "Encounters with the Love of God" exercise in Appendix B. (15 minutes)

- Regather to share about the *visio divina* experience. (10 minutes)

- Pray the "Expanded Jesus Prayer," Practice 8 in Appendix A, aloud together twice. (10 minutes)

- Introduce Chapter 5 theme and homework. (10 minutes)

- Close with a brief psalm, song, benediction, or prayer. (5 minutes)

- Remind group members to pray for one another this month and pass the hat for the childcare and/or meal fund.

Meeting 6

- Gather; open with a psalm or song, etc., pray, and share a meal together. (45 minutes)

- Opening prayer (5 minutes)

- Check in using the "Three Encounters, Two Regrets, One Focus (3, 2, 1)" prompts in section 4 of this chapter. (50 minutes)

- Read Chapter 6 poem aloud (5 minutes)

- Discuss Chapter 5 homework. See review questions from Meeting 2. (30 minutes)

- Pray "The Lord's Prayer in Seven Movements," Practice 10 in Appendix A, with group members taking turns reading each movement. Allow time for members to respond to each movement. (25 minutes)

- Introduce Chapter 6 theme and homework and assign people to Confession and Communion groups with one coordinator for each group. (15 minutes)

- Close with a brief psalm, song, benediction, or prayer. (5 minutes)

- Remind group members to pray for one another this month and pass the hat for the childcare and/or meal fund.

Meeting 7

- Gather; open with a psalm or song, etc., pray, and share a meal together. (45 minutes)

- Opening prayer (5 minutes)

- "Five Minutes of Stillness," Practice 1 in Appendix A. (5 minutes)

- One-minute open check in—"As we gather today, how are you?" (15 minutes)

- Read Chapter 7 poem aloud. (5 minutes)

- Introduce and practice "Contemplative Prayer," Practice 13 in Appendix A. (15 minutes)

- Discuss Chapter 6 homework. See review questions from Meeting 2. (30 minutes)

- Share "Reflection and Journaling" entries from Chapter 6 homework (cf. *The Gift of Being Yourself*, by David Benner, Chapter 5). (45 minutes)

- Introduce Chapter 7 theme and homework. (10 minutes)

- Close with a brief psalm, song, benediction, or prayer. (5 minutes)

- Remind group members to pray for one another this month and pass the hat for the childcare and/or meal fund.

Meeting 8

- Gather; open with a psalm or song, etc., pray, and share a meal together. (45 minutes)

- Opening prayer (5 minutes)

- Prayer of examen and check-in prompt—three words that best describe you right now. (25 minutes)

- Read Chapter 8 poem aloud. (5 minutes)

- Discuss Chapter 7 homework. See review questions from Meeting 2. (30 minutes)

- Introduce "Imaginative Reading of Scripture," Practice 13 in Appendix A. Allot 15 minutes for group members to individually engage with a text selected from *"Encounters with the Love of God"* (Appendix B). Regather to debrief the experience for 10 minutes. (30 minutes)

- Introduce Chapter 8 theme and homework. (10 minutes)

- Take turns praying the "Psalm 90 Blessing" (see Part 5) over one another. (15 minutes)

- Close with a brief psalm, song, benediction, or prayer. (5 minutes)

- Remind group members to pray for one another this month and pass the hat for the childcare and/or meal fund.

Meeting 9

- Gather; open with a psalm or song, etc., pray, and share a meal together. (45 minutes)

- Opening prayer (5 minutes)

- Practice the "Examen of Words," Practice 14 in Appendix A. (15 minutes)

- 3-word check-in, with brief explanation, based on what people noticed in their Examen of Words time. (20 minutes)

- Read Chapter 9 poem aloud. (5 minutes)

- Discuss Chapter 8 homework. See review questions from Meeting 2 above. (30 minutes)

- Invite each group member to find a quiet place to sit and spend 15 minutes in individual contemplative prayer; then regather to debrief the time. (30 minutes)

- Introduce Chapter 9 theme and homework. (10 minutes)

- Break into groups of three or four and pray "A General Blessing" (see section 5 of this chapter) over one another. (15 minutes)

- Have one person close in prayer. (5 minutes)

- Remind group members to pray for one another this month and pass the hat for the childcare and/or meal fund.

Meeting 10

- Gather; open with a psalm or song, etc., pray, and share a meal together. (45 minutes)

- Opening prayer (5 minutes)

- One-minute open check-in—"As we gather today, how are you?" (10 minutes)

- Read Chapter 10 poem aloud. (5 minutes)

- Allow 10 minutes for each group member to share the gift they have prepared for the "Giving Gifts" exercise, Practice 17 in Appendix A. Pause for a few moments of silent savoring after each person shares; then pray a brief prayer of thanksgiving for the person and their gift. (120 minutes. If time runs short, remaining members can share their gifts at the following meeting.)

- If time allows, discuss selected portions of Chapter 9 homework. See review questions from Meeting 2.

- Introduce Chapter 10 theme and homework. (10 minutes)

- Invite one person to close in prayer. (5 minutes)

- Remind group members to pray for one another this month and pass the hat for the childcare and/or meal fund.

Meeting 11

- Gather; open with a psalm or song, etc., pray, and share a meal together. (45 minutes)

- Opening prayer (5 minutes)

- Prayer of examen and check-in prompt—three words that best describe you right now. (20 minutes)

- Read Chapter 11 poem aloud. (5 minutes)

- Have any remaining group members share their "Giving Gifts" offerings. (30 minutes)

- Discuss Chapter 10 homework. See review questions from Meeting 2 above. (30 minutes)

- Freely discuss group members' experience of the group thus far. (20 minutes)

- Introduce both Chapter 11 and Chapter 12 theme and homework, taking time to review "Building for Life," Practice 20 in Appendix A, in more detail. (15 minutes)

- Introduce "Postures of Prayer," Practice 18 in Appendix A, and practice it together as a group. (15 minutes)

- Invite one person to close in prayer. (5 minutes)

- Remind group members to pray for one another this month and pass the hat for the childcare and/or meal fund.

Meeting 12

- Gather; open with a psalm or song, etc., pray, and share a meal together. (45 minutes)

- Opening prayer (5 minutes)

- Prayer of examen and check-in prompt—three words that best describe you right now. (20 minutes)

- Read Chapter 12 poem aloud (5 minutes)

- Discuss the themes, practices, and experiences that have been particularly impactful and beneficial this year. Allow at least 2–3 minutes for each person to share, as well as time for open discussion. (45 minutes)

- Allow 3–4 minutes per person to share life mission statements from the "Building for Life" exercise, Practice 20 in Appendix A, as well as brief reactions to the exercise overall. (45 minutes)

- Pray the "Prayer of Consecration" from Chapter 12 aloud together as a group, allowing group members a few minutes to review it first. (5 minutes)

- Break into groups of three or four and take turns praying the "Prayer of Blessing" from Chapter 12 over one another. (5 minutes)

- Have someone close with the benediction at the end of Chapter 12. (5 minutes)

SECTION 4: Some Resources for Use During Meetings

To open a meeting

- Sing a seasonal song or hymn of your choice.

- Read one of the following psalms, or another psalm of your choice:
    - Psalm 46
    - Psalm 103
    - Psalm 113
    - Psalm 116
    - Psalm 136:1–9, 23–26 (vv. 10–22 optional) —also good as a responsive reading
    - Psalm 145

- Sing the Lord's Prayer. *

- Sing "O Joyous Light." *

- Sing the Doxology. *

* see section 5 of this chapter

For checking-in at the beginning of a meeting

- **Highs and Lows**

    Group members share for 1–2 minutes each regarding one high point and one low point from the past week or so.

- **Consolation and Desolation**

    Group members share one time of consolation (orientation and connection with God) and one time of desolation (disorientation and distance from God) from the past week or so.

- **One-minute Check-in**

    Allow one minute for each group member to answer the question: "As we gather today, how are you?"

- **Three Words**

    Take 3–4 minutes to sit together in the presence of God. Consider the events of the past day or two, ask God to help you notice your thoughts, feelings, and posture of heart. Choose three words that best describe what you notice. Then give 1–2 minutes to each person to share their words and to briefly explain why. After everyone shares, spend 1–2 minutes in silence to recall what each person shared and to quietly hold each one before God in prayer.

- **Three Encounters, Two Regrets, One Focus (3, 2, 1)**

    Take 3–4 minutes to sit together in the presence of God, asking him to help you consider your past week.

    - Recall three times you encountered God. Thank him for those encounters.

    - Recall two times of sorrow or regret for your words, thoughts, actions, or way of being. Seek God for grace and forgiveness in those areas.

    - Finally, identify one area where you sense God inviting you to grow in grace and wisdom. Ask God for help to lay hold of this grace and wisdom.

    - Allow 3–5 minutes to each person to share what they noticed.

    - After everyone shares, take 1–2 more minutes of silence to briefly recall what each 12-for-12 companion shared and to quietly hold each one before God in prayer.

    Note: This exercise typically takes at least 5 minutes per person and will often take a substantial portion of your group time.

To close a meeting

- Sing one of the following liturgical songs or chants from Part 5:
    - The Doxology
    - The Lord's Prayer
    - "O Joyous Light"

- Read or sing one of the following benedictions or write or choose one of your own.
    - Numbers 6:24-26
    - Romans 16:24-27
    - Ephesians 3:20-21
    - 1 Thessalonians 5:23-24
    - 2 Thess. 3:16
    - Hebrews 13:20-21
    - Jude 24-25

- Have one or more group members close the meeting by taking turns reading one of the following psalms or scriptures aloud (or choose one of your own).
    - Psalm 4 (an evening psalm)
    - Psalm 33
    - Psalm 90
    - Psalm 103
    - Psalm 104
    - Psalm 146
    - Psalm 148
    - Luke 1:46-55 (The Magnificat)
    - Luke 2:25-32 (The Prayer of Simeon)

SECTION 5: Some Prayers, Songs, Chants, and Blessings

The Lord's Prayer

Sing the Lord's Prayer using one of the many available traditional or modern melodies, or simply pray the Lord's Prayer aloud together.

Our Father, Who art in heaven,
Hallowed be your name.
Your Kingdom come, your will be done
    on earth as it is in heaven.
Give us this day our daily bread,
And forgive us our trespasses as we forgive
    those who trespass against us.
And lead us not into temptation,
    but deliver us from evil.
For thine is the kingdom and the power and the
    glory forever.

The Doxology

Praise God from whom all blessings flow.
Praise him all creatures here below.
Praise him above ye heavenly hosts.
Praise Father, Son, and Holy Ghost.
Amen.

The Priestly Blessing

The Lord bless you, and keep you; the Lord make His face shine on you, and be gracious to you; the Lord lift up His countenance on you, and give you peace. (Num. 6:24-26 NASB)

The Prayer of Simeon

Sovereign Lord, as you have promised,

you may now dismiss your servant in peace.

For my eyes have seen your salvation, which you have prepared in the sight of all nations:

a light for revelation to the Gentiles,

and the glory of your people Israel.

(Lk. 2:29-32 NIV)

O Joyous Light: An Orthodox liturgical hymn

(Various melodies can be found online)

O Joyous Light of the holy glory, of the immortal, heavenly, holy, blessed Father. O Jesus Christ, now that we have come to the setting (rising, shining) of the sun and behold the light of evening (morning, noonday), we praise God: Father, Son, and Holy Spirit. For meet it is at all times to worship you with voices of praise, O Son of God and Giver of Life. Therefore, all the world glorifies you.

Psalm 90 Blessing

May God give you wisdom to . . .

May God establish the work of your hands.

Glory Be to the Father...

Glory be to the Father, and to the Son,
and to the Holy Spirit,
as it was in the beginning, is now,
and ever shall be,
world without end. Amen.

A General Blessing

A prayer of blessing (for each person to pray over one other person near the close of a meeting)

I bless you, _____, as you step into the month ahead. As you walk through these coming weeks, may you see and savor the Lord's presence and beauty. May God fill you with his Spirit and all wisdom, keep you from sin, and surround you and your family with his peace and love. May he bear good fruit in you and through you as you join him in proclaiming and bringing his kingdom to the world. And as you walk, may his light illumine you in all things, may his joy be yours, may his love overflow through you to everyone you meet, and may quiet, stillness, and his abiding peace accompany you all your days. In the name of the Father and the Son and the Holy Spirit. Amen.

The Apostles' Creed

I believe in God, the Father almighty,
   maker of heaven and earth;
And in Jesus Christ his only Son our Lord;
   who was conceived by the Holy Ghost,
   born of the Virgin Mary,
   suffered under Pontius Pilate,
   was crucified, dead, and buried.
   He descended into hell.
   The third day he rose again from the dead.
   He ascended into heaven,
   and sits on the right hand of God the
   Father almighty.
   From there he shall come to judge the quick
   and the dead.
I believe in the Holy Ghost,
    the holy universal Church,
    the communion of saints,
    the forgiveness of sins,
    the resurrection of the body,
    and the life everlasting. Amen.

RESOURCE 5
Bibliography

Adams, Richard. *Watership Down*. New York: Macmillan, 1972.

Baab, Lynne M. *Sabbath Keeping: Finding Freedom in the Rhythms of Rest*. Downers Grove: InterVarsity Press, 2005.

Barton, Ruth R. *Sacred Rhythms: Arranging Our Lives for Spiritual Transformation*. Downers Grove: InterVarsity Press, 2006.

Bello, Charles. *Prayer as a Place: Spirituality That Transforms*. Choctaw: HGM Publishing, 2008.

Benedict and Timothy Fry. *RB 1980: The Rule of St. Benedict in English*. Collegeville: Liturgical Press, 1981.

Benner, David G. *The Gift of Being Yourself: The Sacred Call to Self-Discovery*. Downers Grove: IVP Books, 2015.

---. *Sacred Companions: The Gift of Spiritual Friendship & Direction*. Downers Grove: InterVarsity Press, 2002.

Bloom, Anthony. *Beginning to Pray*. New York: Paulist Press, 1970.

Bonhoeffer, Dietrich. *Life Together*. Minneapolis: Fortress Press, 2015.

Brother Lawrence. *The Practice of the Presence of God: Based on the Conversations, Letters, Ways, and Spiritual Principles of Brother Lawrence, as Well as on the Writings of Joseph de Beaufort*. Nashville: T. Nelson Publishers, 1982.

Cahill, Thomas. *How the Irish Saved Civilization: The Untold Story of Ireland's Heroic Role from the Fall of Rome to the Rise of Medieval Europe*. New York: Nan A. Talese, 1995.

Calvin, Jean. *Institutes of the Christian Religion*. Philadelphia: Westminster, 1960.

Carmichael, Amy. *Candles in the Dark: Letters of Hope and Encouragement*. Fort Washington, PA: CLC Publications, 2010.

Cather, Willa. *Great Short Works of Willa Cather.* New York: Harper Perennial, 1989.

---. *Death Comes for the Archbishop.* New York: Alfred A. Knopf, 1927.

Daughtry, Darius V. *And the Walls Came Tumbling.* North Miami: Omiokun Books, 2019.

de Caussade, Jean Pierre, translated by Kitty Muggeridge, with an introduction by Richard J. Foster. *Sacrament of the Present Moment.* San Francisco: Harper & Row, 1989.

---. "What can a poem do?" Poetry, June 2021. Chicago: The Poetry Foundation, 2021.

Episcopal Church. *The Book of Common Prayer and Administration of the Sacraments and Other Rites and Ceremonies of the Church: Together with the Psalter or Psalms of David: According to the Use of the Episcopal Church.* New York: Church Hymnal Corp., 1979.

Foster, Richard. *Celebration of Discipline.* London: Hodder & Stoughton, 1989.

Francis. *The Church of Mercy: A Vision for the Church.* Chicago: Loyola Press, 2014.

Hamm, Dennis. "Rummaging for God: Praying Backwards through Your Day." Ignatian Spirituality. July 15, 2023. https://www.ignatianspirituality.com/ignatian-prayer/the-examen/rummaging-for-god-praying-backward-through-your-day/

Hammarskjöld, Dag. *Markings.* New York: Alfred A. Knopf, 1966.

Herndon, William H. and Weik, Jesse W. *Abraham Lincoln, The True Story of a Great Life: The Complete Version with original illustrations.* Amazon Kindle, 2021.

Heschel, Abraham Joshua. *The Sabbath: Its Meaning for Modern Man.* New York: Farrar, Strause and Giroux, 2005.

Hopkins, Gerard Manley. *The Poems of Gerard Manley Hopkins.* London: Oxford University Press, 1967.

Hughes, Langston and Arnold Rampersad, ed. *The Collected Poems of Langston Hughes,* New York: Vintage Classics, 1995.

Ignatius. *The Spiritual Exercises of St. Ignatius of Loyola: With Points for Personal Prayer from Jesuit Spiritual Masters.* Charlotte: TAN Books, 2020.

Keller, Timothy. *Every Good Endeavor: Connecting Your Work to God's Work.* New York: Dutton, 2012.

Kierkegaard, Søren. *Purity of Heart Is to Will One Thing: Spiritual Preparation for the Office of Confession.* New York: Harper, 1956.

Marcel, Gabriel. *The Mystery of Being.* London: Harville Press, 1950-1951.

Marcel, Gabriel and Brendan Sweetman. *A Gabriel Marcel Reader.* South Bend: St. Augustine's Press, 2011.

Pathak, Jay and Dave Runyon. *The Art of Neighboring: Building Genuine Relationships Right outside Your Door.* Grand Rapids: Baker Books, 2012.

Paton, Alan. *Cry, the Beloved Country.* New York: Scribner, 1948.

Peterson, Eugene H. *Eat This Book: A Conversation in the Art of Spiritual Reading.* Grand Rapids: W.B. Eerdmans Pub. Co., 2006.

Philippe, Jacques. *Interior Freedom.* New York: Scepter Publishers, 2007.

---. *Searching for and Maintaining Peace: A Small Treatise on Peace of Heart.* New York: Alba House, 2002.

Summerell, Steve. *"Spiritual Formation."* Class lecture. VIMIN-1000 Spiritual Formation, Vineyard Institute, Columbus, OH, 2012.

Thurman, Howard. *The Disciplines of the Spirit.* New York: Harper & Row, 1963.

---. *The Inward Journey.* New York: Harper, 1961.

Tozer, A. W. *The Knowledge of the Holy: The Attributes of God, Their Meaning in the Christian Life.* San Francisco: Harper & Row, 1961.

Warner, Larry. *Journey with Jesus: Discovering the Spiritual Exercises of Saint Ignatius.* Downers Grove: IVP Books, 2010.

Willard, Dallas. *The Great Omission: Reclaiming Jesus's Essential Teachings on Discipleship.* San Francisco:Harper, 2006.

---. *Renovation of the Heart: Putting on the Character of Christ.* Carol Stream: NavPress, 2002.

---. *The Spirit of the Disciplines: Understanding How God Changes Lives.* San Francisco: HarperOne, 1999.

RB 1980: The Rule of St. Benedict in English (1980), Timothy Fry, Timothy Horner, Imogene Baker, ed.

www.ingramcontent.com/pod-product-compliance
Lightning Source LLC
Chambersburg PA
CBHW040014080526
44586CB00028B/3000